T0327674

Trading VIX Derivatives

Founded in 1807, John Wiley & Sons is the oldest independent publishing company in the United States. With offices in North America, Europe, Australia and Asia, Wiley is globally committed to developing and marketing print and electronic products and services for our customers' professional and personal knowledge and understanding.

The Wiley Trading series features books by traders who have survived the market's ever-changing temperament and have prospered—some by reinventing systems, others by getting back to basics. Whether a novice trader, professional or somewhere in-between, these books will provide the advice and strategies needed to prosper today and well into the future.

For a list of available titles, visit our Web site at www.WileyFinance.com.

Trading VIX Derivatives

Trading and Hedging Strategies
Using VIX Futures, Options, and
Exchange-Traded Notes

RUSSELL RHOADS, CFA

WILEY

John Wiley & Sons, Inc.

Published by John Wiley & Sons, Inc., Hoboken, New Jersey.
Published simultaneously in Canada.

For general information on our other products and services or for technical support, please contact our Customer Care Department within the United States at (800) 762-2974, outside the United States at (317) 572-3993 or fax (317) 572-4002.

Wiley also publishes its books in a variety of electronic formats. Some content that appears in print may not be available in electronic books. For more information about Wiley products, visit our web site at www.wiley.com.

Library of Congress Cataloging-in-Publication Data:

Rhoads, Russell.
    Trading VIX derivatives : trading and hedging strategies using VIX futures, options, and exchange-traded notes / Russell Rhoads.
        p. cm. – (Wiley trading ; 503)
    Includes bibliographical references and index.
    ISBN 978-0-470-93308-4 (hardback); ISBN 978-1-118-11846-7 (ebk);
    ISBN 978-1-118-11847-4 (ebk); ISBN 978-1-118-11848-1 (ebk)
    1. Derivative securities.   2. Hedging (Finance)   3. Options (Finance)   I. Title.
    HG6024.A3R523 2011
    332.64'57–dc22
                                                                            2011014331

Printed in the United States of America

10   9   8   7   6   5   4   3   2   1

Dedicated to Merribeth, who holds down the fort.

Contents

Preface

The current level of the CBOE Volatility Index, or VIX, is part of the litany of information thrown out at a rapid pace on morning business programs. In times of extreme market moves, the VIX gets a bit more attention and possibly a little explanation. That explanation is often that it is a "fear index." Needless to say, the VIX is much more than an index of fear in the stock market.

The VIX emerged from academic work in the early 1990s as a method of determining a consistent level of implied volatility of option contracts trading on the S&P 100 (OEX) Index at the Chicago Board Options Exchange. For almost a decade, this measure was a side note of market activity.

Then, in the early part of the 2000s, the formula was updated to encompass more option contracts and the focus shifted from the S&P 100 to the S&P 500 index. This update, to include more contracts and focus on the S&P 500, was in preparation to offer derivative contracts on volatility.

Futures and then option contracts were developed by the CBOE to allow investors the ability to capitalize on an outlook for market volatility. These contracts witnessed steady growth until the second half of 2008, when, with an explosion in implied volatility, the marketplace realized the benefits of volatility as a diversification tool.

Other exchanges have taken notice of the success of VIX futures and options and have developed their own volatility indexes and derivative products. Volatility indexes and derivatives on gold, oil, currencies, and even soybeans are now calculated and traded by a variety of exchanges.

This book is divided into two sections. The first half of the book is a description and overview of the variety of volatility-related indexes and products currently available. The unique features of many of the derivative contracts are based on implied volatility, and these are touched on throughout the first section. Some of the confusion that novice traders encounter when considering trading VIX products is addressed, along with instructions on how to interpret a variety of indexes.

The second half of this book is devoted to the uses of volatility-related indexes and products. Methods for speculating on the direction of the overall market or just volatility are addressed. Using volatility derivatives as a tool for hedging traditional portfolios is discussed. Also, the emergence of volatility indexes and trading products as forecasting tools is discussed.

Volatility as an asset class and trading tool is a rapidly growing area in the markets. While writing this book, dozens of new indexes and derivative products based on implied volatility were introduced. Trying to keep up with all of them is nearly impossible, and if I'd tried, this book may never have made it to your hands.

Acknowledgments

There are many people throughout my life who have allowed me to reach the point where I look forward to going to work and truly enjoy what I get to do professionally day in and day out.

The primary person is my wife, Merribeth Rhoads. Her support and patience have been a key contribution to the completion of this book in a timely manner.

My daughters, Margaret and Emerson, are a constant inspiration to work hard and accomplish as much as I can to set a proper example for them. My first friend and little pal are the driving force behind all I do.

My father, Richard Rhoads, has always been most supportive when I needed it and offered key pieces of advice at critical points in my career. Also, a special thanks to my Aunt Jean, who has been an excellent matriarch of the Rhoads clan for the past decade or so. I would also like to thank Richard Smith and Margie Johnson, who decided what was best for me well before I could decide myself.

Professionally, the staff of The Options Institute at the Chicago Board Options Exchange is probably the best group of people I have worked with in my life. Alphabetically, I want to thank Taja Beane, Laura Johnson, Barbara Kalicki, Michelle Kaufman, Debra Peters, Pam Quintero, and Felecia Tatum. The other three instructors at The Options Institute—Jim Bittman, Marty Kearney, and Peter Lusk—are the best mix of mentors I could have ever hoped for in my career. Also, Michael Mollet of the CBOE Futures Exchange was very helpful in pointing me in the right direction regarding VIX-related products. The professionals at the brokerage firms I work with on a regular basis have allowed me to maintain a constant enthusiasm for my current position. Finally, a portion of my job is focused on educating college students. Their enthusiasm for and interest in the financial markets rubs off on me.

Also, for a second time around, Meg Freeborn and Kevin Commins of Wiley have been wonderful to work with. I hope to collaborate on more projects with them in the future.

In the time I have been at the Options Institute, I have instructed several thousand individuals who are interested in options trading and strategies. Many of you have challenged me with your questions and inspired me with your interest in the derivative markets. Two chapters in this book directly emanated from discussions and questions that I had with students. To all those who watch webinars or attend classes in person, I truly appreciate the time you give me.

CHAPTER 1

Understanding Implied Volatility

I n this book, we will discuss the ins and outs of a popular market indicator, or index, that is based on implied volatility. The indicator is the CBOE Volatility Index®, widely known by its ticker symbol, VIX. It should come as no surprise that a solid understanding of the index must begin with a solid understanding of what implied volatility is and how it works.

Implied volatility is ultimately determined by the price of option contracts. Since option prices are the result of market forces, or increased levels of buying or selling, implied volatility is determined by the market. An index based on implied volatility of option prices is displaying the market's estimation of volatility of the underlying security in the future.

More advanced option traders who feel they have a solid understanding of implied volatility may consider moving to Chapter 2. That chapter introduces the actual method for determining the VIX. However, as implied volatility is one of the more advanced option pricing concepts, a quick review before diving into the VIX and volatility-related trading vehicles would be worthwhile for most traders.

HISTORICAL VERSUS FORWARD-LOOKING VOLATILITY

There are two main types of volatility discussed relative to securities prices. The first is historical volatility, which may be calculated using recent trading activity for a stock or other security. The historical volatility of a stock is factual and known. Also, the historical volatility does not give any indication about the future movement of a stock. The forward-looking volatility is what is referred to as the implied volatility. This type of volatility results from the market price of options that trade on a stock.

The implied volatility component of option prices is the factor that can give all option traders, novice to expert, the most difficulty. This occurs because the implied volatility of an option may change while all other pricing factors impacting the price of an option remain unchanged. This change may occur as the order flow for options is biased more to buying or selling. A result of increased buying of options by market participants is higher implied volatility. Conversely, when there is net selling of options, the implied volatility indicated by option prices moves lower.

Basically, the nature of order flow dictates the direction of implied volatility. Again, more option buying increases the option price and the result is higher implied volatility. Going back to Economics 101, implied volatility reacts to the supply and demand of the marketplace. Buying pushes it higher, and selling pushes it lower.

The implied volatility of an option is also considered an indication of the risk associated with the underlying security. The risk may be thought of as how much movement may be expected from the underlying stock over the life of an option. This is not the potential direction of the stock price move, just the magnitude of the move. Generally, when thinking of risk, traders think of a stock losing value or the price moving lower. Using implied volatility as a risk measure results in an estimation of a price move in either direction. When the market anticipates that a stock may soon move dramatically, the price of option contracts, both puts and calls, will move higher.

A common example of a known event in the future that may dramatically influence the price of a stock is a company's quarterly earnings report. Four times a year a company will release information to the investing public in the form of its recent earnings results. This earnings release may also include statements regarding business prospects for the company. This information may have a dramatic impact on the share price. As this price move will also impact option prices, the option contracts usually react in advance. Due to the anticipation that will work into option prices, they are generally more expensive as traders and investors buy options before seeing the report.

This increased buying of options results in higher option prices. There are two ways to think about this: the higher price of the option contracts results in higher implied volatility, or because of higher implied volatility option prices are higher. After the earnings report, there is less risk of a big move in the underlying stock and the options become less expensive. This drop in price is due to lower implied volatility levels; implied volatility is now lower due to lower option prices.

A good non-option-oriented example of how implied volatility works may be summed up through this illustration. If you live in Florida, you are familiar with hurricane season. The path of hurricanes can be unpredictable, and at times homeowners have little time to prepare for a storm. Using homeowners insurance as a substitute for an option contract, consider the following situation.

You wake to find out that an evacuation is planned due to a potential hurricane. Before leaving the area, you check whether your homeowners insurance is current. You find you have allowed your coverage to lapse, and so you run down to your agent's office. As he boards up windows and prepares to evacuate inland, he informs you that you may renew, but the cost is going to be $50,000 instead of the $2,000 annual rate you have paid for years. After hearing your objections, he is steadfast. The higher price, he explains, is due to the higher risk associated with the coming storm.

You decide that $50,000 is too much to pay, and you return home to ride out the storm. Fortunately, the storm takes a left turn and misses your neighborhood altogether. Realizing that you have experienced a near miss, you run down to your agent's office with a $50,000 check in hand. Being an honest guy, he tells you the rate is back down to $2,000. Why is this?

The imminent risk level for replacing your home has decreased as there is no known threat bearing down on your property. As the immediate risk of loss or damage has decreased tremendously, so has the cost of protection against loss. When applying this to the option market, risk is actually risk of movement of the underlying security, either higher or lower. This risk is the magnitude of expected movement of the underlying security over the life of an option.

When market participants are expecting a big price move to the upside in the underlying security, there will be net buying of call options in anticipation of this move. As this buying occurs, the price of the call options will increase. This price rise in the options is associated with an increase risk of a large price move, and this increase in risk translates to higher implied volatility.

Also, if there is an expectation of a lower price move, the marketplace may see an increase in put buying. With higher demand for put contracts, the price of puts may increase resulting in higher implied volatility for those options. Finally, if put prices increase, the result is corresponding call prices rising due to a concept known as put-call parity, which will be discussed in the next section.

PUT-CALL PARITY

Put and call prices are linked to each other through the price of the underlying stock through put-call parity. This link exists because combining a stock and put position can result in the same payoff as a position in a call option with the same strike price as the put. If this relationship gets out of line or not in parity, an arbitrage opportunity exits. When one of these opportunities arises, there are trading firms that will quickly buy and sell the securities to attempt to take advantage of this mispricing. This market activity will push the put and call prices back in line with each other.

Put and call prices should remain within a certain price range of each other or arbitragers will enter the market, which results in the prices coming back into parity. Parity between the two also results in a similar implied volatility output resulting from using these prices in a model to determine the implied volatility of the market.

Stated differently, increased demand for a call option will raise the price of that call. As the price of the call moves higher, the corresponding put price should also rise, or the result will be an arbitrage trade that will push the options into line. As the pricing of the option contracts are tied to each other, they will share similar implied volatility levels also.

For a quick and very simple example of how put-call parity works, consider the options and stock in Table 1.1.

Using the XYZ 50 Put combined with XYZ stock, a payout that replicates being long the XYZ 50 Call may be created. The combination of owning stock and owning a put has the same payout structure as a long call option position. With the XYZ 50 Call trading at 1.00 and the XYZ 50 Put priced at 2.00, there may be a mispricing scenario. Table 1.2 compares a long XYZ 50 Call trade with a combined position of long XYZ stock and long a XYZ 50 Put.

The final two columns compare a payout of owning XYZ stock from 50.00 and buying the XYZ 50 Put at 2.00 versus buying an XYZ 50 Call for 1.00. Note that at any price at expiration, the long call position is worth 1.00 more than the combined stock and put position. With this pricing

TABLE 1.1   Put, Call, and Stock Pricing to Illustrate Put-Call Parity

Stock/Option	Price
XYZ Stock	$50.00
XYZ 50 Call	$1.00
XYZ 50 Put	$2.00

TABLE 1.2 Payout Comparison for Long Call and Long Stock + Long Put trade

XYZ at Expiration	Long XYZ Stock	Long XYZ 50 Put	Long Stock + Long Put	Long XYZ 50 Call
45.00	−5.00	3.00	−2.00	−1.00
50.00	0.00	−2.00	−2.00	−1.00
55.00	5.00	−2.00	3.00	4.00

difference, there is the ability to take a short position in the strategy that will be worth less and buy the strategy that will be worth more at expiration. The payout diagram in Figure 1.1 shows how the two positions compare at a variety of prices at expiration.

The lines are parallel throughout this diagram. The higher line represents the profit or loss based on buying the 50 call. The lower line represents the payout for the spread combining a long stock position and a long 50 put position. At any price at expiration, the combined position has less value than the long 50 call. Knowing this outcome, it is possible to benefit from the 1.00 spread, which will exist at any price at expiration for two positions that are basically the same.

Due to put-call parity and the mispricing between the 50 Call and 50 Put, the call may be purchased combined with a short position in the stock and put option. A quick transaction using the prices in the example would result in a profit of 1.00 upon options expiration. This 1.00 profit would be realized regardless of the price of the stock at expiration. Firms would attempt to take advantage of this opportunity through buying the cheaper call option and selling the comparable more expensive put option. The market

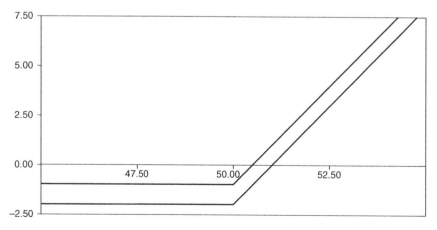

FIGURE 1.1 Payout Diagram Comparison

activity of these participants is what keeps put and call option prices in line with each other and the implied volatility of both put and call contracts at the same level.

ESTIMATING PRICE MOVEMENT

What the implied volatility of an option projects onto the underlying security is the expected range of price movement over a certain period of time. This estimation of price movement is based on statistics and the bell curve. The implied volatility of an option is the projection of an annualized one standard deviation move in the underlying stock over the life of the option. According to statistics and using implied volatility as a guide, the price of a stock should land between up and down one standard deviation at option expiration. The closing price should land in this range 68.2 percent of the time.

This 68.2 percent comes from statistics and what is referred to as a normal distribution. Statistics like this reveal that 68.2 percent of the time a stock should be between up one standard deviation and down one standard deviation a year from today. A formula may also be used to take this annualized number and narrow down the projection to a single day. The normal distribution also indicates that there is a 95.4 percent expectation of the stock landing between up two standard deviations and down two standard deviations. Finally, at three standard deviations, the probability reaches 99.7 percent.

With a stock trading at $50 and the underlying option prices indicating 20 percent implied volatility, the result is a one standard deviation price move equal to $10 (20 percent of $50). In other words, the stock is expected to close between $40 (down $10) and $60 (up $10) with 68.2 percent certainty a year from today. A two standard deviation price move would be equal to $20. This is calculated by simply multiplying 2 times a single standard deviation. Using two standard deviations, it can be projected out that the stock should land between $30 and up $70, with a confidence of 95.4 percent. At three standard deviations, there is a 99.7 percent chance of the stock closing between $20 and $80 a year from the date of the calculation.

VALUING OPTIONS: PRICING CALCULATORS AND OTHER TOOLS

An option pricing calculator is a tool that allows a user the ability to input the pricing variables that determine the value of an option with the result being a theoretical option price. Ultimately the market determines the price of an option through buying and selling forces. However when analyzing and investigating option trades, using an option pricing calculator with certain assumptions gives an idea where an option may be trading in the future. Also, using an option pricing calculator is an excellent way to become familiar with the price action of option contracts. The CBOE has a free option calculator available on its website at www.cboe.com/tradtool; it is a valuable tool for option pricing.

The value of an option contract is derived from a variety of inputs. Inputs into an option pricing model include the price of the underlying security, the strike price of the option, the type of option, dividends, interest rates, and time to option expiration. The final input into an option pricing model is the implied volatility of the option. These inputs may be used in a model to determine the value of an option.

Table 1.3 demonstrates how an option pricing model is used to determine the value of an option. The inputs are at the top of the table, with the value of the option showing up as the only output. Option pricing models calculate a variety of pieces of useful information, such as the impact of changes in pricing factors. These outputs are known as the option Greeks. However, to keep focus on the topic at hand, implied volatility, only the necessary outputs are going to be demonstrated in this example of an option calculator.

The option price in the model is determined from a stock trading at 44.75 with implied volatility of 30 percent and a risk-free interest rate of 1.00 percent. The result is a call option value with a strike price of 45 and 30 days to expiration would be valued at 1.45 based on the inputs used in this model. Keep in mind that this is a pricing model, not the actual market trading price of the option. Again, the inputs in the model are assumptions,

TABLE 1.3 Option Pricing Calculator–Option Value Output

Factor	Input
Call/Put	Call
Underlying Price	44.75
Strike Price	45.00
Implied Volatility	30%
Days to Expiration	30
Interest Rate	1.00%
Dividends	0.00%
Output	**Result**
Option Value	1.45

not just the market price. Just because using these inputs results in a value of 1.45 for this 45 Call does not mean it can be traded at this level. In fact, the market price of this option will vary if the market consensus differs from the inputs used in this model.

The real value of an option at any given time is actually determined by the price that it may be bought or sold in the market. In the case of this 45 Call, even though the inputs into the model result in a 1.45 value, when checking market quotes for this option we find that the current trading price is 1.70. The reason for the difference between our model's value and the market price is the result of different implied volatility levels being used. The previous model, in Table 1.3, takes inputs and the result in a difference in option values based on the inputs.

The pricing factors in an option pricing model are for the most part set in stone. The exception of this is the implied volatility input. For the model, the assumption of 30 percent implied volatility was used. However, the market is pricing in a higher implied volatility level. This is determined before any numbers or formulas have been run just by comparing the option market price and the option value assumption that resulted from the model. The market price of the option is higher than the pricing model output. Seeing this, it is pretty certain that the implied volatility based on market prices is higher than what was entered into the model. There is a direct correlation between high and low relative option prices and higher or lower implied volatility.

Table 1.4 is an option pricing model that uses the market price as an input with the sole output being implied volatility. This implied volatility level is being indicated by the 1.70 market price of the 45 Call. The higher option price here is a higher implied volatility than what was used in the first pricing model. As the option price in this model is higher than the

TABLE 1.4 Option Pricing Calculator—Implied Volatility Output

Factor	Input
Call/Put	Call
Underlying Price	44.75
Strike Price	45.00
Option Price	1.70
Days to Expiration	30
Interest Rate	1.00%
Dividends	0.00
Output	**Result**
Implied Volatility	35%

TABLE 1.5 Impact of a 5 Percent Increase in Implied Volatility		
Implied Volatility	30%	35%
Option Price	1.45	1.70

option value that resulted from a 30 percent implied volatility, the expectation would be a higher implied volatility result. Using 1.70 as the price of the option actually results in the implied volatility that is being projected by this option price to be 35 percent. Professional traders generally start with the market price of an option to calculate implied volatility as that is where the implied volatility of an option is ultimately determined.

Another method of demonstrating the impact of different implied volatility levels on option prices appears in Table 1.5. Instead of a comparison of what the model output was versus the option price based on model outputs, consider the previous option prices in a different way. Consider the two option prices and implied volatility differences as changes based on an increase in demand for the option. Both prices represent the market and the option price increases from 1.45 to 1.70. This option price rise occurs due to an increase in buying of the call option while all other factors that influence the option price stay the same.

Since the price of the option contract has increased, the resulting implied volatility output from an option model has also increased. Higher option prices, whether put or call prices, will result in a higher implied volatility output with no changes in any of the other option pricing factors.

To recap, there is a direct link between the demand for option contracts and their prices in the marketplace. This is regardless of changes occurring in the underlying stock price. With demand in the form of buying pressure pushing option prices higher or an increase in selling occurring due to market participants pushing option prices lower, the implied volatility of an option is dictated by market forces.

FLUCTUATIONS BASED ON SUPPLY AND DEMAND

As mentioned in the first section of this chapter, implied volatility does fluctuate based on supply and demand for options. This leads to the question, "What exactly causes the supply and demand for options to fluctuate?" The short answer is the near-term expected price changes that may occur in the underlying stock. These moves are usually the result of information that has influenced the fundamental outlook for a stock. The best example of this type of information would be a company's quarterly earnings reports.

Every publicly traded company in the United States reports its earnings results four times a year. The date and timing (generally before the market open or after the market close) are usually known well in advance of the actual announcement. Along with the earnings results, other information is disseminated, such as the company's revenues and the source of those revenues. Many companies offer a possible outlook regarding the prospects for their business conditions, and most will hold a public conference call to answer professional investors' questions. These events often have a dramatic impact, either positive or negative, on the price of a stock.

Again, the date that these results are announced is public knowledge and often widely anticipated by analysts and traders. As the date draws near, there is usually trading in the stock and stock options that is based on the anticipated stock price reaction to the earnings announcement. The result is usually net buying of options as there is speculation regarding the potential move of the underlying stock. The net option buying results in higher option prices and an increase in the implied volatility projected by the options that trade on this stock. Usually this increase impacts only the options with the closest expiration and strike prices that are close to where the stock is trading. An excellent example of this can be seen in the option prices and resulting implied volatility levels for Amazon stock shown in Table 1.6.

These are market prices from just before the close of trading on July 22, 2010. Amazon's earnings were reported after the market close on the 22nd with weekly options that expire on the 23rd having only one trading day until expiration after the news was released. The difference in implied volatility between the options that have one trading day left and those that have just under a month left is pretty significant.

TABLE 1.6 Amazon Option Implied Volatility and Option Prices Minutes Prior to an Earnings Announcement

AMZN @ 120.07

Call Strike	July 23 Call	July 23 Call IV	Aug 21 Call	Aug 21 Call IV
115	7.00	163%	9.25	48%
120	3.92	156%	6.25	45%
125	1.82	148%	4.05	45%
Put Strike	**July 23 Put**	**July 23 Put IV**	**Aug 21 Put**	**Aug 21 Put IV**
115	1.92	159%	4.05	48%
120	3.82	155%	6.20	47%
125	6.75	148%	8.90	45%

This difference stems from the options that market participants would use as a short-term trading vehicle related to Amazon's earnings announcement. This would be the same for hedgers and speculators alike. Both would focus on the strike prices that are closest to the trading price of the stock as well as the options with the least amount of time to expiration.

Option contracts that have the closest expiration to a known event that occurs after the event are the contracts that will have the most price reaction before and after the event occurs. With Amazon reporting earnings the evening of July 22 and an option series expiring on July 23, the July 23 options are the contracts that will see the most price action based on the stock price reaction to the earnings release.

The stock price is very close to the 120 strike price when the option first listed and just before the earnings announcement. Using the 120 strike options, implied volatility for both the put and call options that expire the following day is around 155 percent. This indicates that on an annualized basis the option market is pricing in a 155 percent price move over a single day. This is much more dramatic sounding that it is in reality. Annualized implied volatility of 155 percent for an option with a single trading day left translates to a one-day move of around 9.76 percent. The math behind this is (see the following feature on calculating single day implied volatility):

$$9.76\% = 155\%/15.87$$

This single-day implied volatility can be interpreted as being a single standard deviation range of expected price movement of the stock on that day.

CALCULATING SINGLE-DAY IMPLIED VOLATILITY

Assuming there are 252 trading days in a year, the denominator of this formula turns out to be the square root of the number of trading days for the year.

1 Day Movement = Implied Volatility/Square Root of 252

Amazon did report its earnings, and the initial price reaction was pretty close to what the option market was pricing in. The NASDAQ opening price the day after the company reported earnings was down 11.76 percent from the previous day's close. The market was forecasting a 9.76 percent move based on option pricing.

TABLE 1.7 Implied Volatility Changes Approaching Amazon Earnings

Date	AMZN	120 Call	120 Call IV
July 15	120.13	4.80	71%
July 15	122.06	5.92	78%
July 16	118.49	4.00	84%
July 19	119.94	4.33	87%
July 20	120.10	3.95	90%
July 21	117.43	2.73	111%
July 22	120.07	3.92	155%

As a refresher from college statistics: One standard deviation in statistics indicates there is a 68.2 percent chance that an outcome is going to land between up and down one standard deviation. So this single-day implied volatility indicates the market is expecting Amazon's stock to trade within up or down 9.76 percent with a 68.2 percent level of confidence in the next day.

Table 1.7 shows the increase in the implied volatility of the 120 Call projected by Amazon option prices as the earnings announcement approaches. Implied volatility for other options rises in the same way, since 120 is the closest strike to the stock price when the option started trading and just before earnings were announced. Also, the options contract is a weekly expiration option that begins trading on a Thursday morning and expires on the following week's Friday close. This particular option started trading on July 15 with the last trading day being July 23 or is what is called a weekly option that has only eight trading days from listing to expiration.

The first row is the opening price for the weekly option and underlying price for the option. When the option first traded it had an implied volatility level of 71 percent. This compares to non-earnings-period implied volatility levels, which are usually in the mid 30 percent range for Amazon options.

Over the next few days, the earnings announcement draws closer and the stock stays in a fairly tight range. The implied volatility of the option contracts continues to rise as time passes. By the time the announcement is imminent, the implied volatility of the 120 Call has more than doubled.

This illustration of how implied volatility climbs in front of a potentially market-moving event is a bit magnified by the options only having one day of time value remaining before the announcement. However, it is a good illustration of how option prices, through the implied volatility component, discount a potential market-moving event when the timing of this event is a known entity.

THE IMPACT ON OPTION PRICES

Implied volatility is commonly considered an indication as to whether an option is cheap or expensive. This determination may be made through examining past implied volatility levels for the options of a particular stock or index and comparing present values.

Demand for options pushes up the price of an option contract and results in higher implied volatility. However, other factors such as the underlying price, time to expiration, and interest-rate levels also determine the price of an option. These other factors are not impacted through the buying and selling pressure on option contracts. Only implied volatility will fluctuate based on market buying and selling pressure.

The goal of any directional trading strategy should be to buy low and sell high. If the market considers any trading vehicle inexpensive, there will be participants that take advantage of this through purchasing the instrument. On the other hand, if something appears expensive it may be sold. Implied volatility is a measure that option traders use to define whether options are overvalued or undervalued.

As a simple example, take the option prices and implied volatility levels in Table 1.8. The data in this table represent a stock trading at 24.00 per share, and the value of a 25 Call with 90 days until expiration. The different option prices are based on various implied volatility levels. Note that as the option price increases so does the implied volatility of the 25 Call.

If options for the underlying stock usually trade with an implied volatility of 25 percent, then when the option could be purchased for 0.80 it may be considered undervalued or inexpensive. At 0.80 the option had an implied volatility level of 20 percent. When implied volatility rose to 30 percent and the option was trading for 1.30, the option may be considered expensive. At 1.05 with an implied volatility of 25 percent, the historical norm, the 25 Call may be considered fairly valued.

Of course, using implied volatility as a measure of how expensive or cheap an option is must be done in the context of some external factors. Remember, if the company is preparing to announce quarterly earnings, the

TABLE 1.8 Implied Volatility Levels and Option Prices

Stock Price	25 Call	Implied Volatility
24.00	0.80	20%
24.00	1.05	25%
24.00	1.30	30%

implied volatility would be expected to be high relative to other periods of time. In that case, a comparison to implied volatility behavior around previous earnings announcements would be a more accurate analysis of whether the options appear cheap or expensive.

IMPLIED VOLATILITY AND THE VIX

The VIX will be further defined in the next chapter, but the concepts in this chapter should be tied to the VIX before moving forward. The VIX is a measure of the implied volatility being projected through the prices of S&P 500 index options. The VIX can be used to indicate what type of market movement option prices are projecting on the S&P 500 over the next 30 days or even a shorter time. Since the VIX is measuring implied volatility of S&P 500 index options and since implied volatility is a measure of risk projected by option pricing, the VIX is considered a gauge of fear in the overall market.

The remainder of this book explores the VIX index which is based on the concept of implied volatility. With a solid understanding of implied volatility, exploration of the VIX index, methods of using the VIX for market analysis, and ways to directly trade volatility should be easier to comprehend.

CHAPTER 2

About the VIX Index

O fficially known as the CBOE Volatility Index, the VIX is considered by many to be a gauge of fear and greed in the stock market. A more accurate description of what the VIX measures is the implied volatility that is being priced into S&P 500 index options. Through the use of a wide variety of option prices, the index offers an indication of 30-day implied volatility as priced by the S&P 500 index option market.

Before diving further into the calculation that results in the VIX, this chapter will cover the history of exactly how this index was developed followed by an overview of how the VIX is determined. Then for interested parties there is a more in-depth discussion of how the VIX is calculated. The VIX index has historically had an inverse relationship to performance of the S&P 500, and this often results in questions from traders who are new to the VIX. This relationship will be discussed in the context of put-call parity, which was mentioned in Chapter 1.

Finally, there are a handful of VIX-related indexes based on other equity-market indexes. The S&P 100–related VIX is still calculated using the old method to maintain some continuity for historical comparisons. Finally, there are also VIX indexes calculated on options based on the Nasdaq 100, Russell 2000, and Dow Jones Industrial Average, which are discussed toward the end of the chapter.

HISTORY OF THE VIX

The concept behind the VIX index was developed by Dr. Robert Whaley of Vanderbilt University in 1993. His paper "Derivatives on Market

Volatility: Hedging Tools Long Overdue," which appeared in the *Journal of Derivatives*, laid the groundwork for the index. The original VIX was based on pricing of S&P 100 (OEX) options and used only eight option contracts to determine a volatility measure.

At the time, OEX options were the most heavily traded index option series that reflected performance of the stock market in the United States. This volatility index was based on a limited number of options and was slightly disconnected from the overall stock market due to the narrower focus of the S&P 100 versus the S&P 500.

In 2003 there was a new methodology for calculation of the VIX index that was developed through work done by the CBOE and Goldman Sachs. Although the calculation was altered, the most important aspect to this change for individuals is that the underlying options changed from the OEX to options trading on the S&P 500. Another significant change was an increase in the number of options that were used in the index calculation. Through a wider number of option contract prices feeding the formula to calculate the VIX, a true 30-day implied volatility level that is being projected on the S&P 500 by the options market is realized.

The S&P 500 index is considered by professional investors to be the benchmark for the performance of the stock market in the United States. The members of the index are 500 of the largest domestic companies in the United States that meet criteria based on market capitalization, public float, financial viability, liquidity, type of company, and industry sector. Companies are usually dropped from the index when they have violated membership criteria or have ceased to operate due to a merger or acquisition.

The industry representation of the S&P 500 index appears in Table 2.1. With a broad distribution of companies in the index, there is no industry that dominates the index's performance. This diversification

TABLE 2.1 S&P 500 Industry Weightings

Industry	Weighting
Consumer discretionary	9.10%
Consumer staples	11.70%
Energy	11.40%
Financials	15.40%
Health care	13.40%
Industrials	10.00%
Information technology	18.50%
Materials	3.40%
Telecom services	3.30%
Utilities	3.80%

across industries is a major reason the S&P 500 is considered a performance benchmark by most professional investors.

CALCULATING THE VIX

After the VIX index was introduced, the CBOE moved forward with the first exchange listed volatility derivative instruments. Through the CBOE Futures Exchange (CFE®), the CBOE introduced futures contracts based on the VIX. Other instruments have followed, and more are in development.

There are two ways to explain how the VIX is determined. First, it can be explained using simple nonmathematical terms. Then, for those interested in an in-depth discussion of the formula and calculation, a more detailed overview will follow. Having a basic understanding of how the VIX is determined is more than enough to move forward with trading. However, for those with more interest in the VIX calculation, the more comprehensive description is included.

The Nonmathematical Approach

The VIX is an indicator of 30-day implied volatility determined through the use of S&P 500 index option prices. The option price used in the formula is actually the midpoint of the bid-ask spread of relevant at and out of the money actively traded S&P 500 index options. Using the midpoint of the spread is a more accurate price description than the last price for an option contract. Also, the contracts used are the S&P 500 index options that trade to the next two standard expirations with at least eight days to expiration. When a series reaches this eight-day point, it is not used anymore in the calculation and the options that expire farther in the future then start to contribute to the VIX calculation.

All of these S&P 500 options are then used to create a synthetic at the money option that expires exactly 30 days from the very moment of the calculation. This time variable to the formula is constantly being updated to weight the balance of the two expiration series in the formula. Using a wide number of actively quoted S&P 500 index options, a synthetic 30-day option is created and the VIX is the implied volatility of that option. This results in implied volatility of the synthetic option contract, which is then reported as the VIX.

The Formula and Calculations

It is possible to trade the VIX with a cursory understanding of how the index is determined. Those who are satisfied with their understanding of the VIX and what it represents may skip ahead. However, readers who are more interested in how the VIX is calculated should be interested in the remainder of this section.

The input for calculating the VIX index comes from all actively quoted S&P 500 index options for the next two standard option expirations that have at least eight days remaining until expiration. Eliminating the nearer term expiration options that have only a week to expiration takes out some of the end-of-contract volatility that can occur in the market.

The option contracts from these two expiration series are the at and out of the money put and call options. The series of options used extends out of the money until there are two consecutive option strikes that have no bid-ask market posted. Again, the midpoint of the bid-ask spread for the options is used in the calculation.

The time to expiration part of the calculation is very specific, down to the second. This is constantly being updated to change the weighting between the two series of options feeding into the calculation. Although S&P 500 index options cease trading on a Thursday for Friday morning settlement, the time to expiration is based on the market opening time, 8:30 A.M. central time, on the Friday of expiration.

There is also a forward price for the S&P 500 that is calculated using the closest at the money options in conjunction with put-call parity. This S&P 500 forward price is the underlying security price and strike price used to price the synthetic option used in the calculation. The implied volatility of that option is what is quoted at the VIX.

Finally if there is interest in using Microsoft Excel© to replicate calculating the VIX, a paper produced by Tom Arnold and John H. Earl Jr. of the University of Richmond is useful. In a very short study, 10 pages, they lay out the groundwork for using Excel to replicate the calculation of the VIX (to read the full paper, go to http://papers.ssrn.com/sol3/papers.cfm?abstract_id=1103971). Also, once the template has been set up, changing the time frame and underlying instrument is simple. Using the template, the VIX methodology may be applied to a variety of instruments or time frames with little effort.

THE VIX AND PUT-CALL PARITY

Many traders and investors often ask why there appears to be an inverse relationship between the direction of stock prices and the VIX. The relationship may be broken down to the nature of purchasing options. When the market is under pressure, there is a net buying of put options, which will result in higher implied volatility. This rapid increase in demand for put

TABLE 2.2 Prices to Demonstrate Put-Call Parity

Security	Price
XYZ Stock	45.00
XYZ 45 Call	2.50
XYZ 45 Put	2.00

options pushes the implied volatility for both put and call contracts higher; the reason behind this is called put-call parity.

Put-call parity states that the prices of put and call options that have the same strike price and expiration are related. This relationship exists due to the ability to create synthetic positions in one option through combining the other option with the underlying stock. With this possibility, if the price of one option differs enough from the price of the other, an arbitrage opportunity may present itself.

For instance, in a zero-interest-rate environment, a put and call price should have the same value if the stock is trading at the strike price. As the options are related in price, the implied volatility of these options is also related. This is unrealistic, but it is a good method of demonstrating put-call parity. The prices in Table 2.2 may be used to demonstrate what can happen when put-call parity breaks down.

It is possible to replicate the payout of a long call through combining a put option and a stock position. Stated another way, a long stock position along with owning a put will result in the same payout structure as being long a call option. So, if the same payout may be created in two methods, the pricing of these two should be equivalent. If they are not equal, the lower priced one may be bought while the higher priced one is simultaneously sold. This is known as an arbitrage trade, in which an instant profit may be realized through a pricing difference in two equivalent securities.

If the XYZ 45 Put is purchased and shares of XYZ stock are also bought, the resulting position at expiration will be the same as owning the XYZ 45 Call. Above 45.00, the call option would result in a long position in XYZ; below 45.00, the call would not be exercised and there would be no position in XYZ. With a long 45 put position combined with a long position in the stock, if the stock is below 45.00 at expiration the put option will be exercised and the stock sold. The result would be no position in XYZ. Above 45.00, the stock would still be owned, as the XYZ 45 Put would not be exercised. Regardless of the stock price at expiration, the resulting position in XYZ will be the same. Due to the different prices between the 45 Call and

TABLE 2.3 Long XYZ 45 Call versus Long XYZ 45 Put + Long XYZ at Expiration

XYZ	Long XYZ Stock	Long XYZ 45 Put	Long Stock + Long Put	Long XYZ 45 Call
35	−10.00	8.00	−2.00	−2.50
40	−5.00	3.00	−2.00	−2.50
45	0.00	−2.00	−2.00	−2.50
50	5.00	−2.00	3.00	2.50
55	10.00	−2.00	8.00	7.50

45 Put, there is a difference in profit or loss of the position at expiration. Table 2.3 demonstrates this at a variety of price points at expiration.

The column Long Stock + Long Put represents the position payout at expiration of the combined long stock–long put position. Note at all price levels the combined long stock and long put position is worth 0.50 more than the long call position. If at all price levels at expiration the long call position will be worth less than stock plus put position, then an arbitrage opportunity exists.

The arbitrage trade would be to purchase the stock and put option while taking a short position in the call option. At any price level for XYZ at expiration, this trade would result in a profit of 0.50. Table 2.4 displays the outcome through buying XYZ at 45.00 and purchasing the XYZ 45 Put for 2.00 along with selling the XYZ 45 Call at 2.50.

Admittedly this is an overly simplistic example, but the hope here is to get across the idea of put-call parity and what happens when put and call prices get out of line relative to each other. Execution of this combined position with the result of a riskless profit would involve transaction costs and a cost of capital. For individuals this might be prohibitive, but for professional trading firms this is an opportunity. When option prices get out of line to a point where a professional firm may take advantage through placing orders to buy and sell the instrument that are mispriced, then

TABLE 2.4 Long XYZ Stock + versus Long XYZ 45 Put + Short XYZ 45 Call at Expiration

XYZ	Long XYZ Stock	Long XYZ 45 Put	Short XYZ 45 Call	Combined Profit/Loss
35	−10.00	8.00	2.50	0.50
40	−5.00	3.00	2.50	0.50
45	0.00	−2.00	2.50	0.50
50	5.00	−2.00	−2.50	0.50
55	10.00	−2.00	−7.50	0.50

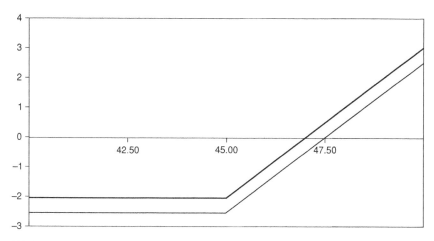

FIGURE 2.1 Payoff Comparison

orders to take advantage of this mispricing will be executed. These trades will quickly push markets back into line and eliminate the arbitrage profit.

Figure 2.1 is a payoff diagram that compares the payout of the long call and combined long put–long stock position. The higher line represents the combined long put–long stock position. The lower line shows the profit or loss for the long call position. Note the lines are parallel—the only difference is the profit or loss. This difference shows an arbitrage profit that may be realized by shorting the long call and buying the other two instruments, then holding the positions to expiration.

The put-call parity formula has many components and is beyond the scope of this book. However, the formulas in Table 2.5 illustrate on a

TABLE 2.5 Variety of Positions Created through Put-Call Parity

Position	Combination
Long call	Long stock + long put
Short call	Short stock + short put
Long put	Short stock + long call
Short put	Long stock + short call
Long stock	Long call + short put
Short stock	Short call + long put

position basis what the equivalent single-position result is from different combinations of a put, call, or stock.

A comparable payout of any single long or short position with a put, call, or stock may be created using a combination of the other two securities. Although it may seem like this does not relate to the VIX, there is a point to this exercise.

The relationship between put and call prices that results in put-call parity does have an impact on the VIX index. The level of the VIX is based on the implied volatility of a variety of both put and call options. The indicated implied volatility of option contracts rises and falls based on market forces. The specific market force that impacts implied volatility is the net buying or selling of options. This increase in demand is not necessarily purchase of either all call or all put options buy just net buying of option contracts. Since strong demand for call options will result in higher put prices and demand for puts will result in higher call prices, higher demand for either type of contract results in higher implied volatility for both put and call contracts.

The VIX has historically had an inverse relationship with the S&P 500 index. The reason behind this inverse relationship relates to the type of option activity that occurs during bullish markets versus bearish markets. When markets rally, there is rarely a rush by investors to purchase call options. Therefore when the market is rising, there is rarely dramatically higher option purchasing versus options selling.

When the S&P 500 comes under pressure, especially in very turbulent times, there is often a panic-like demand for put options. This demand for protection results in increased purchasing of put options. The result is a fast move higher in implied volatility for both S&P 500 put and call options. This higher demand then results in an increase in implied volatility and finally a move higher in the VIX index.

In summary, the VIX moves higher when there is more demand for S&P 500 options, this demand tends to increase when there is nervousness about the overall market. This concern about the market will result in increased demand for put options. Put-call parity is the reason the implied volatility of both types of options moves together. The result of this increased demand for puts is higher implied volatility indicated by the pricing of S&P 500 options and a move higher in the VIX.

THE VIX AND MARKET MOVEMENT

Again, the VIX is a measure of 30-day implied volatility as indicated by the pricing of S&P 500 index options. The VIX is expressed as an annualized volatility measure, but it may actually be used to determined shorter-term market-price movements. Recall the example with Amazon reporting earnings in the previous chapter. The implied volatility of the at the money options that only had a day left to expiration could be used to determine the magnitude of movement expected from Amazon stock the day following the company's earnings release. The implied volatility of those options was expressed as an annualized number.

The VIX is the 30-day implied volatility of the S&P 500, but it is also expressed as an annual figure. When the VIX is quoted at 20, this can be interpreted as SPX options pricing in an annualized move, up or down, of 20 percent in the S&P 500 index over the next 30 days. Using the VIX index, the anticipated movement of the underlying market may also be interpreted. The formula for determining the expected magnitude of market movements based on the VIX index is shown in the section following.

CALCULATING EXPECTED 30-DAY MARKET MOVEMENT

The formula for determining expected 30-day market movement is simple:

30-Day Movement = VIX/Square Root of 12

To determine the anticipated 30-day movement of the stock market as defined by the VIX involves dividing the VIX by the square root of 12. In the previous chapter the implied volatility for a stock was used to interpret the expected one-day move for the stock. The square root of 12 is a convenient number as 30 days is the average month and there are 12 months in the year. In a similar manner to breaking down what implied volatility was indicating about movement in Amazon stock, the VIX may be used to determine the anticipated 30-day move for the S&P 500.

If the VIX is quoted at 20, the result would be the market expecting movement of about 5.77 percent over the next 30 days. Following the formula for determining 30-day market movement, the math would be:

$$5.77\% = 20/3.46$$

At times the VIX has reached some extreme points with the index actually reaching over 100 intraday. Table 2.6 shows what different VIX levels indicate about anticipated stock market movement.

The VIX may also be used as an indication of what magnitude of daily price movement is being expected for the S&P 500. Much like the formula used in Chapter 1 for Amazon stock, the VIX can be taken down to a

TABLE 2.6 VIX and Expected 30-Day Movement of the S&P 500

VIX	Expected 30-Day Move
3.46	1%
6.92	2%
10.40	3%
13.85	4%
17.32	5%
20.78	6%
24.25	7%
27.71	8%
31.18	9%
34.64	10%

single-day estimate of market movement. Instead of repeating the formula from the previous chapter, a trader's rule of thumb about the VIX will be discussed.

In the VIX trading arena, the option and futures traders take the level for the VIX and divide it by 16 to get a rough estimate of what sort of daily move is expected in the stock market based on the level of the VIX. Remember, the denominator of the formula in Chapter 1 was the square root of 252 or about 15.87. The traders round this up to 16 to get their denominator. So the VIX at 16 would indicate S&P 500 index options are anticipating daily price movement of 1 percent (16/16). A VIX of 32 would be interpreted as the S&P 500 option market anticipating a daily price move of 2 percent (32/16).

The math behind this method is not exact, but this is a pretty good rule of thumb. In 2008 when the VIX was trading in the mid-60s, this may be taken as the option market expecting a daily price move of 4 percent. Using a more common stock market index, this translates to the Dow Jones Industrial Average (DJIA) at 10,000 points being expected to trade in a 400-point range on a daily basis. Four-hundred-point days in the DJIA usually result in the stock market getting more than just professional investor's attention during the day. Those sort of moves generally grab headlines.

EQUITY MARKET VOLATILITY INDEXES

In addition to an index based on S&P 500 volatility, the CBOE has developed a handful of other volatility measures based on other common stock market indexes. Table 2.7 is a list of indexes based on index volatility

TABLE 2.7 CBOE Equity Market Volatility Indexes

Index	Ticker	Underlying	Website
CBOE Volatility Index	VIX	SPX	www.cboe.com/vix
CBOE DJIA Volatility Index	VXD	DJX	www.cboe.com/vxd
CBOE NADSAQ-100 Volatility Index	VXN	NDX	www.cboe.com/vxn
CBOE Russell 2000 Volatility Index	RVX	RUT	www.cboe.com/rvx
CBOE S&P 100 Volatility Index	VXO	OEX	www.cboe.com/vxo
Amex QQQ Volatility Index	QQV	QQQ	www.nyse.com

Sources: www.cboe.com and www.nyse.com.

that the CBOE has developed. There are also some quotes and strategy-based and alternative-asset-based volatility indexes the CBOE has developed. Those indexes will be discussed in Chapter 7.

CBOE DJIA Volatility Index

The CBOE DJIA Volatility Index is calculated in a similar fashion as the VIX. Quotes for this index are disseminated using the symbol VXD. The index was created in 2005, and the index was introduced on March 18 of that year. The index indicates the market's expectation of 30-day implied volatility based on index option prices on the Dow Jones Industrial Average (DJX).

The DJX is one of the oldest stock indexes and is one of the most commonly quoted indicators of the overall stock market. Charles Dow, the publisher of the *Wall Street Journal*, created the index in order to bring more attention to his newspaper. The DJIA was first quoted on May 26, 1896. On days the stock market is open, at some point on the national news how the DJX did on the day will be mentioned. Some other common names for the DJX are the DJIA, Dow Jones, or just the Dow. For a person who pays little attention to the stock market or even for most investors, the Dow Jones Industrial Average is what they think of when they think of the stock market.

The DJX is composed of 30 stocks that represent a wide variety of industries and some of the largest companies in the United States. The stocks appear in Table 2.8. The small concentration of companies does take something away from the index being representative of the overall economy, but it continues to be the most commonly quoted index.

Note that although the index is referred to as an industrial index, a variety of industries are represented by the DJX. For example, Wal-Mart and Home Depot are major retailers, Pfizer is a pharmaceutical company,

TABLE 2.8 Members of the Dow Jones Industrial Average

Company	Symbol
Alcoa Inc.	AA
American Express Company	AXP
AT&T Corp.	T
Bank of America Corp.	BAC
Boeing Co.	BA
Caterpillar Inc.	CAT
Chevron Corp.	CVX
Cisco Systems	CSCO
Coca-Cola Co.	KO
E.I. Du Pont de Nemours	DD
Exxon Mobil Corp.	XOM
General Electric Company	GE
Hewlett-Packard Co.	HPQ
Home Depot Inc	HD
Intel Corp.	INTC
International Business Machines Corp.	IBM
Johnson & Johnson	JNJ
J. P. Morgan Chase Company	JPM
Kraft Foods Inc.	KFT
McDonald's Corp.	MCD
Merck & Co. Inc.	MRK
Microsoft Corp.	MSFT
Minnesota Mining & Mfg. Co.	MMM
Pfizer Inc.	PFE
Procter & Gamble Co.	PG
The Travelers Companies	TRV
United Technologies Corp.	UTX
Verizon Communications Inc.	VZ
Wal-Mart Stores Inc.	WMT
Walt Disney Co.	DIS

and The Travelers Companies specializes in financial services. The industry weightings for the DJX appear in Table 2.9.

The highest weighting of stocks in the DJX is represented by industrial companies, but only about a quarter of the performance of the index will be attributed to this market sector. A variety of other industries contribute to the DJX, which does result in an index that is representative of the overall economy in the United States. For instance, when consumer goods and services are combined, this area of the market represents about another quarter of the index's performance.

TABLE 2.9 Dow Jones Industrial Average Industry Weightings

Sector	Weighting
Basic materials	3.75%
Consumer goods	10.52%
Consumer services	13.24%
Financials	10.80%
Health care	7.78%
Industrials	22.46%
Oil and gas	9.83%
Technology	17.64%
Telecommunications	3.98%

Finally, the CFE does not currently trade futures based on the VXD. However, from April 2005 to the middle of 2009 futures contracts based on this index did trade at the exchange.

CBOE NASDAQ-100 Volatility Index

Using quotes for options that trade on the NASDAQ-100 Index (NDX), the CBOE NASDAQ-100 Volatility Index is an indication of implied volatility on the NASDAQ-100 index. Trading with the symbol VXN, the index displays 30-day implied volatility for the NDX.

The NASDAQ-100 is an index composed of the 100 largest companies not involved in the financial sector that trade on the NASDAQ. The NASDAQ marketplace opened in 1971 as an alternative exchange to the traditional floor-based exchanges like the New York Stock Exchange. In 1985 the NASDAQ developed two market indexes to promote their exchange, one of which is the NASDAQ-100.

Table 2.10 shows the industry sector weightings that comprise the NDX. What is unique regarding this market index is the lack of financial and health care stocks in the index. The result is a focus on other industries with a very large weighting in the technology sector. In fact, the index is dominated by technology- and communications-oriented stocks, which when combined make up almost 75 percent of the index. Also, the SPX has approximately a 20 percent weighting in the financial sector, which results in the NDX and SPX having disparate performance at times.

Futures were also traded on the VXN from 2007 to 2009. As this index may experience higher volatility than some other market indexes, the demand for a return of these contracts may result in them being relisted at some point.

TABLE 2.10 NASDAQ-100 Sector Weightings

Sector	Weighting
Basic materials	0.40%
Consumer cyclical	8.40%
Communications	24.40%
Consumer noncyclical	16.80%
Energy	0.50%
Industrial	3.10%
Technology	46.40%

CBOE Russell 2000 Volatility Index

The Russell 2000 Index is composed of the 2,000 smallest companies that are in the Russell 3000 Index. Although representing two-thirds of the companies in the Russell 3000, which is composed of 3,000 of the largest publicly traded companies in the United States, the Russell 2000 only represents about 8 percent of the market capitalization of the Russell 3000. The Russell 2000 index is composed of small-cap companies, which mostly focus on domestic markets. This index has a great niche as a representation of domestic economic trends in the United States.

Russell Investments also calculates the Russell 1000 index, which consists of the 1,000 largest companies in the Russell 3000. The top third of those companies represents 92 percent of the market capitalization of the Russell 3000.

The ticker symbol RUT represents option trading on the index and, like the previous volatility related indexes, the Russell 2000 Volatility Index (RVX) attempts to show what the market is pricing in 30-day implied volatility for the index. At times the Russell 1000, Russell 2000, and Russell 3000 names are not entirely accurate. When, due to an acquisition, merger, or dissolution, a company ceases to exist as it had in the past, it may be replaced by a new company in a market index. These Russell indexes are actually reconfigured once a year at the end of June, with the number of stocks in each index taken back to the proper number.

Also, there is a minimum capitalization level for a company to be a member of the Russell 1000. When the indexes are rebalanced, the number of stocks in the Russell 1000 and Russell 2000 is very close to their respective numbers, but it may not be equal to the expected number of stocks in each index. For instance, after the 2010 rebalance the Russell 1000 consisted of 988 stocks and the Russell 2000 consisted of 2,012 stocks. The total of the two indexes results in all the stocks that make up the Russell 3000. The Russell 3000 makes up 99 percent of the market capitalization of the U.S. stock market.

Between the index restructuring dates, companies that cease to exist will be deleted from the indexes, but no replacement will necessarily be put in their place. However, company spinoffs and initial public offerings may be added between the June reconstruction dates. Those stocks are added on a quarterly basis.

RVX futures traded at the CBOE from 2007 through early 2010.

CBOE S&P 100 Volatility Index

When the VIX was originally quoted by the CBOE, the calculation was based on the implied volatility of the S&P 100 Index (OEX), not the S&P 500. When the calculation was altered in 2003, it was done so with part of the revision resulting in a focus on the S&P 500 as opposed to the S&P 100 index.

The CBOE S&P 100 Volatility Index (VXO) is actually the original VIX index, which was created in 1993. It continues to be calculated using the original methodology based on OEX options. Introduced in 1983 by the CBOE, OEX was the first equity index option product. Originally the index name was the CBOE 100 Index. Loosely translated, OEX could mean Option Exchange 100. The OEX and options listed on the index were so innovative that entire books were written on trading OEX options.

The OEX represents 100 of the largest companies in the United States. This results in the combined components of the OEX being close to 45 percent of the total market capitalization of publicly traded stocks in the United States. Also, almost 60 percent of the S&P 500 market capitalization is represented by the 100 stocks in the OEX.

Even with just 100 names, the OEX is a diversified index with all industry sectors being covered. Table 2.11 is a summary of the industry

TABLE 2.11 S&P 100 Index Industry Weightings

Industry	Weighting
Consumer discretionary	6.25%
Consumer staples	15.32%
Energy	15.86%
Financials	11.06%
Health Care	15.40%
Industrials	10.59%
Information technology	17.35%
Materials	1.03%
Telecom services	5.30%
Utilities	1.86%

weightings of the OEX. Note the industry weightings of the OEX are as diversified as the S&P 500 even though there are fewer stocks in the index.

Amex QQQ Volatility Index

The Amex QQQ Volatility index is another measure of implied volatility of the Nadsaq market. The method behind this index is similar to the original volatility index calculation used for the VXO. The index indicates the forward-looking volatility for the QQQ based on option prices. To get a true option contract value, the midpoint of the bid-ask spread is used as the option price input for the calculation.

The CBOE and CFE currently trade options and futures only on the VIX index. However, these alternate VIX indexes may be used to gain insight into market activity. The VIX and other index-related volatility indexes are excellent representations of what sort of near-term volatility is expected from the overall stock market according to the implied volatility of index options. Each of the indexes that have VIX representation have slightly different components and may indicate that there is higher expected volatility in one sector as opposed to others.

Before we tackle strategies, there are a few chapters dedicated to the derivatives that trade on volatility. These instruments are introduced in Chapter 3. In Chapter 4, options on the VIX index, which started trading at the CBOE in 2006, will be introduced. In late 2010, weekly options that settle in a position in a VIX futures contract began trading on the CFE. These VIX options are discussed in Chapter 5. Finally, in 2009 trading of exchange-traded notes (ETNs) based on the VIX began. These ETNs will be discussed in Chapter 6.

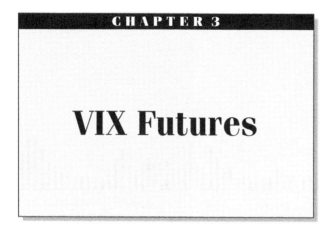

CHAPTER 3

VIX Futures

A fter 2003, when the method used to determine the VIX index was updated, the next step was to introduce products that traded directly on the level of the VIX. On March 26, 2004, the CBOE Futures Exchange began trading futures contracts based on the VIX index. The CBOE Futures Exchange was established for the purpose of trading futures contracts based on the VIX as well as other volatility-related indexes. The VIX futures contracts were quickly recognized through winning the Most Innovative Index Derivative Award at the Super Bowl of Indexing Conference in December 2004.

This chapter will highlight the growth of VIX futures contracts as a trading and hedging vehicle. Then the specifications of these futures contracts will be discussed. Both the VIX and Mini-VIX futures will be discussed along with the settlement process behind VIX futures contracts. Finally, the relationship of VIX futures to the VIX index and the relationship of VIX futures contracts with different expiration dates will be covered.

STEADY GROWTH OF NEW PRODUCTS

Since 2004, the CBOE Futures Exchange has seen steady growth in trading on VIX futures contracts. This growth has been the result of acceptance of volatility as a trading vehicle and asset class by a wide variety of market participants.

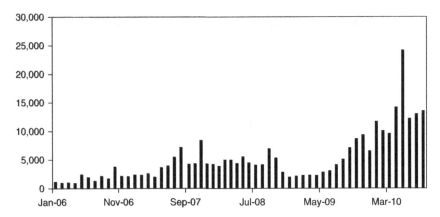

FIGURE 3.1   VIX Futures Average Daily Volume, January 2006–August 2010

Figure 3.1 depicts the average daily volume on a monthly basis for the
VIX futures arena. In the months leading up to September 2010, the volume
started increasing dramatically. In May 2010, a month that experienced
significant market volatility due to what was termed the "flash crash" on
May 6, average daily volume came in at well over 20,000 contracts.

Volume increases in times like May 2010 occur when some sort of market event results in increases in market volatility. Even in lower-volatility
periods, there has been steady growth in VIX futures trading volume. This
growth accompanies the increased acceptance of the VIX futures by the
marketplace. Currently, average daily volume for VIX futures contracts is
equivalent to futures markets that have been around for decades. Unlike
the majority of futures markets, which are open almost 24 hours a day, the
VIX futures are open only on business days from 7:20 A.M. to 3:15 P.M. central time. Therefore, the volume that is being traded is being executed in a
smaller time frame than most futures markets.

Open interest for VIX futures grew quickly, reaching almost 80,000 contracts in the fall of 2007 (Figure 3.2). As market volatility began to decrease
after this peak, the open interest fell over several months, bottoming out in
March 2009. Interestingly, March 2009 was also a period when the overall
stock market tested and held the low levels put in during the fourth quarter
of 2008. After testing support, the market began an uptrend that surprised
many analysts. Although this market uptrend dampened volatility, VIX futures did see a steady increase in open interest. Following this bottoming
out, a new wave of opening contracts and increased volume pushed the
open interest to record highs in May 2010, which coincided with a period
of high volatility. Finally, in August 2010 the open interest for VIX futures

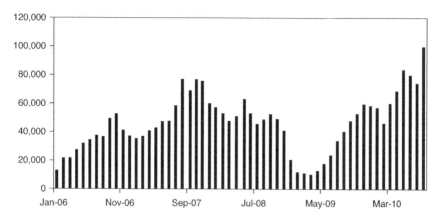

FIGURE 3.2 VIX Futures Average Open Interest, January 2006–Aug 2010

was just shy of 100,000 contracts, in a month where the market did not experience much volatility.

CONTRACT SPECIFICATIONS

Like the VIX calculation, the contract specifications for the VIX futures underwent a change after introduction. In 2007, the contract took on its current form. The most major change was that the value of the contract was divided by 10, so a VIX futures quote of 150 under the old methodology would be comparable to a corrected quote of 15. To avoid confusion, only current contract specs will be discussed here. However, if you're interested in further changes, visit www.cboe.com/vix. Any reference to historical VIX trading that occurred before the contract adjustment will automatically be altered for the new format.

VIX futures contracts can be listed for up to nine consecutive months. As of this writing, the number of contracts listed had expanded from seven consecutive monthly expirations to eight. VIX futures expire on the Wednesday that is 30 days before the following month's standard option expiration date. Standard option expiration is the third Saturday following the third Friday of the month. Backing up 30 days will land on a Wednesday.

Again, standard option contracts expire on the Saturday following the third Friday of the month. For example, December 2010 standard option expiration was December 18, 2010. November VIX futures contracts expire on Wednesday November 17, 2010. VIX futures contracts are settled in cash based on a special VIX calculation that is determined through opening option prices on expiration Wednesday. This pricing is based on a process known as AM settlement, which will be discussed in the next section. AM refers to the settlement price being based on the market opening the follow day which occurs in the morning or in the AM. Conversely, PM settlement is based on afternoon closing prices.

Why the "Third Saturday Following the Third Friday"?

A common question regarding standard option expiration is, "Why do standard option contracts expire on the third Saturday following the third Friday?" First, Saturday expiration was selected to allow firms and the Option Clearing Corporation to handle the paperwork involved in exercised and assignment of open option contracts. As far as the third week goes, this week was chosen because it is least likely to have a market holiday during the week. The only market holiday that may fall during this week is Good Friday, which has been a market holiday since 1908. Good Friday last fell in expiration week in 2008 and is due to happen again in 2014.

The symbol for a VIX futures contract consists of the letters VX, a letter signifying the expiration month, and then a number to indicate the expiration year. This is a common method for identifying futures contracts. Table 3.1 summarizes the standard letters to indicate an expiration month for futures contracts.

For example, the August 2010 VIX future would have the symbol VXQ10. The VX indicates this is a VIX futures contract. Q is the letter

TABLE 3.1 Months and Corresponding Futures Symbol Letters

Month	Symbol
January	F
February	G
March	H
April	J
May	K
June	M
July	N
August	Q
September	U
October	V
November	X
December	Z

symbol for an August expiration. 10 signifies that this is the contract that expires in August 2010. This is a standard description of the method to determine VIX futures. It is possible that different quote systems may have a small deviation to this.

The Logic behind Monthly Future Symbols

The letters that indicate the expiration month for futures contracts may appear to be a bit illogical, but there was some thought behind this method. January uses the letter F, which stands for the first month of the year. The letters continue in order, with letters that may be misconstrued as numbers being excluded. Keep in mind, this method was developed when all orders were handwritten. Letters such as I, L, O, and W could be read as a 1, 1, 0, or sideways 3. December rounds out the list with a corresponding letter of Z. Z is the last letter of the alphabet and matches up with the last month of the year.

Until recent trading hours for VIX futures contracts coincide with the trading hours in the S&P 500 index options pit. Using Chicago time, VIX futures contracts are open from 7:20 A.M. to 3:15 P.M. central time Monday through Friday. The VIX index is based on S&P 500 index options; those products trade from 8:30 A.M. to 3:15 P.M. Chicago time. So for that first hour and ten minutes the futures prices are based on the anticipation of where the VIX price will be when the S&P 500 index option market opens. This is the current trading time for the VIX futures and S&P 500 index options, but with 24-hour trading in many markets, this could eventually change.

The value of a VIX futures contract is determined by multiplying $1,000 times the level of the index. If the November 2010 contract is trading at 25.00, then the value of the contract would be $25,000. The result is that each one-point move in the contract is a gain or loss of $1,000. The minimum price move of a VIX futures contract is .05, which translates into a minimum dollar move of $50 up or down.

VIX futures are cash settled based on this final settlement price. Long positions and short positions are settled through a cash transfer from the position holders based on the value of the contract. Cash settlement is common among many financial futures contracts, specifically contracts that track indexes. In the case of VIX futures, the result is a cash amount based on the settlement value determined for the specific contract. For example, if a VIX futures contract has a settlement value of 25.00, then the value is $25,000.

What Is Cash Settlement?

Many traditional futures contracts are settled in the underlying product. Corn futures contracts that trade at the Chicago Mercantile Exchange are settled through physical delivery of 5,000 bushels of corn. This is normally avoided through closing out contracts before delivery. Cash settlement is a substitute for this process that is applied mostly to financial futures contracts. In 1981, cash settlement was introduced with eurodollar futures contracts.

The final settlement value for the VIX futures is determined through what is known as AM settlement. AM settlement is applied to a variety of index-related derivatives including S&P 500 index futures and options. Using AM settlement, the final value for VIX futures is determined by a special opening quotation (SOQ) process that occurs the day after trading ceases for the contracts. The process involves using the opening prices of relevant S&P 500 index option contracts as opposed to the midpoint of the bid ask for each of these contracts. If there is no opening price, then the midpoint of the bid-ask spread will be used to determine what prices are used to determine an opening price to use in the formula. These prices are then used to calculate a VIX level that is used to settle contracts.

VIX futures contracts trade through the market close on Tuesday and then have settlement determined on Wednesday morning. The process to determine the actual VIX settlement price usually is finalized midmorning on this Wednesday. Once the value has been determined, it is disseminated using the symbol VRO. Most quote services and brokerage firms use this symbol to disseminate the final VIX settlement level.

There is an inverse relationship between the direction of the S&P 500 and movement in the VIX index. Due to this relationship, a large overnight move in the stock market, as depicted by S&P 500 futures contracts, can result in a significant change in the VIX from the previous close. This type of market activity could also have an impact on the VIX settlement process. In the past there have been some cases where the VIX index and VIX futures closes the Tuesday before settlement have been quite different than the eventual VIX settlement price. The next few tables summarize the VIX index and futures closing prices on the Tuesday before AM settlement and the settlement price for the VIX on the following open from January 2007 through September 2010. Table 3.2 shows VIX settlement activity for 2007.

In 2007 the VIX was trading at what would be considered very low levels relative to much higher volatility results from 2008 and 2009. However, the issues of some sort of large overnight stock market move impacting the

TABLE 3.2 2007 VIX Settlement Data

	VIX Settlement	Index Close	Index vs. Settlement	Future Close	Future vs. Settlement
Jan-07	10.71	10.74	0.03	10.59	−0.12
Feb-07	9.95	10.34	0.39	10.43	0.48
Mar-07	12.98	13.27	0.29	13.06	0.08
Apr-07	12.03	12.14	0.11	11.87	−0.16
May-07	13.63	14.01	0.38	13.96	0.33
Jun-07	13.01	12.85	−0.16	12.88	−0.13
Jul-07	16.87	15.63	−1.24	15.57	−1.30
Aug-07	25.05	25.25	0.20	25.24	0.19
Sep-07	20.29	20.35	0.06	20.18	−0.11
Oct-07	18.33	20.02	1.69	20.03	1.70
Nov-07	26.70	24.88	−1.82	25.08	−1.62
Dec-07	22.08	22.64	0.56	22.55	0.47

settlement of VIX derivatives did exist. A couple of times a bearish move in the stock market caused a spike in the VIX, which resulted in a higher VIX settlement level relative to the previous close for both the futures and index.

Specifically, July 2007 and November 2007 VIX settlements resulted in a different bullish outcome relative to where the VIX closed the night before. The Tuesday closing prices for July 2007 settlement were the VIX index at 15.63 and the VIX futures at 15.57. The following day the final settlement level for the July 2007 VIX was 16.87. This was a difference of 1.24 higher than the index close and 1.30 higher than the futures close. On a percentage basis, this resulted in the settlement for the VIX contracts being around 8 percent higher than the previous close of either the VIX index or the VIX futures.

Also, November 2007 settlement resulted in the VIX settlement being much higher than the previous closing price for both the index and the futures contracts. Settlement came in at 26.70 while the index had gone out at 24.88 and the futures closed at 25.08 the previous day. This settlement was a difference of 1.82 higher than the index close and 1.62 higher than the futures close. On a percentage basis, this is a 7 percent move higher relative to the index close and around a 6 percent move higher than the futures contract close.

Remember, when the stock market moves higher overnight, the VIX may actually experience a drop relative to the previous closing prices. A good example of this occurred in October 2007. October 2007 VIX settlement was 18.33. The index closed at 20.02 and the futures contracts closed at 20.03 the previous evening. The resulting settlement was lower by 1.69

TABLE 3.3   2008 VIX Settlement Data

	VIX Settlement	Index Close	Index vs. Settlement	Future Close	Future vs. Settlement
Jan-08	24.18	23.34	−0.84	24.04	−0.14
Feb-08	25.51	25.02	−0.49	26.07	0.56
Mar-08	25.67	25.79	0.12	25.95	0.28
Apr-08	21.78	22.78	1.00	22.87	1.09
May-08	17.16	17.58	0.42	17.37	0.21
Jun-08	21.54	21.13	−0.41	21.05	−0.49
Jul-08	28.40	28.54	0.14	28.43	0.03
Aug-08	20.83	21.28	0.45	21.00	0.17
Sep-08	31.54	30.30	−1.24	29.68	−1.86
Oct-08	63.04	53.11	−9.93	52.80	−10.24
Nov-08	67.22	67.64	0.42	67.04	−0.18
Dec-08	51.29	52.37	1.08	52.44	1.15

than the index and 1.70 than the futures or about an 8.5 percent move relative to both. Table 3.3 shows VIX settlement during 2008.

The kind of market volatility witnessed in 2008 had not been experienced in decades. The result was a move for stock market volatility to levels that would have been considered impossible just a year earlier.

In 2008 the most dramatic case of an overnight difference between the close of the VIX index and VIX futures and the eventual settlement price occurred with October VIX settlement. The day before AM settlement, the VIX index closed at 53.11 and the October futures contracts closed at 52.80. As a result of a big down move in the U.S. stock market, the VIX settlement came in dramatically higher the following day. The settlement price of 63.04 was 9.93 higher than the index close and 10.24 higher than the futures contract closing price. This is a change of 18 percent relative to the index and more than 19 percent higher than the futures close. Table 3.4 shows VIX settlement during 2009.

At the beginning of 2009, there was a carryover of the market activity that emerged in the second half of 2008. In 2009 there were also a couple of surprises related to the settlement of VIX contracts. January brought an instance in which the VIX index and future were both significantly higher than the settlement level that was determined by opening S&P 500 index option prices the following day. Due to a big rally in the underlying stock market, the VIX settlement was sharply lower than where the index and futures closed the previous day.

The index went out at 56.65 and the futures closed at 57.90. Settlement, based on the S&P 500 index option opening prices, came in at 49.88. This

TABLE 3.4 2009 VIX Settlement Data

	VIX Settlement	Index Close	Index vs. Settlement	Future Close	Future vs. Settlement
Jan-09	49.88	56.65	6.77	57.90	8.02
Feb-09	48.40	48.66	0.26	48.00	−0.40
Mar-09	40.62	40.80	0.18	40.05	−0.57
Apr-09	38.20	37.67	−0.53	37.85	−0.35
May-09	27.04	28.80	1.76	28.50	1.46
Jun-09	31.03	32.68	1.65	31.85	0.82
Jul-09	23.48	23.87	0.39	24.05	0.57
Aug-09	28.76	26.18	−2.58	26.35	−2.41
Sep-09	23.64	23.42	−0.22	23.50	−0.14
Oct-09	20.82	20.90	0.08	21.10	0.28
Nov-09	22.54	22.41	−0.13	22.55	0.01
Dec-09	20.84	21.50	0.66	21.35	0.51

was 6.77 lower than the index close and 8.02 lower than the final future price. On a percentage basis, this was a drop of about 12 percent relative to the index and almost 14 percent relative to the futures contracts.

In August the opposite situation occurred. It was not as dramatic on a point basis, but it was still comparable to the magnitude of the January settlement difference on a percentage basis. On a point basis, the VIX had returned to more moderate levels as the stock market experienced a nice uptrend in the spring and summer of 2009.

The August VIX settlement was 28.76, with the index closing at 26.18 and the futures closing at 26.35 the previous day. The index close was 2.58 or about 10 percent lower than the settlement price. The futures close was also about 10 percent lower than the settlement price going out at 26.35. The final table that shows VIX settlement activity is Table 3.5, which depicts what occurred in 2010.

The year 2010 was a relatively tame time period for VIX settlement prices relative to where the index and futures closed the evening before. January, on a percentage basis, was similar to some of the other surprises that occurred in the past, but for the most part this was a relatively calm period.

Again, if a futures contract is held through expiration, the cash settlement is based on the special opening quotation (SOQ) that is determined by opening S&P 500 index option prices. A couple of examples of how this works in the cases of big differences between the closing prices for the VIX and the VIX settlement prices follow.

TABLE 3.5 2010 VIX Settlement Data

	VIX Settlement	Index Close	Index vs. Settlement	Future Close	Future vs. Settlement
Jan-10	18.87	17.58	−1.29	17.85	−1.02
Feb-10	22.50	22.25	−0.25	22.60	0.10
Mar-10	16.68	17.69	1.01	17.45	0.77
Apr-10	15.80	15.73	−0.07	16.00	0.20
May-10	34.53	33.55	−0.98	32.70	−1.83
Jun-10	26.11	25.87	−0.24	25.85	−0.26
Jul-10	23.79	23.93	0.14	24.40	0.61
Aug-10	24.82	24.33	−0.49	24.35	−0.47
Sep-10	22.97	21.56	−1.41	21.70	−1.27
Oct-10	21.41	20.63	−0.78	20.95	−0.46
Nov-10	22.21	22.58	0.37	22.25	0.04
Dec-10	16.01	16.49	0.48	16.75	0.74

Using the VIX settlement situation from January 2009, the settlement value of the January VIX futures contract was 49.88 or on a dollar basis $49,880. The previous closing price for the January VIX futures contract was 57.90, which is a dollar value of $57,900. So a financial instrument that was valued at $57,900 based on a closing price was worth $49,880 when cash settled the following day. This sort of result would be a windfall for a short position holder and an unpleasant experience for a long contract holder.

Figure 3.3 depicts the price action of the January 2009 futures contract in the final few weeks until expiration. The final date on the chart is January 21, 2009, which is the settlement date of the contract. The small tick at the

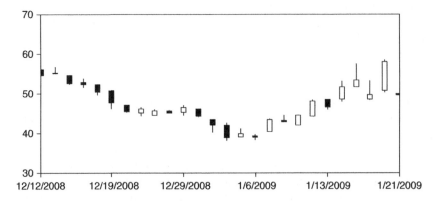

FIGURE 3.3 January 2009 VIX Future Trading into Settlement

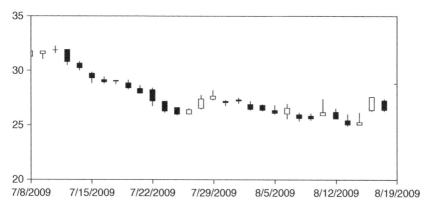

FIGURE 3.4 August 2009 VIX Future Trading into Settlement

right of the chart shows the settlement price level. In the final three days of trading leading up to settlement the majority of the price action appears to occur above the settlement level. The final day of trading actually had a low price of 50.30. This means 100 percent of the price action the day before settlement occurred above the final settlement price of 49.88.

The opposite situation occurred in August 2009, when the VIX settlement was 28.76 while the futures contract closed at 26.35 the day before. Again, that means the settlement value for a contract that was worth $26,350 on the close resulted in a value of $28,760. In this case, a nice surprise occurred for the long contract holder while a short position realized a negative impact of $2,410 per contract.

Figure 3.4 is a chart showing several weeks' trading leading up to August settlement on August 19, 2009. Although not as dramatic a difference between the last day of trading and the January settlement, August 2009 is an interesting case. Note that on the far right of the chart, the final settlement price for this contract is much higher than the previous closing price.

The last time the August 2009 VIX futures contract traded above the settlement value of 28.76 was almost a month before settlement on July 20, 2009. This is an interesting outcome, as any short position held through expiration that was initiated after July 20 would have been a losing trade. This would not be the case using the final trading price on August 18 of 26.35, but is the case when cash settlement was determined Wednesday morning.

The lesson behind the changes of the AM settlement level for the VIX relative to the previous closing prices is this. If a trader wants some sort of certainty as to their profit or loss on a VIX trade, the best course of action would be to close out the trade and not take the risk of some sort of market movement that results in a different (hopefully favorable) outcome to the trade.

MINI-VIX FUTURES

On March 2, 2009, the CBOE Futures Exchange introduced trading in CBOE Mini-VIX futures contracts. The symbol for these contracts is VM, as opposed to VX for the VIX futures. These contracts are also based on the VIX, but have different contract specifications than the standard VIX futures contracts.

Each point for the Mini-VIX futures represents $100, as opposed to $1,000 for the standard contract. The result is the contract specifications for the Mini-VIX futures are one-tenth of the standard contract. Like the big VIX futures contracts, the minimum price tick change is 0.05, but each tick change represents $5 gain or loss instead of $50.

The base symbol for the Mini-VIX futures contracts is VM and the contracts use the same standard symbols for expiration months as the full-size VIX futures contracts. Using the monthly futures symbols from Table 3.1 in this chapter, an August 2010 Mini-VIX contract would be quoted with the symbol VMQ10. The components break out to VM for the contract, Q representing August expiration, and 10 representing the year 2010.

Another difference between the VIX futures and Mini-VIX futures is the number of expiration months trading. The VIX futures have contracts expiring for the next eight consecutive months, while the Mini-VIX futures have contracts that expire for only the next three months. So if today were August 1, 2010, then August, September, and October Mini-VIX futures contracts would be available for trading.

The settlement process for the Mini-VIX futures is exactly the same as the VIX futures. This involves AM settlement with a special opening quotation formula determining the settlement price. The issue discussed in the previous section with there being a difference between the final trading price for the mini-VIX futures relative to the eventual settlement price is determined by the SOQ. Be aware that the potential overnight risk issue that exists for the full-size VIX contract is the same for the Mini-VIX future.

PRICING RELATIONSHIP BETWEEN VIX FUTURES AND THE INDEX

An interesting aspect regarding the VIX futures contracts is the pricing relationship to the VIX index. As VIX futures settle based on where the VIX is upon expiration, a VIX futures trade is placed with the anticipation of where the VIX index will be on expiration. Additionally, a shorter-term trade would be based on what direction the trader felt the index was going to move, but this trade would also be based on where the VIX futures are trading relative to the index.

Trading in VIX futures is a bit different than many financially oriented futures contracts. For instance, when the stock market is open, the S&P 500 futures contracts trade in a range that is related to the underlying S&P 500 index. This is referred to as the fair value of S&P 500 futures related to the underlying index. This fair value exists due to arbitrage situations that may arise if the S&P 500 futures become mispriced relative to the S&P 500 index.

The mechanics behind this arbitrage exist due to the ability to buy or sell the S&P 500 index in the form of a basket of stocks that would replicate the performance of the S&P 500. Then an offsetting position opposite of the position in the basket of stocks would be entered in S&P 500 futures contracts. At expiration, the S&P 500 futures and index prices are expected to converge. Through having a long position in an instrument and a short position in another instrument that are expected to have the same value at expiration, the arbitrage opportunity in S&P 500 stocks and futures exists.

For example, the S&P 500 index is trading at 1,100 and the S&P 500 futures contracts are being quoted at 1,125. If a basket of stocks that replicate the S&P 500 are purchased and simultaneously the S&P 500 futures are sold in equal dollar amounts, a profit of 25 points is locked in. At expiration the two values should converge for this profit. Due to this relationship and the trading that occurs to attempt to take advantage of this, the S&P 500 futures contracts tend to trade around the underlying index within a defined range.

With respect to VIX futures, there is no underlying basket of securities that may replicate owning the VIX index. Since there is no underlying basket of securities that may be used to replicate the VIX index, no relationship exists that holds the VIX futures in a fair value range around the VIX index based on arbitrage trades.

The VIX futures trade in anticipation of the future price of the VIX index and at times may trade at premium to the index and at times may trade at a discount to the index. This relationship is a bit unusual for financial futures and may be a reason some traders shy away from trading VIX futures. Figure 3.5 shows the relationship between the VIX futures contracts and the VIX index.

This chart depicts the final few closing prices of the November 2009 VIX futures contract relative to the VIX index. The solid line represents the index, while the dashed line is the November futures contract. Note at the beginning of the chart the futures contracts close at a premium to the underlying index. Then after a move higher from the index, the futures are

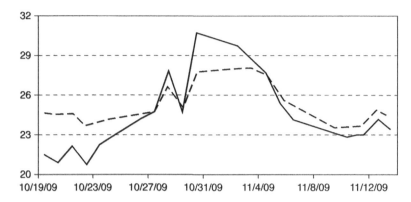

FIGURE 3.5 VIX Futures versus VIX Index

now at a discount to the index. As expiration approaches, the futures and index start to stay in a very close range.

It is possible over the course of hours for the VIX futures contracts to trade both above and below the VIX index. The chart in Figure 3.6 shows just this.

This chart is a five-minute chart of the VIX index and the June 2010 VIX futures contract on May 26, 2010. Again, the dashed line represents the futures contract while the solid line represents the index. Due to high volatility in the S&P 500 index on this day, the VIX index climbed from just over 31 to slightly over 35. The futures rose, but not nearly as much as the underlying index. Through the middle of the morning, the index was at a discount to the futures, but starting around 10:30 A.M. Chicago time and for the remainder of the day the index traded at a premium.

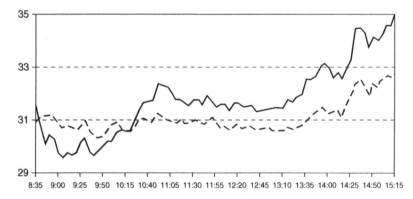

FIGURE 3.6 Intraday VIX Futures versus VIX Index

TABLE 3.6 Percent Days That VIX Futures Are at a Premium to VIX Index

	First Month Greater Than Index	Second Month Greater Than Index	Third Month Greater Than Index	Fourth Month Greater Than Index
2007	65.74%	70.92%	70.92%	69.32%
2008	56.13%	55.34%	51.38%	48.22%
2009	79.37%	79.37%	72.62%	70.63%
2010	77.25%	82.63%	86.23%	86.23%
Total	**68.91%**	**71.07%**	**68.80%**	**66.96%**

Historically the VIX futures contracts have been at a premium to the VIX index more often than at a discount. Using closing prices from January 1, 2007, through August 31, 2010, closing prices for the first four expiration months were compared to the closing price for the VIX index. The results appear in Table 3.6.

The table shows the percentage of days that the first- through fourth-month contracts close at a premium to the VIX index. For instance, if a VIX futures contract closes at 31.00 and the VIX index closes at 30.00, then the futures are at a 1-point premium to the index. Each year that contributes to the overall data, 2007–2010, are also broken out. The data for 2010 were compiled for only the first eight months of the year. Also, although VIX futures have been trading since 2004, 2007 data are used as the starting point for contract availability and liquidity reasons.

The contract representing the first month is the nearest expiring VIX futures contract. This contract is rolled into the next contract on the close of the last Friday the contract is trading before expiration. Then the following month becomes the first month. For example, the March 2009 contract would be the first month until the Friday before March VIX expiration and then the April 2009 contract would become the first month.

The year 2008 was an interesting one for the equity markets due to a variety of factors. The results of this study for that year are interesting. The closing of VIX futures relative to the VIX index was at a discount much more often than in any of the other three years in the study. In fact, the fourth month in 2008 closed at a discount more often than at a premium to the index. This can be attributed to the very high level of the underlying index during a good part of 2008.

The other years in this table have results that are consistent with a more normal market environment. That is the expectation of higher implied volatility in the future. This expectation is shown by the futures contracts being at a premium to the index a majority of trading days.

FUTURES' RELATIONSHIP TO EACH OTHER

As VIX futures contracts may trade at a premium or discount to the underlying VIX index, VIX futures will also trade at a premium or discount to each other at times. This premium or discount represents the market's outlook for volatility over different time periods. Table 3.7 compares the second-, third-, and fourth-month expirations to the closing prices of the first month.

The table uses the same method as Table 3.6. The difference is this is a comparison of the second, third, and fourth months to the first-month closing price. Note the results are similar to the table comparing the futures to the spot index. This year, 2008, is an outlier, with the more distant expiration months closing at a discount more often than closing at a premium to the first-month futures contract.

For instance, if today were July 1, 2010, there would be contracts with expirations for July 2010 through January 2011 trading. If there is an expectation that the stock market will experience increased volatility in the September-to-November period, the VIX futures expiring in this time period may be trading at a significant premium to the July and August contracts.

Conversely, if today were March 1, 2011, there would be contracts with expirations for March 2011 through the fall of 2011 trading. If the market expects lower volatility in the summer of 2011, then the July 2011 contract may be trading lower than the March, April, and May contracts.

A variety of factors can contribute to the pricing differences between different VIX futures contracts, and trades may be placed based on an outlook for market volatility over certain periods. Trading the price difference

TABLE 3.7   Percent Days That VIX Future Are at a Premium to VIX First-Month Future

Year	Second Month Greater Than First Month	Third Month Greater Than First Month	Fourth Month Greater Than First Month
2007	68.53%	66.53%	65.34%
2008	49.80%	43.87%	39.92%
2009	69.84%	66.67%	65.48%
2010	90.42%	90.42%	92.22%
Total	67.71%	64.68%	63.27%

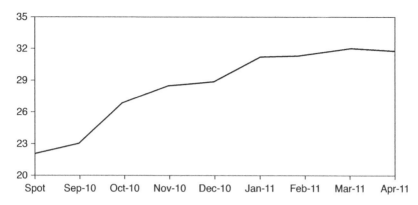

FIGURE 3.7 VIX Futures Closing Prices

between various VIX futures expirations will be discussed further in Chapter 12.

Another way to approach this is comparing VIX future prices to a yield curve. The VIX futures will coincide with what is referred to as the *term structure of volatility*. Figure 3.7 is an example of how volatility expectations based on futures closing prices may be shown.

In this chart the VIX is steadily higher from expiration to expiration indicating the market expects higher volatility in the stock market. Utilizing the term structure of VIX futures may also result in an indicator for the overall future direction of the stock market which will be discussed in Chapter 9.

VIX FUTURES DATA

The data used to create all the daily charts in this chapter came directly from the CBOE's web site. All closing data for VIX futures are available for download from the CBOE Futures Exchange's web site. The data can easily be downloaded into Microsoft Excel or Access for analysis. For each day that a futures contract traded, the Open, High, Low, Close, Settlement, Volume, and Open Interest are available. This data are available for all futures contracts (not just the VIX) that trade at the CFE. All closing data can be found at www.cfe.cboe.com/Data/HistoricalData.aspx. Also, all settlement values for VIX futures and options may be found on the CBOE website at www.cfe.cboe.com/Data/Settlement.aspx.

CHAPTER 4

VIX Options

A t this point, you should have a solid understanding of the VIX futures markets. VIX option prices are directly related to the corresponding VIX futures contracts. If you have a strong interest in VIX options and skipped directly to this chapter without reading Chapter 3, please back up a few pages. There are some important characteristics that the VIX futures and VIX options share—specifically, anticipatory pricing and the settlement process for each. A solid understanding of the information in Chapter 3 is essential before moving forward with this chapter.

Index options based on the CBOE Volatility Index were introduced on February 24, 2006. Less than a year later, the Super Bowl of Indexing Conference named VIX index options the most Innovative Index Derivative Product of 2006. The introduction of VIX options came about two years after VIX futures started trading at the CFE, but their popularity, based on volume, has surpassed the futures contracts. Institutions have found that at times VIX options offer the ability to hedge an equity portfolio better than other index option products, even products that directly trade based on a portfolio's benchmark index. This use of VIX options as a cheap hedging vehicle has led to the quick growth in trading volume.

As mentioned, acceptance of VIX options by traders, investors, and portfolio managers as a trading and hedging vehicle has caught on quickly over the course of just four years. Figure 4.1 displays the open interest of VIX index options at the end of each month since inception to August 2010. Note the tremendous growth in the open interest, which topped 3.5 million contracts at the end of May 2010.

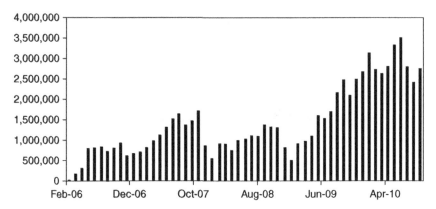

FIGURE 4.1 VIX Options Monthly Open Interest

Some of the peaks and valleys that have occurred in open interest for VIX options have coincided with increases and decreases in market volatility. For instance, the peak in May 2010 coincided with a dramatic increase in stock market uncertainty that resulted from the flash crash on May 6, 2010. Increased trading in VIX options often coincides with uncertainty regarding the stock market. At that time, the financial community was definitely uncertain of what was going on in early May 2010.

The Flash Crash of 2010

On May 6, 2010, with just over an hour left in the trading day, the Dow Jones Industrial Average quickly dropped 600 points. The market had been under pressure most of the day, with the DJIA already down 400 points at the time of the "event."

Due to a variety of factors, the market witnessed the largest point swing in history that day. Months later the exact reasons behind the drop have not been fully determined, but the exchanges have taken steps to attempt to ensure that there is not a repeat of the volatility seen that day.

Figure 4.2 shows the average daily volume by month of VIX options traded at the CBOE from inception to August 2010. Starting from a nonexistent product, the average daily volume in May 2010 surpassed 300,000 contracts a day. This has resulted in the VIX index option series being the second most actively traded index option series at the CBOE. This volume total trails only the S&P 500 index option series. The number varies on a monthly basis, but typically VIX option trading accounts for about

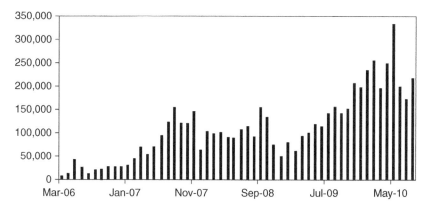

FIGURE 4.2 VIX Options Average Daily Volume by Month

25 percent of the daily index option trading at the CBOE, while SPX options account for about 50 percent of index trading volume.

The high open interest and growth in volume for VIX options is a direct result of the ability to use VIX options for hedging and speculating on the direction of the overall stock market. As more institutional investors become knowledgeable and comfortable with volatility as an asset class, this growth is certain to continue. There are several studies relating to using VIX futures and options in hedging programs, a few of which are discussed in Chapter 11.

Note that VIX option volume on a contract basis is much higher than the volume depicted for the VIX futures contracts that was displayed in the previous chapter. For instance, average VIX futures volume in May 2010 was about 24,000 contracts, while the average VIX option volume was over 300,000 contracts. However a direct comparison does not tell the whole story. Remember, a VIX futures contract represents $1,000 times the level of the VIX index. A single VIX option contract represents $100 times the VIX index. Therefore the relationship between the two is 10 to 1.

CONTRACT SPECIFICATIONS

The expiration date for VIX options is determined in the same manner as expiration for the VIX futures contracts. The options expire the morning of the Wednesday that is 30 days before the following month's standard equity option expiration Friday. An option expiration calendar that includes expiration dates for all option products including VIX options may be found at www.cboe.com/TradTool/ExpirationCalendar.aspx.

TABLE 4.1 Option Expiration Cycles	
Cycle	**Expiration Months**
January	January, April, July, October
February	February, May, August, November
March	March, June, September, December

VIX index options trade the next three expiration months. In addition, there are usually three more expiration months based on what is referred to as the February expiration cycle. The February cycle refers to having options that expire in February, May, August, and November. Equity options are on a cycle that involves starting with January, February, or March and always having expiration in three-month intervals based on the first month. The naming of the cycle is based on which month occurs first in the year for the respective cycle. Table 4.1 summarizes the three expiration cycles.

As mentioned toward the end of the previous section, the multiplier for a VIX option contract is 100, so a VIX option contract represents 100 times the quoted price of the option. This is the same price conversion as a standard equity option contract. The VIX futures contracts have a multiplier of 1,000, so remember that a VIX option contract actually represents 1/10th the value of a VIX futures contract.

VIX options are cash-settled instruments. The settlement for an in the money option will result in a cash transfer between the short position holder and the long position holder in the option. For instance, if a VIX 30 Call is open at settlement and the VIX settlement price is 31.00, the option is 1.00 in the money. This results in a $100 transfer from the holder of a short position in this option to the holder of a long position.

The settlement price for VIX options is determined using the SOQ discussed in the previous chapter. There are also the same issues that arise holding a VIX futures position until AM settlement for VIX options. However, the approach a trader may take leading up to expiration may be different with the options than with the futures contracts. VIX options are European-style options, which may be exercised only at expiration.

A VIX option contract value can change tremendously based on an overnight move in the stock market that impacts the final VIX settlement level. In what may be a positive case for an option holder, an option can change from being out of the money to in the money based on the difference between the AM settlement price and the VIX index closing price the previous day. The profit or loss associated with an option position may change based on a difference between the closing price of the VIX index on the Tuesday before settlement and the final VIX settlement level that results on Wednesday morning.

TABLE 4.2 October 2008 VIX Settlement Data

	VIX Settlement	Index Close	Index Settlement	Future Close	Future Settlement
Oct-08	63.04	53.11	−9.93	52.80	−10.24

This potential change in option value is a double-edged sword, as a move in the markets may also cause an option that has some intrinsic value based on the index and futures close to being out of the money based on a price move. A large overnight move in the markets could actually cause what would have been an expected profit from an option position to be a complete loss.

Table 4.2 was taken from a table in the previous chapter. VIX settlement for the October 2008 option contracts is an example of circumstances changing dramatically for traders with positions held through expiration. Specifically, both the VIX Oct 55 and VIX Oct 60 strike put and call options. Other strikes were also impacted, but as the closing index price was lower than both these strike prices and the settlement was higher, these options realized the most dramatic impact. Table 4.3 summarizes the call option settlement values based on both the VIX index close and the final VIX settlement price.

To add an in the money option to the example, the 50 Call has been included in the table. More than just these three strikes were trading on the VIX at October expiration, but the value of these three was dramatically impacted by the difference between the VIX index close of 53.11 on Tuesday and the VIX settlement level of 63.04 on the following day. Using the VIX index close as an assumption of where settlement would be, the Oct 50 Call had some value at 3.11. When the settlement quote was determined the following morning, the option value jumped almost 10 points to 13.04. Considering that VIX options have a multiplier of $100 per point, the result was almost an additional $1,000 benefit to the option holder. The option goes from a dollar value of $311 (3.11 × $100) to $1,304 (13.04 × $100).

TABLE 4.3 October 2008 VIX Option Settlement Impact on Call Option Values

	Value at VIX Index Close 53.11	Value at VIX Settlement 63.04
50 Call	3.11	13.04
55 Call	0.00	8.04
60 Call	0.00	3.04

Long holders of positions in the Oct 55 and Oct 60 Call options were in for quite a positive surprise. Neither contract was in the money based on the index close of 53.11. However, once the settlement level was determined these two options had some intrinsic value. Based on index closing price versus the eventual VIX settlement level, the Oct 55 Call went from being out of the money by 1.89 to 8.04 points in the money with the settlement price. Therefore, a credit of $804 was paid to a holder of an option that was worthless the previous day. The Oct 60 Call also ended up going from out of the money, almost 7 points out of the money, to 3.04 of value or $304 to the holder.

So far, focus has been on the long holders of these options. These long positions all benefited from a change in value based on a new settlement price. For every winner in these situations, there is actually a loser. A trader that had a short position in either the Oct 55 or Oct 60 Call would have expected their options to expire out of the money based on the index close. With the stock market move that resulted in a much higher settlement price versus the VIX index's previous close, the options were now in the money.

Instead of an option expiring with no value, the result was a cash debit for short positions in those options. A short position in the Oct 55 Call would have resulted in a debit of $804 per contract and a short position in the Oct 60 Call would have resulted in a debit of $304 per contract.

The October put options were also impacted by the settlement value of the VIX. Table 4.4 shows three put option values based on the VIX index close and then the final value based on the VIX settlement level. These options were actually impacted in a different way. The VIX settlement was higher than the index close which results in a lower value for put options as opposed to a higher value for call options. The VIX Oct 55 Put and VIX Oct 60 Put options both went from being in the money, using the index close, to being out of the money based on settlement the following morning. Long put holders that may have been expecting a payout were disappointed once settlement was determined. Two of the options on the table expired with no value, the Oct 65 Put did end up with some intrinsic value, but this value went from 11.89 using the index close to only 1.96 at final settlement.

TABLE 4.4   October 2008 VIX Option Settlement Impact on Put Option Values

	Value at VIX Index Close 53.11	Value at VIX Settlement 63.04
Oct 55 Put	1.89	0.00
Oct 60 Put	6.89	0.00
Oct 65 Put	11.89	1.96

For every long put position there was a short put position. The traders with a short put position saw some benefit in the pricing difference that resulted at settlement. Short positions in the Oct 55 and Oct 60 Put options ended up being short positions in options that expired out of the money. The result was the holder of the position ended up experiencing no account debit at expiration. A short position in the VIX Oct 65 Put would have resulted in a debit of $1,189 at settlement based on the index closing price. Due to the overnight movement in the markets, the result was a much higher settlement value and a debit of $191.

The approach to avoiding a negative surprise at expiration with VIX futures was to exit a position before settlement. Exiting would ensure that the profit or loss from a trade is realized and not subjected to an unexpected difference between the market close and the settlement price. With options, this would hold true when there is an option that is in the money at expiration. When there is intrinsic value in an option, whether a positive value for a long option holder or a negative value for a short position, closing out the position may be the best course of action. At minimum the risk around settlement will be eliminated and the profit or loss on the trade will be certain.

For out of the money options that may have strike prices slightly out of the money relative to the index, a different approach may be in order. For long option holders, the option may be trading for a very small premium. The ability to exit the position and salvage the trade from being a total loss may be tempting. However, as the option may benefit from a big move in the overnight, holding the position may result in a profit if the settlement level moves enough to result in the option being in the money.

For example, today is the Tuesday before Wednesday January 2011 VIX expiration. The VIX index is trading at 29.75 a couple of hours before the close, and it may still be possible to sell a VIX Jan 30 Call for a small credit of .05 or possibly .10. However, after commissions the premium received for selling the option may not be worth the effort. Although some proceeds may result from selling the option, at this point it may make sense to hold the option and see if something occurs between the Tuesday U.S. stock market close and Wednesday open when VIX settlement levels would be determined through opening S&P 500 index option prices.

As far as a short option position with a strike that is slightly out of the money, it may be prudent to buy back the option to avoid the risk of the option resulting in an account debit. This would occur in cases where the settlement price differs to the point of the option having intrinsic value.

For every open long option position, there is a corresponding short option position. Consider the previous situation, with the VIX index trading around 29.75 with a couple of hours to go in trading, as a big overnight move could result in a costly situation for a short position in the Jan 30 Call.

To avoid a negative surprise due to an overnight market move, it may actually make sense for traders with a short position to try to close out their exposure. If the following day VIX settlement comes in much higher than the previous closing price for the VIX index, this may result in a debit to the account for a short option position. If the short VIX Jan 30 Call were covered maybe for a cost of $10 or $15 plus commissions, this possibility would not be of any concern. In a situation where the VIX settlement moves in a direction that would have resulted in a costly surprise to the short option holder, this may be money well spent.

RELATIONSHIP TO VIX INDEX

When traders who are inexperienced in VIX options first look at VIX option quotes, they may be discouraged from trading them as they may appear mispriced. Much like VIX futures, the VIX option prices are anticipatory based on where the market believes the VIX will be at expiration. For instance, it is possible to see a VIX Call option with a 30 strike priced at 1.00 while the VIX index quoted at 35.00. On first glance, it appears that this VIX option is underpriced, but the reason may be that there is an expectation of lower market volatility by expiration of this option.

If there is a market expectation of a lower VIX, then the VIX futures contract that expires on the same date as the VIX option would be trading at a discount to the VIX index. This VIX future would also be the proper underlying instrument to value VIX options that have the same expiration date. Both the option and futures prices that share expiration are based on the same market expectation of the direction of volatility.

In this case, the VIX future may be trading at 30.50 with the VIX 30 Call at 1.00. The price of 1.00 for a call option with a 30 strike price is much more reasonable with the underlying trading at 30.50 than if the underlying were trading up at 35.00. Table 4.5 displays these prices along with the intrinsic and time value of the call based on the index and the corresponding futures.

When the market anticipates an increase in market volatility, often the result is much higher VIX futures prices than where the VIX index is trading. VIX put options may appear to be dramatically mispriced if the index

TABLE 4.5 Call Option Value Based on VIX Future and VIX Index

	Price	30 Call	Intrinsic Value	Time Value
VIX Future	30.50	1.00	0.50	0.50
VIX Index	35.00	1.00	−4.00	0.00

TABLE 4.6 Put Option Value Based on VIX Future and VIX Index

	Price	35 Put	Intrinsic Value	Time Value
VIX Index	30.00	0.75	−4.25	0.00
VIX Future	35.00	0.75	0.00	0.75

is being erroneously viewed as the underlying instrument. For instance, if the VIX index is trading at 30.00 while the VIX futures are trading at 35.00, the quote for the corresponding VIX put option that has a 35 strike may be something much less than 5.00. It could easily be something less than 1.00 such as a price like 0.75. A difference of 5.00 represents what the expected intrinsic value of this put option would be when comparing the strike of the option (35) to the level of the spot index (30.00). Again, the more appropriate underlying price to use for the VIX put option is the future contract, which is trading at 35.00. Table 4.6 shows how the put option appears using the future price and the index price as the underlying.

RELATIONSHIP TO VIX FUTURES

As mentioned in the previous section, the best underlying security to compare VIX option price to is the corresponding VIX future price. However, unlike equity options, where the underlying stock may be traded in a round lot of 100 shares for a perfect match with a single standard equity option, the VIX futures do not match up as well. A VIX futures contract has a multiplier of 1,000 and the VIX options have a multiplier of 100.

A common trade that involves the underlying stock and a corresponding option contract is the covered call. A covered call involves having a long position in 100 shares of stock and selling a single call option that represents 100 shares against this holding of stock.

If the equivalent of a covered call were created with a long VIX futures contract and short VIX options, 10 VIX option contracts would need to be shorted for each VIX futures contract owned or purchased. The full-size VIX futures contract is the most liquid hedging vehicle for market makers in the VIX pit at the CBOE. However, the mismatch can make it slightly more difficult for market makers trying to limit their exposure to the VIX when posting VIX option markets. Still the best underlying price for valuing a VIX option is the VIX futures contract, not the spot index.

The mini-VIX futures contracts match up one for one with the VIX options. Remember, a mini-VIX future contract has a multiplier of 100, which matches up perfectly with a VIX option contract. For traders considering a strategy that would combine a VIX option and VIX future for a unique payout, the CFE recently introduced option contracts that are more closely associated with VIX futures. These instruments are covered in Chapter 5.

VIX BINARY OPTIONS

A binary option is an option contract that results in an all-or-none payoff at expiration based on the settlement price of the underlying security. In 2007 the Options Clearing Corporation developed rules that allow standardized binary option trading. In 2008 the CBOE introduced exchange-traded binary options on products including the VIX. Quotes for binary options on the VIX may be found using the ticker BVZ, and the link to find out all information on these instruments is www.cboe.com/bvz. More general information on binary options may be found at www.cboe.com/binaries.

VIX binary options are cash settled like other VIX index options. The holder of a VIX binary option that is in the money option at expiration would receive $100, while the holder of an out of the money option would receive $0. VIX binary options are European-style options and may be exercised only at expiration. European-style is a trait shared among all exchange-traded binary options.

VIX binary options expire in the same manner as the regular VIX options and futures contracts. This involves AM settlement on the Wednesday 30 days prior to the following month's standard option expiration day on the third Saturday following the third Friday of the month. Currently VIX binary options are listed for the following three expirations series. If today were August 1, then August, September, and October option series would be trading.

The quoted price for a VIX binary option will range between 0.00 and 1.00 with the minimum price change being 0.01. The contract multiplier is 100 times an option, and a price quote of 1.00 would result in a contract value of $100. This is also the maximum value of the contract at expiration.

A binary call option at expiration would pay $100 if the VIX settlement price is equal to or greater than the strike price of the call option. In cases where settlement is lower than the strike price, there is no cash payout to the option holder and the option would expire with no value. The seller of a binary option that expires out of the money would profit from the premium received for selling this option.

A binary put option at expiration would pay $100 if the VIX settlement price is less than the strike price of the put option. In cases where the settlement is equal to or greater than the strike price, there would be no cash payout and the put option would expire.

TABLE 4.7 August 2009 VIX Settlement Data

	VIX Settlement	Index Close	Index Settlement	Future Close	Future Settlement
Aug-09	28.76	26.18	−2.58	26.35	−2.41

The issue of VIX settlement prices varying from the close the previous day can have a dramatic impact on VIX binary options. Take for example the case in August 2009 where the previous close for the VIX index was 26.18 and the eventual settlement price turned out to be 28.76. The settlement data for August 2009 appears in Table 4.7. The values for the 27.50 strike call and put options changed very dramatically with overnight shift in volatility.

Assuming VIX settlement would be very close to the VIX index closing price of 26.18, the Aug 27.50 Call would be expected to expire with no value. However, as VIX settlement ended up much higher at 28.76 the following morning, the option paid out $100 per contract based on settlement being higher than the 27.50 strike price. On the other end of the spectrum, the Aug 27.50 Put holders went from believing they would receive a payout of $100 per contract to having options that expired with no value. This scenario is summarized in Table 4.8.

Since binary options are priced between 0.00 and 1.00 with the payout at expiration being 1.00, their prices may be used in an interesting way. The price of the option may also be interpreted as the market placing a percentage chance of the option being in the money at expiration. Another way to consider the price of a binary option is as the odds the option contract will pay out at expiration.

As an example, if a binary VIX 30 Call option is trading for 0.50, then the market is stating that there is a 50 percent chance the VIX will settle above 30 at expiration. If a binary VIX 25 Put option is priced at 0.10, then the market is giving this option only a 10 percent chance of paying out at expiration. Another term for this is that the market is predicting a 10 percent chance of payout, the binary option market being a prediction market.

TABLE 4.8 August 2009 VIX Option Settlement Impact on Put Option Values

	Value at VIX Index Close 26.18	Value at VIX Settlement 28.76
BVZ 27.50 Call	0.00	1.00
BVZ 27.50 Put	1.00	0.00

A final interesting aspect of binary options relative to standard options is the margin requirement for a short position. When short an option contract, there is an obligation taken on to fulfill the right the option holder has purchased. In the case of a binary VIX option, the right is a payment of $100 if the option is in the money at expiration. Since the maximum potential risk of a short binary VIX option would involve a payment of $100, the margin requirement is limited.

For example, a binary option is sold short for 0.40 with $40.00 being taken in upon execution of the trade. The margin requirement would be the difference between the maximum option value at expiration and the income taken in upon execution of the trade. For this trade the result would be a margin requirement of $60.00. An example of margin requirement for VIX Binary Option (BVZ) follows:

Sell 1 BVZ Aug 30 Call @ 0.40 ($40.00 Income)

Margin Requirement:
Maximum Potential Loss − Income from Sale = Margin
$100.00 − $40.00 = $60.00

Binary VIX options have an all-or-none payout structure and are useful as tools to determine what level the market is pricing on option expiration for the VIX index. Additionally, they may be combined with other VIX instruments to create unique strategies relative to the direction of the VIX index.

CHAPTER 5

Weekly Options on CBOE Volatility Index Futures

During the summer of 2010, the CBOE introduced weekly options on stocks and exchange-traded funds, which quickly caught on among traders and investors. The evidence of this acceptance was dramatic volume and open interest levels for weekly options just a few weeks after they were introduced. Although the CBOE had been trading index options with weekly expirations for some time, strong interest in these options was realized after they were available on stocks and ETFs. Due to the success of stock and ETF weekly options, the exchange decided to develop weekly options on the VIX.

Weekly options on indexes, stocks, and exchange-traded funds settle in the exact same manner as their standard expiration counterparts. The only difference is that the expiration may not occur on the third Saturday following the third Friday of the month. In fact, the official expiration date for weekly options is the Friday they cease trading. Due to the unique nature of the VIX index, the exchange decided to take a different route for shorter-term VIX options.

Instead of just creating a VIX option that was based on the weekly closing price of the VIX index or an AM settlement product based on the opening prices of S&P 500 index options, the exchange took a different approach. This approach involves options that settle in positions in the underlying VIX futures contracts. In fact, the VIX weekly options actually are futures options that trade on the CBOE Futures Exchange (CFE).

As the weekly VIX futures options are relatively new products there are not volume statistics to discuss. However, with the success of weekly equity options along with the strong volume in the VIX index option market, it is very possible that these new option products should experience similar market acceptance.

CONTRACT SPECIFICATIONS

As stated in the previous chapter, standard VIX options are cash-settled based on the special opening quotation the Wednesday 30 days before the next standard option expiration date. Weekly options on CBOE Volatility Index Futures actually settle in a position in the nearest-term VIX futures expiration. The weekly settlement for these VIX options is actually based on the relevant future contract's closing price on the Friday of each week. In the event the markets are not open on a Friday, the settlement will be based on the previous trading day's closing prices.

The underlying instrument for a weekly option on VIX futures is a VIX futures contract. The specific contract will be the next VIX futures contract expiration that follows the expiration of the VIX futures options. Therefore, in the same month, options that represent two different VIX future contracts will be trading. For instance, Table 5.1 shows the weekly VIX futures options available for trading in November 2010.

There are four Fridays in November, so there will be four weekly option series. Each option contract expires on corresponding Fridays. The settlement product for the options will be different depending on the expiration date. This is based on when the November VIX futures contracts expire. The expiration date for the November 2010 VIX futures contracts was November 17, 2010. Any weekly VIX futures options that expire in November before November 17 will settle in a position in the November contract. This holds true for the first two weekly options series. The other two expirations occur after November 17 and will be settled in the next contract expiration for the VIX futures or the December 2010 contract.

When pricing any weekly VIX futures options based on an underlying, care should be taken when determining the correct underlying contract. Using the example in Table 5.1, the correct underlying for determining the

TABLE 5.1 November 2010 Weekly VIX Options Settlement Date and Contract

Week	Symbol	Expiration Date	Settlement Contract
1	Nov VO1	Nov 5	Nov VIX Future
2	Nov VO2	Nov 12	Nov VIX Future
3	Nov VO3	Nov 19	Dec VIX Future
4	Nov VO4	Nov 26	Dec VIX Future

price of the first two November expirations would be the November VIX future, while the correct underlying for the last two November expirations would be the December VIX futures. Time spreads with VIX derivatives will be covered more fully in Chapters 12 and 13, but for comparing near-term expirations, be aware that options expiring in the same month may have values based on different futures contracts.

As with the VIX futures contracts the minimum price change for a weekly VIX futures option contract is 0.05, which translates to $50. Exchange rules stipulate the strike prices for these options will differ by no less than 0.50. Initially strikes were at minimum 1.00 apart.

WEEKLY OPTIONS AND INDEX OPTIONS

There are several differences between the VIX weekly options and the VIX index options that have been trading for a few years. Before diving into the differences, there is a similarity between the two option contract types. This common trait is using VIX futures contracts as the underlying pricing mechanism.

VIX index options settle in cash and share their expiration date with corresponding futures contracts. As discussed in Chapter 4, when pricing these options, the correct underlying instrument is the futures contract that shares expiration with the option contracts. The weekly VIX futures options do not share expiration dates with VIX futures contracts, but do settle in the next expiring futures contract. Because the weekly VIX options settle in the futures, this results in the pricing of the options being tied directly to a futures contract price.

Table 5.2 summarizes the difference between the VIX weekly and VIX index option contracts.

TABLE 5.2 Weekly VIX Options versus VIX Index Options

	VIX Index Options	**Weekly VIX Options**
Expiration days	30 days before standard option expiration date	Every Friday and Wednesday
Settlement	Cash	Physical delivery
Exercise	American	European
Settlement pricing	PM	AM
Contract value	$100	$1,000
Option Life	Several months	Approximately one month

As a reminder, Weekly VIX options have a contract that will expire every Friday. That means that every week is expiration week for these contracts. VIX index options have only one expiration date a month, occurring on a Wednesday that falls 30 days before the following month's standard option expiration date.

The settlement process for the two types of options is also very different. Weekly VIX options that are in the money at expiration result in a purchase or sale of the next expiring VIX futures contract. In the case of VIX index options, settlement occurs with a cash transfer between those short in the money options and individuals holding long positions.

Another interesting aspect to weekly VIX futures options relative to the standard VIX index options is the exercise style. VIX index options are European-style options, which are exercised upon option expiration. Weekly VIX futures options are American-style options. As a reminder, American-style options may be exercised anytime until and upon expiration.

The method of determining settlement of an option contract differs between the two types of options. VIX weekly options are in the money if the closing price of the underlying futures contract is at least 0.01 in the money. For VIX index options, settlement is determined through a special calculation of the VIX index that is based on opening prices of S&P 500 index options the day following the last trading day for these options. The AM settlement process was discussed in Chapters 3 and 4.

Each VIX futures contract represents $1,000 times the value of the VIX index. This holds true for weekly VIX options also. The dollar amount of a weekly VIX option is equal to $1,000 times the price of the option. This is 10 times the size of VIX Index options which have a multiplier of $100. In addition to VIX Index options not settling in VIX Futures contract positions, this 10-to-1 difference is also something that sets the index options apart from the weekly options.

VIX index options are issued for monthly expirations going out as far as nine months at a time. The weekly VIX options are listed for more than one week at a time. Approval has been given by the Commodity Futures Trading Commission for up to 13 consecutive weeks of VIX weekly option series to trade at a time, but initial plans call for just four weeks' trading.

The latter part of this book will explore a variety of trading strategies that incorporate the instruments introduced in the first few chapters. However, a strategy that is unique to the weekly VIX options will be introduced in this chapter.

WEEKLY OPTION STRATEGY

Common thinking, especially among stock investors and traders, is of the risk of a sharp move to the downside. That is, when there is a large move in the stock market it is to the downside, not to the upside. An old Wall Street saying goes something like, "The market takes the stairs up and the elevator down." If this adage is true, then it may be said the VIX takes the stairs down and a rocketship up.

The VIX generally has an inverse relationship with the stock market as measured by the S&P 500 index. When the S&P 500 moves lower, the VIX usually moves higher. This move in the VIX is usually at a much higher magnitude than the S&P 500 index's move lower. Table 5.3 shows the 10 worst days for the S&P 500, based on percent lost, along with the VIX index change and front month VIX future percent change on those days.

Only once during those 10 trading days was the magnitude of the VIX index's move higher less than the percent lost by the S&P 500 index. Also, only on one occasion did the nearest expiring futures contract gain more on a percentage basis than the S&P 500 index lost. In fact, when looking at the 100 worst days for the S&P 500 index since January 1, 2004, the VIX was up less in magnitude only 12 times than the value lost in the S&P 500.

A protective put is a common option strategy used by traders and investors to protect a long position against a quick and dramatic loss in value. This strategy involves using a long position in a put option to protect against a bearish price move in a security. Since the perceived risk of a position in VIX futures is more to the upside, or a bullish move, than a quick move to the downside, short positions in VIX futures are considered

TABLE 5.3 10 Worst Days in S&P 500 since 2004 and VIX Reaction

Date	SPX % Change	VIX Index % Change	VIX Future % Change
10/15/2008	−9.03%	25.61%	18.61%
12/1/2008	−8.93%	23.93%	13.61%
9/29/2008	−8.81%	34.48%	14.14%
10/9/2008	−7.62%	11.11%	14.79%
11/20/2008	−6.71%	8.89%	5.29%
11/19/2008	−6.12%	9.79%	9.79%
10/22/2008	−6.10%	31.14%	10.34%
10/7/2008	−5.74%	3.13%	11.93%
1/20/2009	−5.28%	22.86%	10.09%
11/5/2008	−5.27%	14.31%	8.12%

too risky for many traders to consider. Now with VIX weekly options available, there is a method of limiting the damage caused by a spike in volatility when a short position in VIX futures is held.

For example, a trader has a short position in the November 2010 VIX futures on October 1. He has held this position since late August with an entry price of 32.50. October is a month that has seen its share of increases in volatility or bearish market moves. With this concern, he would like some protection in case of a market event that pushes market volatility and the VIX futures higher. Finally, he believes this futures contract should continue trending lower if there is no market shock over the next month. Part of this analysis is based on the VIX index trading at 22.50.

To protect against a move higher in the November VIX futures contract he takes a look at purchasing a call option. As he wants protection just for October, the focus in on weekly VIX options that expire on Friday, October 29, which is the last trading day of the month. Table 5.4 shows the current bid-ask quotes for a variety of weekly VIX options that expire on October 29.

After checking quotes he decides to purchase one VIX Oct 29 Weekly 30 Call for 1.80. The cost of this option offsets some of the unrealized profit from his short position in the November VIX futures contract, but it also provides protection against a move higher in the November VIX futures contract. A term for this combined position could be a *protective call*.

Remember that the November VIX futures contract will still be actively traded for a couple of weeks once this call option expires. These option contracts expire on October 29, while the underlying future contract

TABLE 5.4 VIX Weekly October 29, 2010, Option Quotes

	Bid	Ask
18 Call	9.35	10.30
20 Call	7.55	8.10
22 Call	5.70	6.25
24 Call	4.05	4.60
25 Call	3.40	3.90
26 Call	2.85	3.30
28 Call	1.95	2.40
30 Call	**1.45**	**1.80**
32 Call	1.00	1.45
34 Call	0.70	1.00
36 Call	0.45	0.80
38 Call	0.30	0.65
40 Call	0.20	0.50

TABLE 5.5 Protective Call Profit or Loss at Option Expiration

	VIX Futures P/L	30 Call P/L	30 Call Premium	Position P/L
20.00	7.80	0.00	1.80	6.00
22.50	5.30	0.00	−1.80	3.50
25.00	2.80	0.00	−1.80	1.00
27.50	0.30	0.00	−1.80	−1.50
30.00	−2.20	0.00	−1.80	−4.00
32.50	−4.70	2.50	−1.80	−4.00
35.00	−7.20	5.00	−1.80	−4.00

expires on November 17. Table 5.5 is the payoff for this new position based on the current November VIX futures price and the cost of the protective call option.

Through purchasing the call option, the maximum potential loss on this trade is now 4.00, at least until the option expires on October 29. For this protection against a move higher in the VIX futures, a premium of 1.80 has been paid out. The payoff diagram for this combined trade appears in Figure 5.1.

The dashed line on this diagram shows where a short position with no hedge would be based on the price of the November VIX futures contract at expiration. The solid line shows the payout based on combining the long call that expires at the end of October with a 30 strike price with the short position in the futures contract. The break-even level is better for the short futures position, but there is unlimited risk associated with a higher move in the VIX futures. Using the VIX weekly call option to hedge the risk associated with the short futures position results in a lower break-even level,

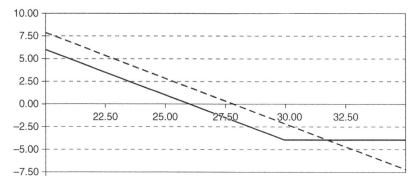

FIGURE 5.1 Protective Call Profit or Loss at Option Expiration Payoff Diagram

but protection against a move higher in the VIX futures contract. Or, the long call is protecting the short futures position from unlimited losses.

VIX weekly options are the first options to settle directly in a position in VIX futures contracts. With settlement in a future contract that has time left until expiration, VIX weekly options offer interesting strategy opportunities. These options have filled a good niche that expanded investor ability to hedge.

CHAPTER 6

Volatility-Related Exchange-Traded Notes

The iShares division of Barclays Bank introduced VIX-related exchange-traded notes in early 2009. One product was based on exposure to shorter-term VIX futures, with the other targeting performance of intermediate-term VIX futures contracts. Before jumping into the specifics of these two products, we offer a quick note on what exchange-traded notes are and how they differ from exchange-traded funds. After covering the specifics of both the iShares ETNs, there is a quick comparison of the two as well as a look at how they perform relative to the S&P 500 index.

In addition, there are other publicly exchange-traded securities basing performance off of the VIX. First, Barclays also has introduced an inverse ETF based on the same index as one of its ETN products. Also, there is a VIX-based exchange-traded fund listed on the London Stock Exchange, but it trades in dollars.

WHAT ARE EXCHANGE-TRADED NOTES?

An exchange-traded note (ETN) is a debt security that is backed by the credit rating of the issuer. The goal of an ETN is to replicate an investment strategy or performance of another investment vehicle. Exchange-traded notes trade in the same manner at exchange-traded funds (ETF) but have a slightly different structure. Again, ETNs are debt securities that attempt to replicate a market index or particular strategy. Barclays Bank has issued a variety of ETN products that replicate anything from investing in commodity products to the performance of a systematic buy-write strategy.

One factor that does play into an exchange-traded note relative to an exchange-traded fund is that there is credit risk associated with the ETN. An ETN is backed by the financial institution that issues the security. The financial crisis of 2008 is a prime example of the economy taking a toll on large financial firms that would in normal times be considered safe investments. Exchange-traded funds will hold a basket of securities to replicate the performance the ETF was created to replicate. Since there are securities held, the risk is not with the issuer, but in the securities held. With an ETN, the viability and potential default of an ETN is tied to the health of its issuer.

Although there is a much different structure backing ETNs and ETFs, they both trade on exchanges in the same manner as stocks. A final difference between the two relates to the potential tax liability of an ETF versus an ETN. ETFs will distribute taxable gains and short-term capital gains on a regular basis. This distribution may create a tax liability even if there has been no transaction in the ETF during the year. ETNs have an advantage in this as the only taxable events are when a position is exited.

iPATH S&P 500 VIX SHORT-TERM FUTURES ETN

The iPath® S&P 500 VIX Short-Term Futures™ ETN (VXX) was the first VIX-related equity-like exchange-traded product. The VXX started trading on the New York Stock Exchange on January 29, 2009. As of this writing, the VXX has been in existence for only about 18 months. Although it is a relatively new product, its volume growth has been tremendous. Figure 6.1 is a chart of the average daily volume by month for the VXX since February 2009.

Like most volatility-oriented trading vehicles, the peak average volume for the VXX occurred in May 2010, which is when the market event termed the "flash crash" occurred. Average daily volume surged to just over 40 million shares a day for that month. This is fairly impressive considering it is a trading product that was nonexistent just a year before. Although the volume subsided a bit after reacting to the volatility associated with the market action in May 2010, an average daily volume of over 20 million shares is pretty impressive.

The goal of the VXX ETN is to mirror an investment in the S&P 500 VIX Short-Term Futures Index. This index is maintained by Standard & Poor's

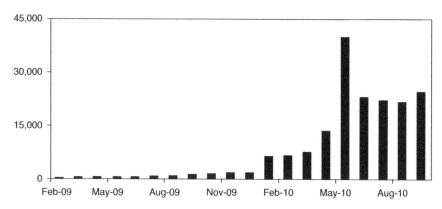

FIGURE 6.1 Average Daily Volume for the VXX (in 1,000s)

as a measure of returns from investing in a long position consisting of the first- and second-month VIX futures contracts. The balance between the two is being adjusted daily.

At the end of May 2010 the CBOE introduced options on the VXX. These options trade just like they do on any other ETN or ETF. The standard VXX option contract represents 100 shares of the VXX ETN. They are American-style options that settle in a long or short position in the VXX. Standard VXX options expire on the third Saturday following the third Friday of the month.

VXX options quickly gained acceptance as a trading vehicle, becoming one of the more actively traded option series at the CBOE. In addition, the CBOE introduced weekly options on stocks and exchange-traded funds in June 2010. These options begin trading on a Thursday with the final day of trading occurring Friday of the following week. For instance, weekly options that are listed on Thursday, September 16, 2010, will trade through Friday, September 24, 2010. Information on weekly options, along with a list of the securities with weekly options available, may be found at www.cboe.com/weekly.

The list of which stocks or exchange-traded fund products have weekly options listed may change from week to week. More newsworthy or volatile stocks tend to show up on the list each week. In late August 2010, the VXX began to regularly show on the list of securities with weekly options available. In early October 2010, the open interest for options on the VXX that had only seven trading days over the life of the contract was over 17,000 contracts. This is an indication of the quick acceptance of trading options on the VXX. As a final example, in early October 2010 the open

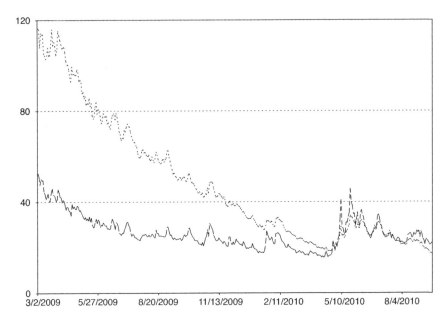

FIGURE 6.2   VXX versus VIX Index

interest for all available VXX options was over 400,000 contracts. That's a pretty impressive level considering these contracts had been trading for just over four months.

The VXX ETN was created to offer an equity-like exchange-traded product that allows investors exposure to stock market volatility. Figure 6.2 compares the price performance of the VXX versus the VIX index from shortly after launching in early 2009 through September 2010. The darker dotted line represents the VXX performance, and the lighter dashed line depicts the VIX index.

Note that the direction of the trend is fairly similar between the two indexes. The VXX commenced trading during a period of high implied volatility for the equity markets, so lower performance would be expected. However, to get a better perspective on the VXX and the VIX index, look to Figure 6.3. In this chart, the VXX and VIX index performance are both indexed to 100 for side-by-side comparison.

It is interesting that in a period where the VIX is trending, the VXX and VIX index experienced fairly similar performance. As the VIX entered a period of range-bound performance, the VXX performance appears to disconnect some from the price movements of the VIX index.

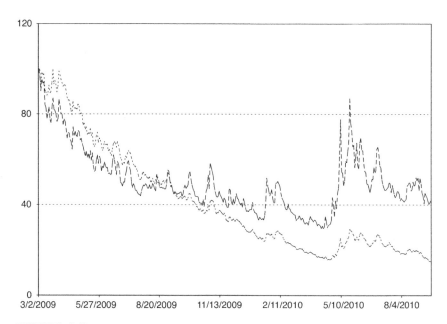

FIGURE 6.3 VXX versus VIX Index Indexed to 100

iPATH S&P 500 VIX MID-TERM FUTURES ETN

The iPath® S&P 500 VIX Mid-Term Futures™ ETN (VXZ) began trading a few weeks after the VXX on February 20, 2009. It also trades on the New York Stock Exchange and has experienced solid volume growth. Its acceptance has not been quite the same as the VXX's, but liquidity should not be a barrier to trading the VXZ. Figure 6.4 shows the average daily volume by month for the VXZ since February 2009.

May 2010 also resulted in a spike in volume for the VXZ. Average daily volume for the month was a solid 750,000 shares. With a calmer stock market, volume backed off a little, coming in under 500,000 shares a day in June 2010. Even at just a small fraction of the VXX volume, the VXZ is also a viable liquid trading vehicle.

Like the VXX, the VXZ also attempts to mirror the performance of an index. The VXZ was created to track the S&P 500 VIX Mid-Term Futures Index. This index measures a return for a long position in the fourth- through seventh-month VIX futures contracts.

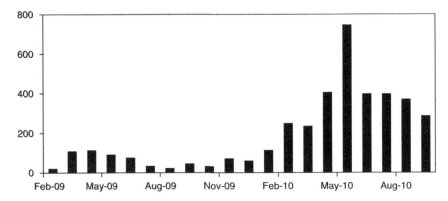

FIGURE 6.4 Average Daily Volume for the VXZ (in 1,000s)

Options also are listed on the VXZ. These options have the same characteristics of other equity-related option contracts. They are American-style options, which may be exercised any time up to and upon expiration. Each contract represents 100 shares of the VXZ, and the contracts are settled in the underlying ETN.

The contract open interest and volume are solid. However, similar to the volume in the underlying ETN, the volume in VXZ options has not quite kept pace with the rapid growth of the VXX ETN.

Figure 6.5 shows the VXZ price performance versus the VIX index from its inception in early 2009 through the middle of September 2010. As the VXZ began trading during a period of high implied volatility, the ETN has lost value since introduction. The trend in this chart is down for both the VXZ and the VIX index.

The VXZ is focused on VIX futures contracts that have four to seven months until expiration. VIX futures contracts with less time to expiration have price performance that tracks the movement underlying VIX index more closely than the futures contracts that expire further in the future.

For a slightly difference perspective on the VXZ and the VIX index performance, see the chart in Figure 6.6. The two instruments are indexed to 100 to get a better perspective on how their prices trade relative to each other.

The difference in performance is more dramatic in this second chart. The VXZ is not designed to track the VIX index. The goal is to focus on a basket of futures with a farther expiration, and with this focus there is a difference between the VXZ and the underlying VIX index performance.

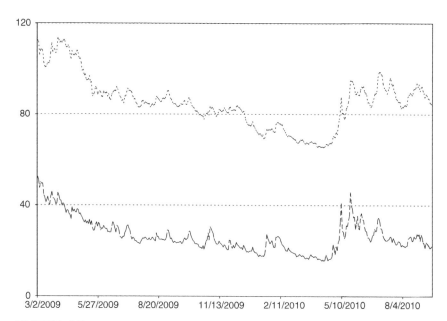

FIGURE 6.5 VXZ versus VIX Index

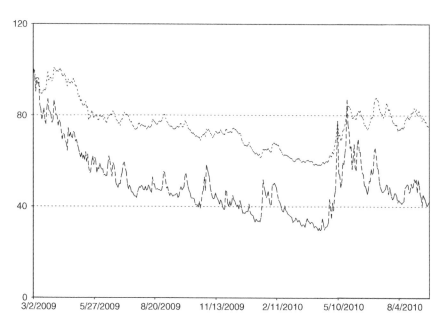

FIGURE 6.6 VXZ versus VIX Index Indexed to 100

COMPARING THE VXX AND VXZ PERFORMANCE

Although there is limited history, the VXX and VXZ have had pretty different price performance since their introduction. The VXX has traded down significantly, while the VXZ has actually held its value better since being introduced. Both the VXX and VXZ had the misfortune of being introduced during a period of high stock market volatility. Figure 6.7 depicts the price difference between the two.

The chart shows a daily price history of the VXX and VXZ from the end of February 2009 through the middle of September 2010. At the end of February, both exchange-traded notes were trading just over 108. Over the next few weeks, the VXX and VXZ tended to trade in line with each other. Starting in April 2009, the prices of the two ETNs diverged.

The dotted line that trades lower on this chart represents the daily closing prices of the VXX. Remember, the VXX focuses on replicating an investment in near-term VIX futures contract. This focus is on a rolling position in the first- and second-month VIX futures contracts. Also, the VXX is the ETN focusing on the VIX that has experienced rapid volume growth.

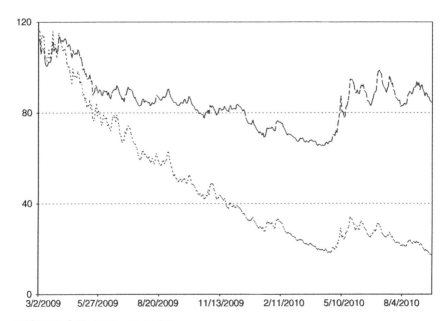

FIGURE 6.7 VXX versus VXZ

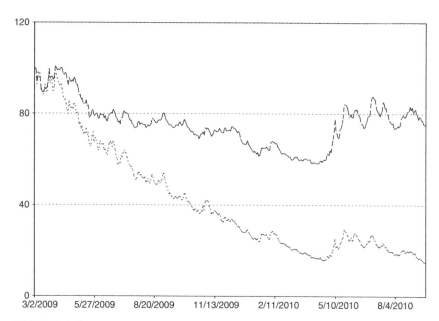

FIGURE 6.8 VXX versus VXZ Indexed to 100

Figure 6.8 shows the performance of the two ETNs through indexing both to 100 at the beginning of the chart. A position in the VXZ over this period would result in a loss of about 25 percent of value. Purchasing the VXX would result in a loss of close to 85 percent over the same time period. The performance of these two ETNs compares to a drop of about 60 percent in the VIX index.

This performance difference between the two ETNs can be attributed to the structure they are both attempting the replicate. The VXX is holding positions in the front two months' futures contracts. The goal is to replicate a portfolio holding a balance of VIX futures with an average expiration of 30 days. To maintain this, the near-term future is being sold and the longer-term future contract is being purchased. This market activity contributes to the underperformance of the VXX.

Consider the closing prices for the VIX futures on September 7, 2010, which appear in Table 6.1. As is often the case, the near-term front month VIX futures contracts are trading at a discount to the contract expiring further in the future. The result is selling the lower-priced future and buying the higher-priced contract. Whenever the further month is trading at a premium to the near month, a lower-priced contract is being sold and a higher-priced one is being purchased. This would involve selling

TABLE 6.1 VIX Futures Closing
Prices—September 7, 2010

Index	23.80
Sep 10	24.45
Oct 10	28.60
Nov 10	29.60
Dec 10	29.90
Jan 11	32.10
Feb 11	32.20
Mar 11	32.55
Apr 11	32.25

September VIX futures at 24.45 and buying October VIX futures for 28.60 or buying expensive contracts relative to the contracts that are sold.

As the futures contracts converge with the VIX index over time and both are trading at a premium to the index, this often means a contract with a lower price is being sold and a contract with a higher price is being purchased. While this trading activity is going on, both instruments may be trending in the direction of the index. This type of market activity results in the VXX's not tracking the VIX index particularly well.

Both these ETNs do trend in the same direction as the VIX, and due to this they also have an inverse relationship with the direction of the stock market. Only on about 16 percent of trading days since inception did both the S&P 500 and VXX move in the same price direction. So, 84 percent of the time when the S&P 500 moves higher, the VXX would be expected to move lower and if the S&P 500 moves lower the VXX should move up in value.

This inverse relationship between the VXX and the S&P 500 can be seen in Figure 6.9. The chart in this figure shows the performance of the VXX, represented by the down trending dotted line versus the S&P 500, which is shown by the dashed line that trends higher. This is an absolute price chart, and the opposite direction of the two is fairly obvious.

The next chart, Figure 6.10, shows the same two instruments as the previous chart, but with each indexed to 100 at the start of the period covered. By indexing the VXX and S&P 500 to 100, the opposite trend of the two is much more apparent.

The correlation of price change between the S&P 500 and both the VXX and VXZ is close to −0.80. This means that there is a pretty significant inverse relationship between both ETNs and price changes of the S&P 500. Figure 6.11 shows the absolute price relationship between the VXZ and S&P 500.

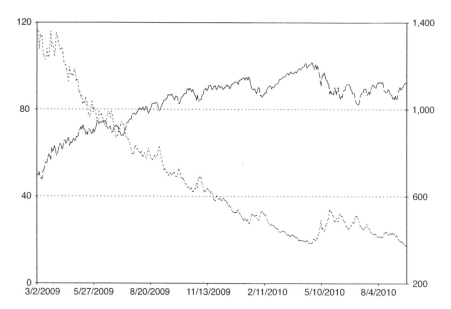

FIGURE 6.9 VXX versus S&P 500 Index

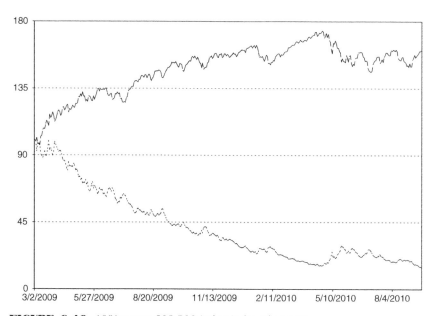

FIGURE 6.10 VXX versus S&P 500 Index Indexed to 100

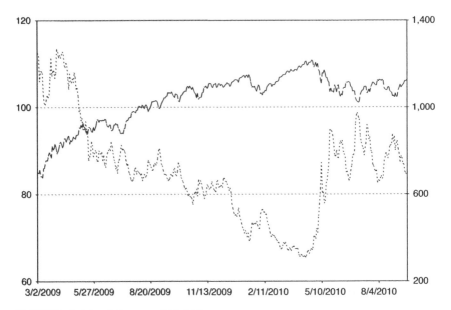

FIGURE 6.11   VXZ versus S&P 500

The chart is similar to the comparison of the S&P 500 and the VXX, but more price movement in the VXZ is apparent due to the scale of the chart. Since performance for the VXZ has been superior to that of the VXX, there is not as wide a price range covered for the ETN in this chart. Indexing both the S&P 500 and VXZ to 100 is a better representation of the performance of the VXZ versus the S&P 500. Figure 6.12 depicts the two instruments in this manner.

Both the VXX and VXZ have an inverse relationship to the movement of stocks as measured by the S&P 500 index. Each has different underlying components that react to changes in volatility in different ways.

BARCLAYS ETN+ INVERSE S&P 500 VIX SHORT-TERM FUTURES ETN

In August 2010, Barclays introduced the first inverse ETN based on the direction of stock market volatility. An inverse ETN attempts to replicate a short position in an underlying security. The Barclays ETN+ Inverse S&P 500 VIX Short-Term Futures™ ETN (XXV) was created to allow investors and traders the opportunity to take a short position on U.S. stock market volatility.

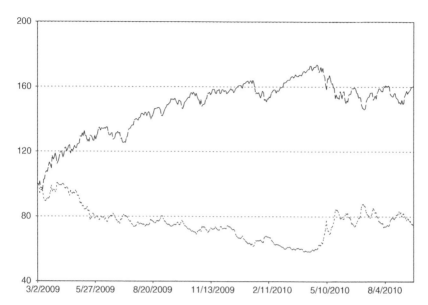

FIGURE 6.12 VXZ versus S&P 500 Index Indexed to 100

The goal of the XXV is to replicate a rolling short position in the front two VIX futures contracts. This is the opposite structure of the VXX discussed previously in this chapter.

Volume in the first month of trading for the XXV was pretty impressive. The XXV actually had a trading session in which volume exceeded a million shares. Figure 6.13 shows the daily volume during the first month of trading for the XXV.

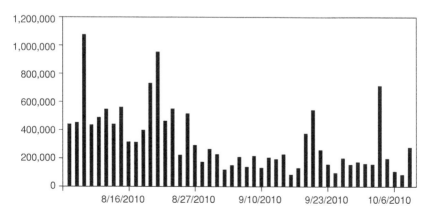

FIGURE 6.13 Daily Volume for the XXV

There is limited history on the XXV, but on a liquidity basis, it appears to be a viable trading tool. With strong volume right out of the box, it will most likely not be the last ETN or ETF based on taking a short position in volatility.

BARCLAYS ETN+ S&P VEQTOR ETN

In addition to inverse or short related exchange-traded funds and notes, there has been an emergence of strategy-based products. The Barclays ETN+ S&P VEQTOR™ ETN (VQT) is the first ETN to incorporate exposure to market volatility. The VQT was designed to offer returns sited to the S&P 500 Dynamic VEQTOR Total Return Index.

This index measures exposure to the S&P 500 Total Return Index and the S&P 500 VIX Short-Term Futures Index. Remember the VXX and XXV are also ETNs that offer exposure to the S&P 500 VIX Short-Term Futures Index.

As an active strategy, the VQT will increase exposure to volatility during low volatility periods. This is based on a fairly complex set of rules that dictate what the weighting should be in volatility derivatives relative to exposure to the equity market. The weighting scale ranges from 10 percent volatility/90 percent stocks to 40 percent volatility/60 percent stocks. Also, there is a stop-loss component to the index.

In a case where the index has lost 2 percent over a five-day period, the index will go 100 percent to cash. The index will stay in cash until the five-day performance is greater than a 2 percent loss. The number of days can vary based on the number of days involved in the negative performance that results in the stop loss being triggered.

S&P 500 VIX FUTURES SOURCE ETF

The S&P 500 VIX Futures Source ETF is an exchange-traded fund offered on the London Stock Exchange. The symbol may vary by quote service, but the ticker is VIXS. The VIXS ETF has the same objective as the VXX ETN that trades in New York. The VIXS began trading on June 18, 2010.

The VIXS marks the first international security to trade based on volatility. It is doubtful that this will be the last, as many exchanges have been exploring development of their own volatility-related indexes to be followed by the development of tradable instruments based on these indexes.

CHAPTER 7

Alternate Equity Volatility and Strategy Indexes

I n addition to the VIX, the CBOE calculates and publishes index data on a variety of volatility-related equity indexes. This chapter will give a quick overview of each of these equity-related volatility indexes along with a comparison of each to relevant markets.

The first index is an extension of the VIX that focuses on longer-dated options, and the result is a longer time horizon for implied volatility. After this index, the remaining indexes are based on a variety of strategies using VIX derivative instruments on a systematic basis. These indexes that represent a strategy will perform differently in different market environments. The result of studying the history of these indexes may be insight into the type of market environment that will benefit different systematic trading strategies. Also, due to the inverse relationship between the S&P 500 index and the VIX, the indexes described in this chapter have a pricing relationship to the S&P 500. These relationships are still developing, but it is starting to be interpreted by some traders as a market forecasting method.

CBOE S&P 500 3-MONTH VOLATILITY INDEX (VXV)

The CBOE S&P 500 3-Month Volatility Index® (VXV®) is similar to the VIX but with a longer time horizon. It was developed to determine implied volatility indicated by longer-dated S&P 500 index options. This index achieves this by focusing on calculating 93-day implied volatility. The

83

calculation uses a combination of S&P 500 index options expiring before and after the targeted 93-day period.

The VXV has a calculation methodology similar to the VIX's, with one major difference. The input for the VIX, which focuses on 30-day implied volatility, involves options that expire over the next two expiration dates, but have at least 8 days remaining until expiration. However, the VXV will use more than just two expiration dates in determining a three-month implied volatility measure. The VXV calculation takes into account S&P 500 index option contracts that expire before and after the targeted 93-day period and use a formula that weights these inputs to determine at the money 93-day implied volatility indicated by S&P 500 index options prices.

Some option contracts will be included in the calculation for both the shorter-term VIX and longer-focused VXV. Additionally, the VXV and VIX both measure volatility on the same index. With some of the same options in both calculations and a similar focus, there is an overlap between the inputs for the two indexes. The following charts depict performance of the VIX and VXV indexes over a handful of time periods.

Figure 7.1 shows the VXV and VIX indexes over the tumultuous period from August 2008 to April 2009. The solid line shows the VIX, which approached the 80 mark during the financial crisis that impacted the markets in late 2008. Note the VXV, during periods of high near-term volatility, tends to not react with the same price magnitude as the VIX.

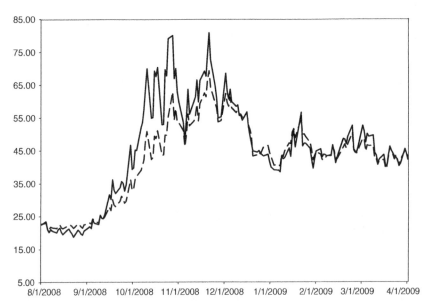

FIGURE 7.1 VXV versus VIX, 8/1/2008–4/1/2009

This period where the VIX moves to historically high levels was an unusual time for the financial markets and lasted only a few weeks. The VXV was often lower than the VIX. This is an indication of the market pricing in lower implied volatility further into the future than over the near term. A move to lower implied volatility would also indicate that the market expects a rebound for the S&P 500 index.

Chapter 3 discussed the relationship of VIX futures contracts to each other. Generally, VIX futures contracts with longer-dated expiration dates trade at a premium to shorter-dated VIX futures contracts. This relationship will often become inverted during periods of market volatility. In these periods, demand for shorter-dated S&P 500 index options, specifically put options, will increase, resulting in higher implied volatility. This increased demand will push implied volatility on near-dated options high relative to the longer-dated option contracts. The effect can be seen in the futures markets, and it also shows up with the relationship of the VIX and VXV.

Figure 7.2 shows the VXV and VIX indexes during a nine-month period in 2009. The dashed line represents the VXV, while the VIX is shown using the solid line. With the exception of a couple of spikes in the VIX, the VXV is consistently at a premium to the VIX.

Figure 7.3 shows the VXV and VIX during the majority of 2010. Note the spikes in the VIX in the middle of this chart, where the VIX is quoted at a premium to the VXV for short periods. These spikes can be attributed

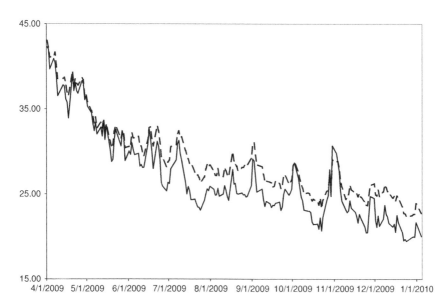

FIGURE 7.2 VXV versus VIX, 4/1/2009–1/1/2010

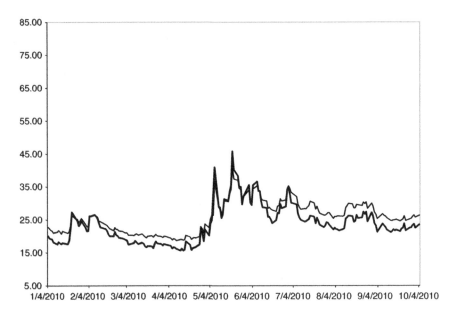

FIGURE 7.3   VXV versus VIX, 1/4/2010–10/4/2010

to the increases in market volatility that occurred around the flash crash of May 2010. Note that the VXV, representing longer-term implied volatility, again reacted in a less volatile manner than the VIX. Note that during this period, the VIX futures contracts were consistently at premium to the spot VIX index.

In Chapter 9, the relationship between the VIX index and futures contracts is shown to be a useful technical analysis tool. The basis of using VIX futures versus the index as an indicator is that the futures contract prices anticipate the direction of the VIX index and consequently the stock market as represented by the S&P 500. The VXV has a longer time-frame focus than the VIX, so the VXV is focused on longer-term implied volatility. The VIX can be considered short-term volatility and the VXV longer-term volatility.

When the VXV is higher than the VIX, near-term volatility is expected to be lower than the potential for longer term market volatility. This is the same as the term structure of VIX futures being in what is referred to as a "normal" curve. When the VXV is at a discount to the VIX, the market is usually reacting to increases in near-term volatility and the result is a rise in the VIX that surpasses a rise in the VXV. Since lower volatility is associated with rising stock prices when the market expects low volatility for the near term, the anticipation is rising stock prices.

TABLE 7.1 VXV versus VIX, January 2004–December 2010

Year	Days that VXV > VIX	Total Trading Days	% Trading Days	S&P 500 Annual Performance
2004	245	252	97%	8.99%
2005	240	252	95%	3.00%
2006	223	251	89%	13.62%
2007	188	251	75%	3.53%
2008	135	253	53%	−38.49%
2009	214	252	85%	23.45%
2010	230	252	91%	12.78%

Table 7.1 is a summary of the VXV relative to the VIX from January 2004 through November 2010. In addition to information about the VXV and VIX, the annual performance of the S&P 500 index is included. Note that on the majority of trading days the VXV closes at a premium to the VIX. This holds true for about 83 percent of trading days in this period.

The period when the VXV was at a discount to the VIX occurred mostly around the financial crisis of 2008. In 2008 the VXV was at a discount to the VIX almost 50 percent of trading days; this disconnect from a normal relationship resulted from the negative performance of the S&P 500 index. The anticipation of lower volatility can be considered an indication of a bullish stock market over a longer time horizon. This secondary relationship between the performance of stocks and implied volatility is the philosophy behind using volatility as a sort of technical indicator.

Figure 7.4 is a chart of the S&P 500 index and a ratio of the VXV and VIX. The top line is a chart of the S&P 500 index, and the bottom line is a

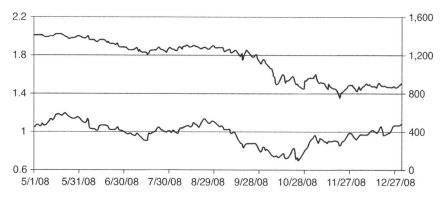

FIGURE 7.4 VXV/VIX Ratio versus the S&P 500 Index, May 2008–December 2008

ratio of the VXV to the VIX index. When the ratio is above 1.00, the VXV is at a premium to the VIX, and when the ratio is below 1.00, the VXV is at a discount to the VIX, indicating that longer-dated options are pricing in lower implied volatility than near-dated option contracts.

VIX PREMIUM STRATEGY INDEX (VPD)

The VIX Premium Strategy Index® (VPD®) is the first strategy-related volatility index discussed in this chapter. The goal of the VPD is to track a consistent program of selling volatility futures contracts. Specifically, the index is based on selling VIX futures contracts on a monthly basis combined with funds deposited in a money market account. The number of contracts sold is limited to sustaining a loss of 25 percent of the account if the VIX futures were to rise 25 points. When the index was created in 2007, historical data going back to 1986 was analyzed. This analysis resulted in the risk control method of using a 25-point maximum potential loss. A 25-point rise in the VIX based on this historical analysis would have occurred about 0.34 percent of the time.

The CBOE began calculating and disseminating the VPD index each day after the equity market closing in 2007. However, the exchange calculated historical closing prices going back to 2004. Figure 7.5 shows the VPD compared to the VIX index from June 2004 through October 2010. The upper line on this chart shows the performance of the VPD, with the lower line representing the VIX. The scale on the right applies to the VPD, and the scale on the left applies to the VIX. As with many equity market–related indexes, the market activity around late 2008 early 2009 stands out on this

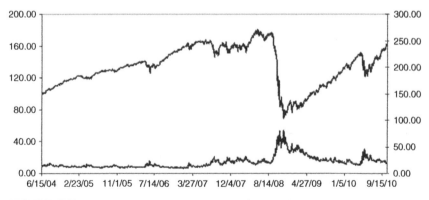

FIGURE 7.5 VPD versus VIX, June 2004–October 2010

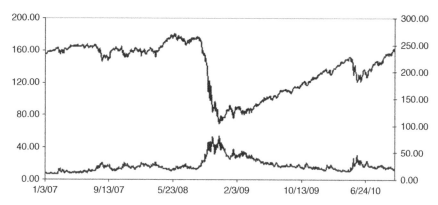

FIGURE 7.6 VPD versus VIX, January 2007–October 2010

chart. The VPD is tracking a short position in VIX futures, which worked well until the dramatic rise in volatility that accompanied the dramatic drop in the equity markets in 2008.

Figure 7.6 narrows the time period down some to highlight the drop in the VPD that resulted from higher VIX prices in 2008. On the last day of August 2008, the VIX closed at 20.57 and the VPD closed at 176.09. On the final trade day of 2008 the VIX stood at 40.00 and the VPD had dropped to 89.19. The result was a VIX that was just under 100 percent higher and a VPD that had lost about 50 percent of value.

Next, we overlay the VPD with a chart of the S&P 500 index to make an interesting comparison. Figure 7.7 compares these two indexes using data from June 2004 to October 2010, with the higher line representing the VPD and lower line the S&P 500. Note the high visual correlation between the two. In periods of bullish market activity, VIX futures contracts

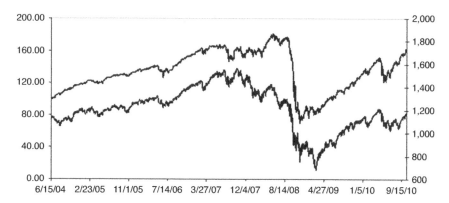

FIGURE 7.7 VPD versus SPX, June 2004–October 2010

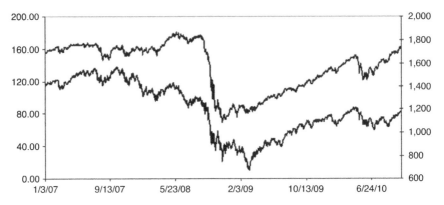

FIGURE 7.8 VPD versus SPX, 1/3/07–10/8/10

generally trade at a premium to the VIX index. The futures contract is cash settled in the index, and the VIX index would be relatively flat or trending lower in a bullish market. A short position in VIX futures, especially when the index is at a discount to the futures, would benefit from lower VIX and the future contract trending down to the index into expiration. The result is positive performance in the strategy that is behind the VPD calculation when the equity market is in a bullish phase.

Finally, Figure 7.8 narrows down the view to highlight the price action around 2008. In that critical period from August 2008 to the end of 2008, the two indexes experienced similar drops with the VPD down around 50 percent and the S&P 500 losing close to 40 percent.

Selling VIX futures to benefit from the drift that comes during a "normal" market environment where the VIX futures are at a premium to the VIX index is a viable strategy. However, the VPD depicts selling VIX futures on a consistent basis regardless of the proximity of the underlying index. Also, the only risk control behind the systematic approach behind the VPD involves limiting risk based on the infrequent occurrence of a 25-point rise in the VIX. The next index in this section uses a different type of risk management to this basic premise.

CAPPED VIX PREMIUM STRATEGY INDEX (VPN)

The Capped VIX Premium Strategy Index® (VPN®) follows the same investment method as the VPD. The VPN is based on a systematic program of selling VIX futures, but with a different risk control in place. This risk

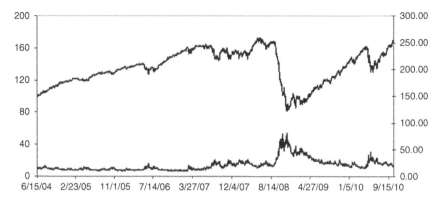

FIGURE 7.9 VPN versus VIX, 6/15/04–10/8/10

control involves the purchase of VIX call options to limit the impact of a spike in volatility. The VPD index limited exposure through assuming a 25-point increase in volatility would be extremely rare. The VPN also uses this 25-point level, but instead of weighting short futures exposure, the VPD buys call options with strike prices at this 25-point threshold. The result is underperformance relative to the VPD when the protection is not needed and outperformance when there is a spike in implied volatility.

There are similar results from this premium selling program with out of the money call options as a hedge as opposed to a weighting based on past levels of volatility spikes. Figure 7.9 shows the VPN versus the performance of the VIX between mid-2004 and late 2010. The chart is very similar to that of the VPD versus the VIX, with a big drop in performance in 2008.

Figure 7.10 narrows the time frame for the VPN and VIX to show performance leading up to and following the equity market setback in 2008.

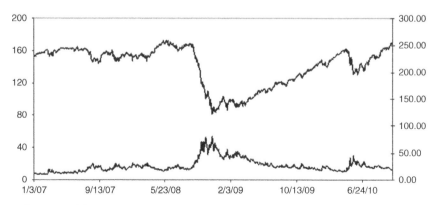

FIGURE 7.10 VPN versus VIX, 1/3/07–10/8/10

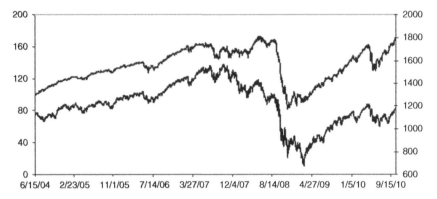

FIGURE 7.11   VPN versus SPX, 6/15/04–10/8/10

The VIX gained almost 100 percent over the last four months of 2008. During this same period, the VPN dropped from 163.74 to 100.44, or just under 40 percent. This drop in the VPN compares favorably to the VPD loss of around 50 percent. This performance difference over this time period is attributable to the two risk control methods applied to each index.

In Figure 7.11, similar performance between the S&P 500 index and the VPN is apparent. The upper line shows the VPD performance, while the bottom line is the performance of the S&P 500 index. As in the comparison between the VPD and the S&P 500, normal or bullish market phases are ideal times to sell the VIX future premium. The result is similar performance between this strategy and the equity market.

Figure 7.12 shows the VPN and S&P 500 from 2007 to late 2010. Note in 2008 the drop in both indexes, which coincides with the market weakness

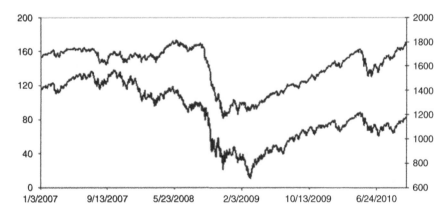

FIGURE 7.12   VPN versus SPX, 1/3/07–10/8/10

that year. The interesting feature of this chart relative to the same period for the VPD is that the VPN does not experience as much of a drop. This relative outperformance of the VPN related to the VPD involves the risk control measure that the VPN implements through buying out of the money call options to hedge against a dramatic rise in volatility.

S&P 500 VARB-X STRATEGY BENCHMARK

The name of the CBOE S&P 500 VARB-X Strategy Benchmark comes from the strategy that it represents. VARB-X, quoted with the symbol VTY, emanates from the words *volatility arbitrage*. The index represents a strategy taking advantage of the historical spread between implied and realized volatility. Core to index is a strategy taking a short position in three-month variance futures that trade on the CBOE Futures Exchange. On a quarterly basis, this position is rolled to a contract expiring three months in the future.

In addition to a rolling short position in three-month variance futures, risk management controls are in place. The hypothetical portfolio that is used to calculate the index will take a position that is equal to 25 percent of available capital. Taking 25 percent of the available capital and dividing by the notional value of the futures contracts results in the number of contracts that will be sold short. Also, the number of contracts sold short may be limited based on contract settlement 25 points higher than the short-selling value of the contracts.

Figure 7.13 shows the VTY versus the VIX from June 2004 to October 2010. Note that the strategy behind the VTY shows consistent performance

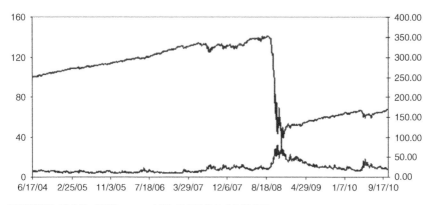

FIGURE 7.13 VTY versus VIX, 6/17/04–10/8/10

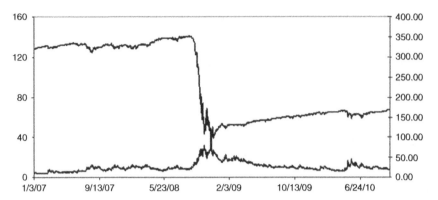

FIGURE 7.14 VTY versus VIX, 1/3/07–10/8/10

until the VIX rallied tremendously in 2008. Being effectively short implied volatility in a leveraged format had a detrimental impact on the VTY index during this period. Upon a return to a normal market and implied volatility environment, the consistent performance behind this strategy returned.

Figure 7.14 narrows down the time frame of the VTY versus VIX comparison to highlight the drop in the VTY due to the rally in the VIX in the latter months of 2008. Note on this chart that the time period leading up to this drop has a flat performance for the VTY.

Figure 7.15 compares the VTY to the performance of the S&P 500 index from June 2004 to October 2010. With the exception of the period in late 2008 where there is a dramatic drop in this index, the strategy worked well over the course of this chart. Regardless of the direction of the stock market, there is a nice steady uptrend in the performance of the VTY.

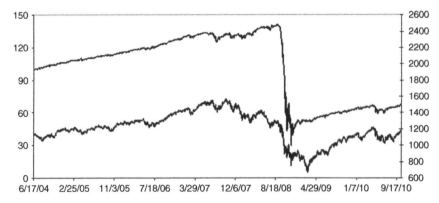

FIGURE 7.15 VTY versus SPX, 6/17/04–10/8/10

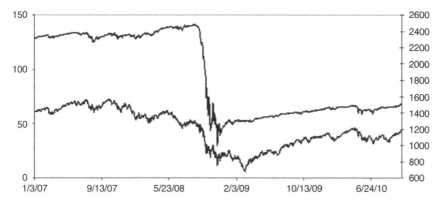

FIGURE 7.16 VTY versus SPX, 1/3/07–10/8/10

Figure 7.16 narrows down the time frame of the previous chart to focus more on the underperformance of this strategy during 2008.

Both charts show the VTY in comparison to the S&P 500 index. Note that the VTY strategy seems to have low correlation with the S&P 500 index during nontumultuous periods in the market. However, the magnitude of the drop in the VTY relative to the S&P 500 during bear markets can be dramatic.

S&P 500 IMPLIED CORRELATION INDEX

The final equity volatility related index quoted by the CBOE is the S&P 500 Implied Correlation Index. This index provides an approach for monitoring the implied volatility of the S&P 500 index in comparison with the implied volatility of a basket of stocks that should closely track the performance of the S&P 500. Many arbitrage firms will create a basket of stocks to replicate performance of the S&P 500 index as opposed to trading in all 500 stocks in the index.

The implied volatility of option contracts on individual stocks is usually higher than the implied volatility of options on a broad-based index. The options on a broad-based index such as the S&P 500 will have a lower implied volatility than that of an individual stock due to the lower risk of a large move in the index. When individual stocks are combined into a portfolio or index, the volatility of these instruments will naturally have lower volatility than the individual components of the portfolio or index.

The Implied Correlation Index measures the correlation of the implied volatility of S&P 500 index options with the implied volatility of the

TABLE 7.2 Beginning and Ending Dates for Implied Correlation Indexes

Index	First Quoted Date	Last Quoted Date
January 2008	January 3, 2007	November 16, 2007
January 2009	January 3, 2007	November 21, 2008
January 2010	November 19, 2007	November 23, 2009
January 2011	November 24, 2008	November 19, 2010
January 2012	November 26, 2009	November 18, 2011
January 2013	November 22, 2010	November 16, 2012

portfolio of selected stocks. A disparity between the two implied volatilities may indicate that the market is overpricing the risk of the overall stock market relative to the risk applied to the individual components of the index. The implied volatility of the individual components is combined to create a portfolio volatility to compare to the S&P 500 index.

Implied correlation indexes are created with a specific January expiration date. This date coincides with Long-term Equity AnticiPation Securities or LEAPS expiration dates. At any time there will be two Implied Correlation Indexes being calculated and quoted by the CBOE.

Table 7.2 shows the beginning and ending dates for a few Implied Correlation Indexes. The first quoted date for the January 2008 and January 2009 Implied Correlation Indexes is January 3, 2007, which is the date from which the CBOE has provided historical data. The other indexes commence quotes the Monday following standard option expiration in November. This follows the final quoted date for the near-dated index, which is the third Friday of November or standard option expiration. For example, on Friday, November 23, 2009, the January 2010 index ceased being quoted and on Monday, November 26, 2009, an implied correlation index for January 2012 began being calculated and quoted.

Figure 7.17 compares the January 2009 Implied Correlation Index to the VIX index. This index was quoted from January 2007 through November 21, 2008, which was a tumultuous time for the overall market. The lower line on the chart is the VIX, with the upper line representing the Correlation Index. Note that they tend to move in lockstep. This is to be expected as they are both measures of risk in the stock market as indicated by S&P 500 index option prices.

Figure 7.18 shows the January 2009 Implied Correlation Index in comparison to the S&P 500 performance. The upper line on this chart represents the S&P 500 index, and the lower line shows the Implied Correlation Index. As with comparison of the S&P 500 and the VIX, there is a definitive inverse relationship between the two.

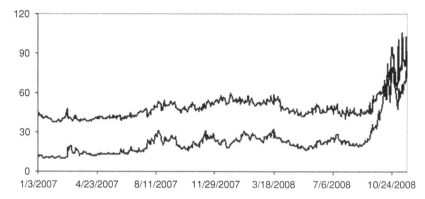

FIGURE 7.17 January 2009 Implied Correlation Index versus VIX

Figure 7.19 takes the January 2010 Implied Correlation Index and overlays performance of this index with the VIX. The lower line on this chart is the VIX, with the higher line being the Implied Correlation Index.

Finally, Figure 7.20 compares the January 2010 Implied Correlation Index to the S&P 500 index. The inverse relationship that was apparent in the January 2009 index is not as obvious on this chart. Although the correlation index is a measure of risk, it is relative to the risk being priced in for individual stock options. The difference in the risk price by index options relative to that of individual stock options was not as dramatic over the life of this index is at was for the January 2009 index.

The Implied Correlation Index is a very specific measure of risk that takes the risk priced into individual stock options in comparison with the risk priced in by S&P 500 index options. Through this comparison, at times the premiums of index options may be considered expensive or cheap

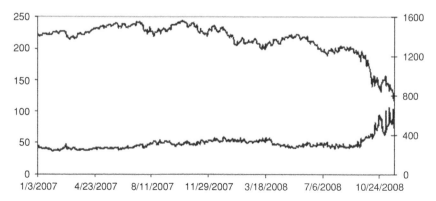

FIGURE 7.18 January 2009 Implied Correlation Index versus S&P 500

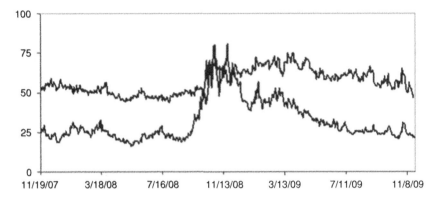

FIGURE 7.19 January 2010 Implied Correlation Index versus VIX

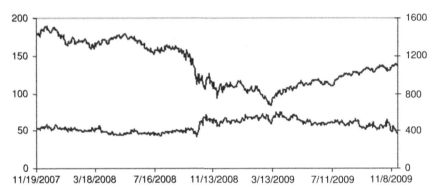

FIGURE 7.20 January 2010 Implied Correlation Index versus S&P 500

relative to the premiums of options trading on the individual components of the index. A use of this index by many professional firms is to determine whether implied volatility in the market is relatively high or low compared to the components of the index.

Each of the indexes in this chapter has implied volatility of the overall stock market as their primary determination of value. Implied volatility tends to rise with drops in the stock market and will often move lower as the stock market enters a bullish phase. This inverse relationship between the stock market and implied volatility had led some market observers to consider the VIX and VIX-related indexes as market forecasting tools. This may be also said for the indexes in this chapter, as they derive their valuations from the same basic premise as the VIX index. Chapter 9 dives more into using the VIX as a market indicator, but the indexes in this section may also qualify as forecasting tools in their own right.

CHAPTER 8

Volatility Indexes on Alternative Assets

In addition to volatility indexes on a variety of equity market indexes, a handful of indexes are based on the implied volatility of other assets. As using volatility as an asset class continues to gain market acceptance, the result should be an expansion of trading in derivatives based on these indexes.

Currently, the CBOE tracks volatility on gold, oil, and the euro based on option trading on securities that trade these respective markets. Each of these markets has unique volatility characteristics that will make derivative products on their volatility levels unique in their own right.

Through an agreement with the CME Group, the CBOE has licensed its VIX methodology for use in the development of volatility-related indexes based on CME Group products. Volatility indexes on oil, gold, soybeans, and corn have been developed. These indexes are based on options on futures on each of these commodities. The long-term plan for these indexes calls for introduction of derivative trading at the exchange based on these indexes. Introduction of oil and gold volatility futures by the CME Group was the first step toward an expansion of volatility-related derivatives. Finally, the CME Group has also started work toward an alternative currency volatility measure known as indexes on realized volatility. This chapter finishes with a description of these realized volatility indexes.

CBOE GOLD VOLATILITY INDEX

The CBOE Gold Volatility Index® trades with the symbol GVZ and was introduced in June 2008 although historical prices are available going back to 2007. The GVZ is designed to depict 30-day implied volatility for the spot gold market.

The level of the GVZ index is determined through using the prices on options that trade on the SPDR Gold Shares exchange-traded fund (GLD). The GLD represents ownership in spot gold based on the cost of an ounce of gold. The GLD is quoted at 1/10th the price of gold, so a GLD price of 110.00 per share would equate spot gold at $1,100 an ounce.

Figure 8.1 shows the performance of the GLD versus the spot price of gold. The upper line on this chart represents the spot gold price, while the bottom line is the daily closing price for the GLD. The scales were adjusted so that the lines did not overlap and appear as a single market. Note the ETF does a excellent job tracking the daily spot price of gold, which is a statement that cannot be made for all exchange-traded funds. As a proxy for owning physical gold, the GLD ETF has become a good substitute and an opportunity for equity investors to directly benefit from higher or lower gold prices.

Popularity in options on the GLD has also grown evident by high open interest and daily trading volume. Further evidence of the acceptance of the GLD comes from the introduction of weekly GLD options. The instruments chosen to have weekly options listed on them are always among the most liquid option series. The GVZ is calculated based on the price of these options that have become a common trading instrument for hedging and speculating on the price of gold.

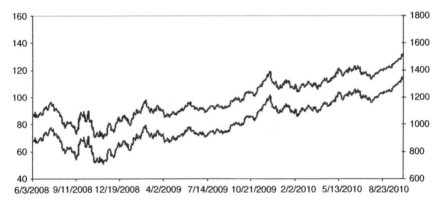

FIGURE 8.1 GLD versus Spot Gold Prices

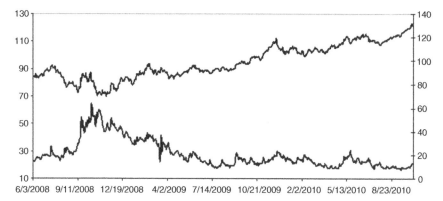

FIGURE 8.2 GVZ versus GLD ETF

Figure 8.2 shows the level of gold implied volatility in the form of the GVZ index in comparison to the price fluctuations in the GLD. The bottom line on this chart represents the GVZ, or 30-day forward-looking implied volatility of the price of gold based on the GLD ETF. The charts appear to be somewhat of a mirror of each other, but the correlation between the two is actually 0.09, indicating that on a daily basis the two are not necessarily negatively correlated.

Finally, Figure 8.3 shows the GVZ versus spot gold. Since the GLD tracks the price of gold so closely, the appearance of this chart is very similar to the chart comparing the GLD to the GVZ. The correlation or lack of correlation between the two instruments is very similar to that of the previous comparison.

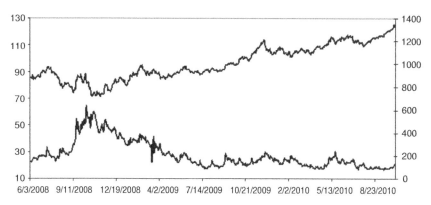

FIGURE 8.3 GVZ versus Spot Gold

The unusual relationship between the implied volatility of GLD options and the price of gold may stem from what market forces are influencing the price of gold. Gold is considered a hedge against inflation, but it also comes under pressure during economic slowdowns. What may be considered negative economic news could have a dramatic impact on gold prices. This impact could result in the price moving higher or lower depending on the nature of the news. Therefore, gold implied volatility may spike with higher gold prices as well as lower gold prices.

As this book was being completed, the CBOE introduced option and futures trading on the GVZ. More information about these products may be found at www.cboe.com/gvz.

CBOE CRUDE OIL VOLATILITY INDEX

The CBOE Crude Oil Volatility Index® is quoted with the symbol OVX. The OVX is the market projection of 30-day implied volatility on the spot price of oil. This index is determined through the implied volatility indicated through the prices of options on the United States Oil Fund, LP or USO. The goal of the USO ETF is to track oil prices through mirroring the price of light sweet crude oil. Light sweet crude is also the underlying for the most actively traded and commonly quoted oil futures contract, specifically the NYMEX crude oil futures contracts.

The USO exchange-traded fund attempts to achieve performance that mirrors the price of oil through investing in oil futures contracts. Figure 8.4 shows the USO versus the spot price of oil. The spot price of oil is based on West Texas light sweet crude closing prices, which is the underlying for the NYMEX contracts. The lower solid line shows the USO, with the upper broken line depicting closing spot oil prices. They tend to trend together, but they appear disconnected somewhat in a flat oil-pricing environment. The USO appears to mirror the price of oil better in a trending environment, both higher and lower, than in a range-bound trading environment for the price of oil. Although there appears to be a divergence of price performance, there is still an 86 percent price correlation between the two during 2009 and 2010.

Figure 8.5 shows how oil volatility, as represented by the OVX, compares to price changes in the USO. The USO is represented by the dashed line, while the OVX is the solid line. The implied volatility of options on the USO appear to go through periods of high and low volatility that do not necessarily correspond to the performance of the USO.

Figure 8.6 takes the OVX and compares it to the spot price of oil. Again the OVX is shown as a solid line, while the spot price of oil is depicted by a

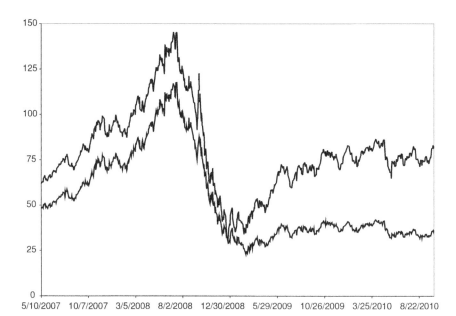

FIGURE 8.4 USO versus West Texas Light Sweet Crude Oil

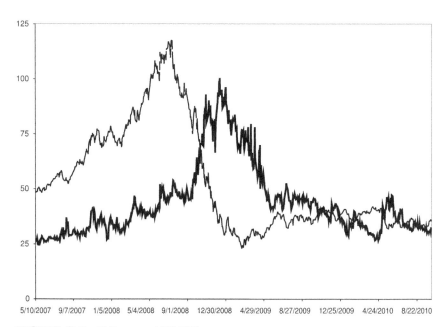

FIGURE 8.5 OVX versus USO ETF

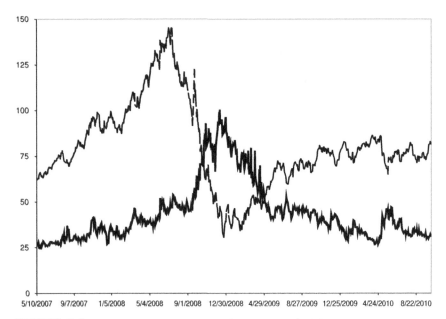

FIGURE 8.6 OVX versus West Texas Light Sweet Crude Oil

dashed line. As in the chart comparing volatility to the USO, the OVX goes through high and low periods of volatility that do not necessarily reflect the spot price of oil.

The OVX is not correlated, negatively or positively, relative to the two representatives for the price of oil. This may stem from the same factors that cause implied volatility of gold to disconnect at times from the price action surrounding gold. At times, higher trending oil prices may be considered a positive development. This would be reflecting a period of economic growth. However, a rapid rise or fall in the price of oil may be considered a negative due to either signaling geopolitical unrest or lack of demand due to a sagging economic environment.

CBOE EUROCURRENCY VOLATILITY INDEX

The CBOE EuroCurrency Volatility Index® is an indication of the markets expected 30-day implied volatility for price movement in the euro currency versus the U.S. dollar. The symbol for the Euro VIX is EVZ and the pricing

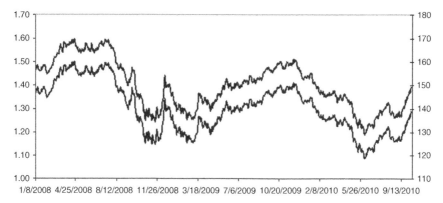

FIGURE 8.7 FXE versus Euro Currency Exchange Rate

is based on option-implied volatility indicated by options trading on the Currencyshares Euro Trust ETF, symbol FXE.

The FXE is an exchange-traded fund that was developed to mirror the performance of the euro versus the dollar. It is quoted at 100 times the rate of the euro as quoted versus the dollar. For instance, if the euro is quoted at 1.25 per dollar, then the FXE would be quoted at 125.00 per share.

Figure 8.7 shows the ability of the FXE to track the change of the euro versus the dollar. The upper line represents the exchange rate between the euro and the dollar. The lower line represents the iShares FXE exchange-traded fund. In order to show the relationship between the two, the scales were offset so the lines did not completely overlap.

The chart shows a high correlation between the two instruments. In fact, the correlation between daily price changes from January 2008 through September 2009 is very high. A quick statistical analysis between the exchange rate and the FXE results in a correlation of .97 which can be translated as the FXE and euro currency moving practically in lockstep with each other.

Implied volatility of the FXE options in the form of the CBOE EuroCurrency Volatility Index is shown versus the performance of the FXE in Figure 8.8. The upper line represents the performance of the FXE ETF, while the lower line shows the daily performance of the EVZ index. Note that the FXE ETF has a wide price range, trading between 110 and 160 over the two years covered by this chart. The EVZ covered a price range of below 10 to just over 30 during this same period.

Figure 8.9 shows the EVZ versus spot euro exchange rate. Again the lower line is the EVZ while the upper line shows the closing spot euro

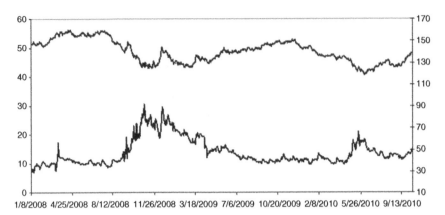

FIGURE 8.8   EVZ versus FXE ETF

prices. As there is a high correlation between the euro exchange rate and the FXE, this chart appears very similar to the one in Figure 8.8. The slight inverse correlation that exists between the EVZ and FXE is also present when comparing the euro exchange rate and the EuroCurrency Volatility Index.

Unlike the gold- and oil-related volatility indexes, the EVZ relationship to the price of its underlying instrument is more like what is seen when comparing the VIX and the S&P 500 index. Although not quite as much an inverse relationship, the implied volatility for options trading on the FXE ETF does appear to rise when there is a downtrend in the level of the euro relative to the dollar.

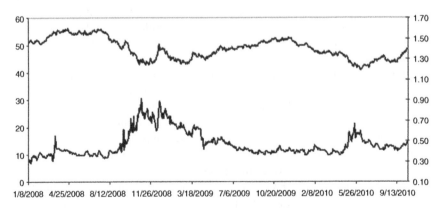

FIGURE 8.9   EVZ versus Euro Currency Exchange Rate

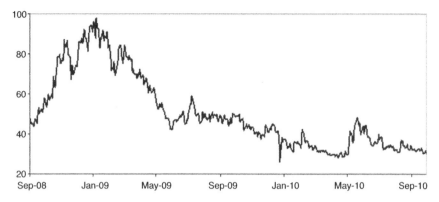

FIGURE 8.10 OIV, September 2008–October 2010

CBOE/NYMEX CRUDE OIL (WTI) VOLATILITY INDEX

NYMEX Crude Oil (WTI) Volatility Index was developed by the CBOE in a licensing agreement with the CME Group, which is the parent company of the NYMEX. This index is quoted with the symbol OIV. The OIV index is based on implied volatility of options that trade on crude oil future contracts with the base symbol OL.

The CME offers historical data on the OIV going back to September 2008. The chart in Figure 8.10 shows the OIV over this period. This chart appears similar to the OVX chart from earlier in this chapter. They are influenced by the same market forces, but they are based on different actual trading instruments. A quick analysis showed over a 97 percent correlation between the OVX and OIV.

The CME Group commenced futures trading on the OIV index in late 2010 under the symbol CVF. The contract specifications for these futures appear in Table 8.1.

Futures on the OIV trade under the base symbol CVF. These futures are quoted electronically by the CME Group and with some small breaks trade practically 24 hours a day from Sunday evening to Friday afternoon. Contracts are quoted a year into the future with monthly expiration.

CBOE/COMEX GOLD VOLATILITY INDEX

CBOE/COMEX Gold Volatility Index was also developed by the CBOE through a partnership with the CME Group, which is the parent of the

TABLE 8.1 CVF Futures Contract Specifications

Symbol	CVF
1 Point =	$500
Tick =	0.01
Settlement	Cash
Expiration	30 days prior to next option expiration
Contracts available	12 consecutive months
Trading hours	Sunday–Friday 5:00 P.M. to 4:15 P.M. Central

COMEX, the primary market for gold futures contracts. This index is quoted under the symbol GVX.

The GVX index is based on implied volatility of options that trade on gold futures with the symbol OG. The standard VIX-related index will calculate 30-day implied volatility. The GVX index determines 60-day implied volatility on gold due to the nature of the options used in the calculation of the GVX. Since the underlying gold options expire every other month, there are not contracts available to formulate a 30-day implied volatility. Therefore the GVX is a quote of 60-day implied volatility, not 30-day.

Figure 8.11 is a chart of the GVX from September 2008 to October 2010. Even through the GVX is measuring 60-day implied volatility and the GVZ results in a measure of 30-day volatility, the two indexes are strongly correlated. Like the two oil volatility indexes, the GVX and GVZ have a correlation of over 0.97.

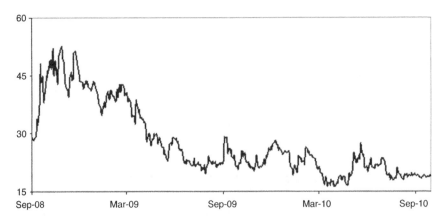

FIGURE 8.11 GVX, September 2008–October 2010

TABLE 8.2 GVF Futures Contract Specifications

Symbol	GVF
1 Point =	$500
Tick =	0.01
Settlement	Cash
Expiration	30 days prior to next option expiration
Contracts available	6 months (Feb, Apr, Jun, Oct, Dec)
Trading hours	Sunday–Friday 5:00 P.M. to 4:15 P.M. Central

In late 2010 the CME Group commenced trading on futures contracts on the GVX index quoted under the symbol GVF. The contract specifications for these futures appear in Table 8.2.

Futures on gold volatility trade under the symbol GVF at the CME group and like the oil-volatility futures, basically trade 24 hours a day from Sunday evening to Friday afternoon. These contracts have the same specifications as the OIV-related futures, but they have only six contracts available for trading. Each contract is spaced out two months apart and this is a function of the GVX being based on 60-day implied volatility.

CBOE/CBOT GRAIN VOLATILITY INDEXES

The CBOE/CBOT Soybean Volatility Index is another volatility index created by the CBOE for use by the CME Group. The CBOT is another of the exchanges that comes under the CME Group of exchanges and has been the home for trading soybean futures for well over a century. This index is quoted with the symbol SIV and is based on soybean options on futures that trade with the symbol OZS.

The CBOE/CBOT Corn Volatility Index was also created by the CBOE for use by the CME Group. This index measures the implied volatility of options that trade on corn futures with the symbol OZC. This index is quoted with the symbol CIV.

FX REALIZED VOLATILITY INDEXES

The CME Group, working with the Volatility Exchange, plans to begin futures trading based on the realized volatility on six currency pairs in 2011. The Volatility Exchange developed a method of calculating realized

TABLE 8.3 FX Realized Volatility Pairs

Currency	Symbol
Euro FX	EUR/USD
Japanese yen	JPY/USD
British pound	GPB/USD
Canadian dollar	CAD/USD
Swiss franc	CHF/USD
Australian dollar	AUD/USD

volatility, which the CME Group uses to calculate indexes to base futures on realized volatility. These currency pairs appear in Table 8.3.

The CME Group method of calculating the realized volatility for each of these pairs involves using the 2:00 P.M. central time fixing price. The prices are based on the currency futures contracts that trade at the CME. Using these prices an index is formulated, and from this index a realized, or known, volatility is calculated. The major difference between this and implied volatility is that implied volatility is an expectation of the market while the realized volatility is a known level of volatility calculated using past price action.

The fixing price is not a closing price for the currency future contract, but instead a volume-weighted price average for the currency futures contracts. This volume-weighted price involves trading over a 30-second period leading up to the two reported times. The CME Group disseminates this information twice a day, at 9:00 A.M. and 2:00 P.M., with the 2:00 P.M. price being the input into the index.

The index will be representing volatility which is expressed in terms of a percent. Like the VIX where implied volatility of 20 percent is quoted

TABLE 8.4 Proposed Monthly Realized Volatility Futures Contract Specifications

Underlying Price	Futures Settlement on Serial or Monthly Underlying Contract
Contract size	$1,000 times index
Tick size	0.01 = $10
Contract months	First 3 consecutive calendar months including 1 March cycle months
Settlement	Cash settled
Last trading day	2nd Friday preceding 3rd Wednesday of contract month
Final settlement	1-month realized volatility
Trading hours	Sunday–Friday 5:00 P.M. to 4:15 P.M. central

TABLE 8.5 Quarterly Realized Volatility Futures Contract Specifications

Underlying Price	Futures Settlement on Serial or Monthly Underlying Contract
Contract size	$1,000 times index
Tick size	0.01 = $10
Contract months	First 3 consecutive months in March cycle
Settlement	Cash settled
Last trading day	2nd Friday preceding 3rd Wednesday of contract month
Final settlement	1-month realized volatility
Trading hours	Sunday–Friday 5:00 P.M. to 4:15 P.M. central

at 20.00, the CME realized volatility indexes and futures will also be expressed in whole numbers. For example, if the monthly realized volatility on the euro currency is 10.5 percent, the index would be displayed at 10.50.

Table 8.4 shows the proposed contract specifications for the monthly version of realized volatility futures expected to trade at the CME. The futures contracts will be valued at $1,000 times the index. Sticking with the euro example, a quote of 10.50 would result in a contract value of $10,500. The minimum price change for this contract will be 0.01 or $10 per tick. Listing of the monthly version of these contracts will include the next two months not on the March cycle (March, June, September, and December) along with the following month on this cycle. Settlement will be in cash based on the level of the index at 2:00 P.M. central on the second Friday before the third Wednesday of the contract month.

Table 8.5 shows the contract specifications for the quarterly version of this product. The terms are the same with the exception of the months that will be available for trading. This contract will have only quarterly expirations available. The next three months in the March cycle will be listed.

CHAPTER 9

The VIX as a Stock Market Indicator

The high level of the VIX is often cited on the business networks when the overall stock market is under pressure. Usually the VIX level is cited and the term *fear and greed index* are associated with it. However, a good explanation of why the VIX tends to rise when the overall stock market is under pressure is not often shared. The implied volatility of option prices rises when there is more demand for than supply of option contracts. When the market comes under pressure, there is often a resulting increase in demand for option contracts. The relationship between increased demand for option contracts in times of panic will be discussed further. Then this concept will be taken another step, and how some traders apply the VIX as a technical indicator will be introduced.

Following the exploration of the relationship of the S&P 500 and VIX indexes, some other methods that have developed involving the VIX will be explored. Specifically, we will examine the VIX index alone, the VIX index combined with other volatility indexes, combining the VIX index with VIX futures trading, and an analysis of the VIX and gold prices. Finally, we'll discuss how to use the put-call ratio calculated through VIX option activity.

By no means should the sample strategies presented in this chapter be taken as absolute recommendations. They are simply basic examples of how powerful the VIX and VIX-related trading activity can be in analyzing market activity. The point behind this chapter is to demonstrate to traders who use technical or quantitative trading strategies that they may want to consider adding the VIX and other volatility-related securities to their technical toolbox.

THE INVERSE RELATIONSHIP BETWEEN THE VIX AND THE S&P 500

The inverse relationship between the stock market and the VIX requires a little explanation. This relationship is in place mainly due to the type of option trading that occurs in times of market weakness. When investors are most concerned regarding the direction of the S&P 500 index or overall market, they tend to seek out protection. One common strategy, to hedge in times of panic, is the purchase of S&P 500 index put options. In times of greater concern regarding the stock market, the purchase of put contracts may be more aggressive. This aggressive purchasing of S&P 500 index put options would result in a rise in implied volatility of S&P 500 index options. The VIX measures implied volatility of S&P 500 index options, so the VIX tends to rise when the overall stock market falls. In times of dramatic market weakness, the VIX will often rise at a magnitude that is greater than the drop in the market. For instance, Table 9.1 shows this relationship based on the 10 worst days for the S&P 500 since 1990.

The CBOE has applied the VIX calculation, which was developed in 2003, to existing data and has the index available from the beginning of 1990. Comparing that data to the daily performance of the S&P 500 index results in the data in Table 9.1. Note that on each of the 10 worst-performing days for the S&P 500 the VIX index was up more, on a percentage basis, than the market was down.

Also, comparing the size of a VIX move to the upside relative to the loss in the S&P 500 index over other periods yields interesting results. Table 9.2 shows the number of times the move to the upside in the VIX has been less than the loss in the S&P 500 index over a variety of days. Also included is

TABLE 9.1 Percent Change of the S&P 500 and VIX Index on the 10 Worst Days from 1/1/1990 to 10/31/2010

	S&P 500 Index	VIX Index
10/15/2008	−9.03%	25.61%
12/1/2008	−8.93%	23.93%
9/29/2008	−8.81%	34.48%
10/9/2008	−7.62%	11.11%
10/27/1997	−6.87%	34.31%
8/31/1998	−6.80%	11.82%
11/20/2008	−6.71%	8.89%
11/19/2008	−6.12%	9.79%
10/22/2008	−6.10%	31.14%
4/14/2000	−5.83%	13.91%

TABLE 9.2 Incidents of VIX Magnitude Being Lower Than S&P 500 Performance from 1/1/1990 to 10/31/2010

Days	Day S&P 500 Performance	VIX Move Less Than S&P 500	Percent VIX Move Less Than S&P 500
10	−5.83%	0	0.0%
25	−4.17%	1	4.0%
50	−3.23%	1	2.0%
100	−2.58%	6	6.0%
250	−1.82%	24	9.6%
500	−1.27%	41	8.2%
1000	−0.71%	132	13.2%

the performance for the cutoff day in each example. For instance, the first row, which shows what occurred over the 10 worst days for the S&P 500 index, shows that the S&P 500 index lost 5.83 percent on the 10th day.

On only one of the worst 50 performance days for the S&P 500 index was the VIX up less in magnitude than the S&P 500 was down. The 50th worst day was down over 3 percent. A 3 percent down move in the stock market is usually a newsworthy event for the day and one that will keep traders at their screens. The worst single day in this worst 50 of days was October 8, 2008, when the stock market lost over 5 percent, but the VIX was only up a little over 3 percent.

As the number of days increases, the magnitude of the drop of the S&P 500 index decreases. The result is smaller down days are included in the study, and the frequency of a VIX move to the upside being more than the loss for the S&P 500 index is lower. Note on the 500th day the market was down only 1.27 percent and on the 1,000th worst day the market loss less than 1 percent (down 0.71 percent). A loss of around 1 percent for the S&P 500 index is not exactly the kind of market activity that results in urgent buying of S&P 500 put options for protection. However, for the 500 worst days of performance, volatility actually increased more than the S&P 500 lost over 90 percent of the time. Even with the 1,000 worst days being measured, over 85 percent of the time volatility increases more than the market loses.

VIX INDEX AS AN INDICATOR

Before discussing the value of the VIX index as an indicator, look to a chart of the VIX versus the S&P 500 from 1990 to late 2010 in Figure 9.1.

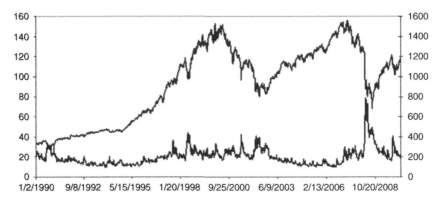

FIGURE 9.1 Weekly Chart of the VIX Index versus the S&P 500 Index, 1/1/1990 to 10/25/2010

On January 2, 1990, the VIX closed at 20.11. Almost 20 years later, the VIX closed at 21.20. The path the VIX took over that long period ranged from an intraday high of 89.53 to a low of 9.31. Over the same period the S&P 500 rose from 352.20 to 1,183.26. Although the VIX is basically flat and the S&P 500 has risen tremendously, the shorter-term inverse relationship between the S&P 500 and the VIX may be used to predict the future direction of stock prices.

For instance, consider using a 20-, 50-, and 200-day moving average for the S&P 500 as the only criteria to be long the index. As long as the S&P 500 closes above these moving averages, there is a long position in the index. When the closing price for the S&P 500 index is below the respective moving average, the system keeps investors on the sidelines and out of the market. For each of these moving averages, a profit would be made through being long the index. Now, if we add a filter that involves the VIX index, there is improvement for each of these moving average rules except for the 200-day moving average system. Table 9.3 shows the results

TABLE 9.3 S&P 500 Moving Averages Combined with VIX Indicator Results

Moving Average	Stand-Alone S&P 500 Result	S&P 500 MA + VIX MA Result
20	95.65	140.22
50	331.83	370.66
200	847.73	626.10

from a simple S&P 500 index moving average and a system combining an S&P 500 moving average system and a VIX index moving average filter.

This test takes each of the moving averages from October 1990 to October 2010 and analyzes the performance of being long the S&P 500 as long as the index closes over the respective moving average. Then a VIX filter is added that involves only being long the S&P 500 in cases where the index is over the respective moving average and the VIX index close is below the same moving average.

The VIX as a filter improves using a 20-day moving average by about 45 S&P points and then it adds about 40 points of value when a 50-day moving average is applied. As the length of the moving average is increased, the effectiveness of using VIX decreases. The idea here is that VIX is much more of a short-term than a long-term market indicator. Spikes in volatility happen quickly, and then the market returns to normal over time. Therefore, as a long-term indicator, the VIX does not appear to be a useful supplement to an S&P 500 moving average system.

Also, it should be noted that buying and holding the S&P 500 index over the same period results in a gain of 880 points for the S&P 500. Admittedly, buy and hold would have outperformed any of these systematic trading approaches. The goal was to display that the VIX index is better over the short term as a market tool as opposed to the long term.

Some of the best buying opportunities for stocks over the decades has occurred when the market appears to be at its worst. Another way to think of this is the best time to buy may be when there is so much fear in the market that there is nothing but sellers in the market. In those times, the result is high implied volatility. Combining market weakness and VIX strength has an interesting outcome.

As a basic analysis of this, buying the S&P for a one-day hold when the market is down 1 percent was tested. Then doing so only when the VIX had a day where it was higher was added to the mix. The result of each approach appears in Table 9.4.

Buying the S&P 500 only when it is down 1 percent or more and holding until the next day's close yields a return of 921.48 S&P 500 points. There is an assumption that there are no transaction costs involved in this system and that a long position mirroring the S&P 500 index may be entered and exited with no slippage. This is a short-term strategy, so adding the VIX

TABLE 9.4 Results of Buying the S&P 500 after a 1 Percent Drop Combined with a VIX-Related Filter

	S&P Down 1%	w/VIX Up 3%
Points gained	921.48	1,060.48

index into the mix actually improves the results a bit. To determine whether there is really fear in the marketplace, a filter of the VIX being up at least 3 percent on the same days was tested. This method takes into account only days on which the VIX moves in a larger magnitude than the S&P 500 index, indicating that fear in stocks combined with increased S&P 500 index option implied volatility based on aggressive option purchases. The result is an extra 120 S&P points over just buying daily weakness.

VIX FUTURES AS AN INDICATOR

A more useful tool to use in market forecasting may be the VIX futures prices versus the VIX index. Also, the relationship between different VIX futures prices has shown promise as a market indicator. A VIX futures contract price is based on the market's outlook for volatility up to and on the expiration date of that contract. Stated another way, VIX futures anticipate the direction and level of the VIX index or the implied volatility of the overall market. With no financial relationship between the spot index and futures contract prices, the result is an indirect market prediction.

This indirect market outlook given by VIX futures works due to the inverse relationship between the S&P 500 and the VIX index. Since the VIX is expected to rally when the stock market moves lower and the VIX would be expected to trend lower during a market upturn, a prediction of where the VIX will be at a certain time in the future is also a bet on what will happen to the S&P 500 index.

If traders expect the S&P to rally, they should sell VIX futures. If they expect the S&P will sell off dramatically, they would take a long position in VIX futures. When VIX futures prices are at a discount to the VIX index, this indicates VIX futures traders believe the S&P 500 index should trade higher and the VIX index should move lower. Conversely, when VIX futures contracts are at a dramatic premium to the VIX index, traders may be anticipating weakness from the overall stock market.

The front month future relative to the VIX index is usually the most active VIX future contract and also the best indicator of the market's expectation of volatility over a short period. This contract will settle in a special calculation of the VIX index, so as time approaches the future contract will trend closer to the value of the index. To eliminate this trend from analyzing the nearest expiring future contract, for testing purposes a new front month is designated the Friday before expiration.

For example, November 12, 2010, is the Friday before November VIX expiration. On this date, even though the November futures contract still

TABLE 9.5 The S&P 500 Index and VIX Front Month Futures Performance on the 10 Worst Days for the S&P 500 Since 1/1/2007

Date	S&P 500 Percent Change	VIX Front Month Percent Change
10/15/2008	−9.03%	18.61%
12/1/2008	−8.93%	13.61%
9/29/2008	−8.81%	14.14%
10/9/2008	−7.62%	14.79%
11/20/2008	−6.71%	5.29%
11/19/2008	−6.12%	9.79%
10/22/2008	−6.10%	10.34%
10/7/2008	−5.74%	11.93%
1/20/2009	−5.28%	12.63%
11/5/2008	−5.27%	8.12%

has a few more days until expiration, the December 2010 contract becomes the front month for analysis purposes.

Any test or analysis using VIX futures contracts will originate only at the beginning of 2007. VIX futures trading has been taking place at the CBOE Futures Exchange since 2004, but the data starting in 2007 has more integrity than going back to the beginning of VIX futures trading. Also, there is a consistency of months available since 2007 that allows for comparisons between contracts. Comparing the worst days for the S&P 500 since the beginning of 2007 with the performance for the tradable front month VIX futures contract yields similar results to the comparison of the S&P 500 and VIX index. Table 9.5 shows this performance comparison.

In 9 out of the 10 worst days for the S&P 500 since 2007, the VIX future contract was up more in magnitude than the S&P 500 index lost. This could be considered more significant than comparing the S&P 500 performance to spot VIX index. The significance comes from the ability to actually trade the VIX future contract and benefit from this price move. The VIX future change is based on traders' anticipation of what may occur in the overall market. When traders buy VIX futures based on the market moving lower, they are anticipating that this trend may continue. Of interest from this table is the day where the S&P 500 lost more on a percentage basis than the VIX future contract rose.

On November 20, 2008, the S&P 500 dropped from 806.58 to 752.44, a loss of 6.71 percent. The same day, the December 2008 VIX future contract gained 5.29 percent, rising from 62.90 to 66.23. Also, the spot VIX index was up from 74.26 to 80.86, a gain of 8.89 percent. Note that the index rose more than the S&P 500 lost, but the future contract did not follow suit. This disparity between the VIX futures, the VIX index, and the S&P 500

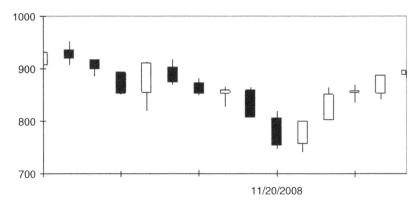

FIGURE 9.2 The S&P 500 Index, November 2008

resulted in an interesting few days following November 20. This interesting response can be seen in Figure 9.2.

November 20 turned out to be a short-term bottom for the overall stock market. The S&P 500 index was up over 15 percent over the next four trading days following this divergence day, when the VIX futures market was not up as much as the S&P 500 was down. Table 9.6 is an overview of the number of times the S&P 500 was down more than the near-term VIX future contract was up on the day for a variety of look-back periods.

This table has pretty consistent results across the board as far as the VIX future contract being up more than the S&P is down about 10 percent of the time. This also translates into the VIX futures rising more than the S&P 500 lost around 90 percent of the time on bearish days. A bearish day in the stock market could easily be considered down more than 2.5 percent on the day, so using the 100 worst days is a fairly logical choice.

TABLE 9.6 Incidents of VIX Futures Magnitude Being Lower Than S&P 500 Performance from 1/1/2007 to 10/31/2010

Tests	Day S&P 500 Performance	VIX Future Move Less Than S&P 500	Percent VIX Move Less Than S&P 500
10	−5.27%	1	10%
25	−3.48%	2	8%
50	−3.23%	5	10%
100	−2.58%	13	13%

A MODIFIED VIX FUTURES CONTRACT

Using the VIX futures contract as an indicator does lead to issues related to time to expiration. As the VIX futures contract approaches expiration, the price gap between the future and the index continues to narrow. To adjust for this, a modified contract price based on the front two months has been created.

The method of developing a VIX reading based on futures to use for technical analysis follows. First, the next two expiration date settlement prices are determined. Then a weighted average of the two contracts is calculated. As time passes, the near-term contract is given less weighting and the longer-term contract is given more, based on their proportion of the combined time to expiration of both contracts.

The following steps would be taken to determine the weighted VIX futures calculation on August 18, 2010. First, the next two expirations would be determined, in this case September 2010 and October 2010. Next, the roll date for each contract is determined with September 23 days off and October 58 days. Finally, the prices of these two contracts will be needed.

CALCULATING A MODIFIED VIX FUTURES CONTRACT

Use the following key and steps to calculate a modified VIX futures contract.

Key

FMD Front month days to roll
BMD Back month days to roll
FMC Front month close price
BMC Back month close price

1. Determine total number of days (TD).

$$TD = FMD + BMD$$

2. $((FMD/TD) \times FMC) + ((BMD/TD) \times BMC)$

As an example of determining the modified VIX futures contract, let's use the closing prices on August 18, 2010:

FMD = 23
BMD = 58
FMC = 29.00
BMC = 31.10

1. TD = 81
2. $(23/81) \times 29.00 + (58/81) \times 31.10 = 30.50$

By taking the two closing prices and weighting them in this manner, the outcome is a closing price of 30.50. This sort of smoothing of the data will allow a better comparison of the closing price of the VIX with the underlying index. As this sort of comparison eliminates the time factor, this calculation creates a better futures-based reading to use as an indicator.

Figure 9.3 is a quick comparison of the spot VIX index and the VIX futures closing prices on a monthly basis from the beginning of 2007 to October 2010. Note that throughout the time period, the futures are at times at a premium or at a discount to the index, depending on the market's outlook for S&P 500 implied volatility.

The modified VIX futures contract is a useful method of smoothing VIX futures. When comparing the front month to the VIX index, the time to expiration may be a factor. Creating a modified contract analysis when comparing the future and index is more useful. The result is the comparison of futures trading versus the index—an easier process.

COMBINING VIX FUTURES AND THE VIX INDEX

Comparing the modified VIX future closing price to the index is a good indication of what the market place expects over the next few weeks regarding the direction of volatility. This comparison results in a prediction of where

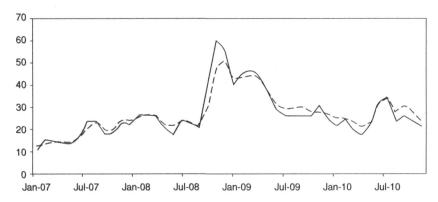

FIGURE 9.3 Monthly Modified VIX Future versus VIX Index, January 2007 to October 2010

TABLE 9.7 Percent of Times the Closing VIX Futures Are at a Premium to the VIX Index

Year	Trading Days Futures above Index	Total Trading Days	% Trading Days above Index	S&P 500 Index Return
2007	177	251	70.5%	3.53%
2008	143	253	56.5%	−38.49%
2009	202	252	80.2%	23.45%
2010	180	209	86.1%	6.11%

the S&P 500 is expected to go over the next few weeks. Table 9.7 shows the percentage of days that the VIX futures are at a premium to the index each year starting with 2007. This data was compiled before the end of 2010 so 2010 represents a partial year.

Note that in 2008 the S&P 500 index lost over 38 percent and the VIX futures closed at a discount much more frequently than in the other three years. The other years, with the futures at a premium more often than not, resulted in a positive year for the S&P 500. However, using the futures relative to the index may be useful in gauging when it is time to buy in moments of panic.

Using the futures price relative to the index as an oversold or panic indicator would result in better performance relative to the S&P since 2007. Table 9.8 shows the performance of the S&P 500 index along with being only long the S&P 500 when the VIX future is at a discount to the VIX index. Also, the final column of this table shows applying a buffer of 5 percent to the VIX index versus the future contract.

Using the VIX futures relative to the index improves performance versus just holding the S&P 500 index. Although underperforming two years

TABLE 9.8 S&P 500 Returns Using the VIX Future versus the VIX Index as a Signal

Year	S&P 500 Performance	Long VIX Future Less Than VIX Index	VIX Future Less Than 95% VIX Index
2007	3.53%	14.79%	17.98%
2008	−38.49%	−11.47%	−6.51%
2009	23.45%	14.34%	9.69%
2010	6.11%	1.70%	2.73%
Average	−1.35%	4.84%	5.97%

and outperforming in a couple of years, trading in this manner results in a return of about 5 percent per year.

The buffer of 5 percent also results in better results than just buying and holding for the S&P 500. Averaging the per-year returns results in an annual return of just about 6 percent per year. This 6 percent return beats the buy-and-hold strategy and is a slight improvement on the nonbuffered return.

VIX INDEX AND GOLD PRICE INDICATOR

A financially related instrument that has been historically associated with market fear is the price of gold. It is an asset that will appreciate in times of turbulence, just like volatility and the VIX. As gold and the VIX have similar reactions to crisis, it makes sense that using them together or related to each other may result in a useful market indicator.

To test the validity of using the price of gold and volatility, the GLD exchange-traded fund is used along with the spot VIX index to represent volatility. Pricing for the GLD goes back as far as late 2004, so testing runs from the beginning of 2005 through late 2010. Figure 9.4 is a price chart comparing the GLD and the VIX monthly closing prices from 2005 to late 2010.

The top line on this chart represents the monthly closing price of the GLD, with the lower line representing the VIX. It appears there are times when they track each other and times when there is some disparity in the direction of the two instruments. A specific time that stands out on this

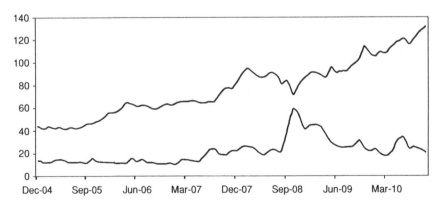

FIGURE 9.4 Monthly GLD versus VIX Index, January 2005 to October 2010

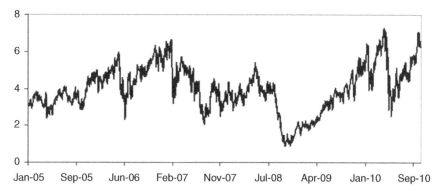

FIGURE 9.5 Ratio of GLD ETF and VIX Index, January 2005 to October 2010

chart is late 2008. As there are times when there is a disconnection between gold and VIX prices, a ratio of the price of gold versus volatility was plotted.

Figure 9.5 shows the ratio of the GLD to the VIX over almost five years. Note that the range fluctuates from a low just below 1.00 to a high that breaches 7.00 a few times. There are times when the price of gold and the VIX index are in sync, but at other times they go in opposite directions.

Before exploring the benefit of this ratio as an indicator, Figure 9.6 shows this ratio compared to the S&P 500 index from January 2005 to October 2010. The lower line represents the GLD/VIX ratio, while the upper line shows the performance of the S&P 500 index over almost five years. Note there appears to be a closer correlation between this ratio and the S&P 500. Both tend to rise and fall in sync.

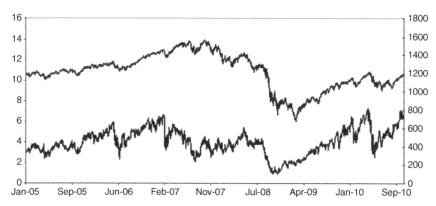

FIGURE 9.6 Ratio of GLD ETF to VIX Index versus S&P 500 Index, January 2005 to October 2010

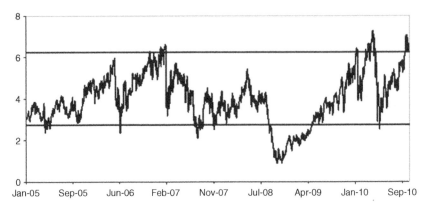

FIGURE 9.7 Ratio of GLD ETF to VIX Index January 2005 to October 2010 with Signal Levels Delineated

Applying this ratio as an indicator has some interesting results. This is a simple strategy, but it demonstrates the usefulness of comparing gold prices to implied volatility to create a market indicator. A buy signal on the S&P 500 index occurs when the GLD/VIX ratio crosses from under 2.75 to above 2.75. A sell signal occurs when the ratio crosses from a reading above 6.25 to below 6.25. The system enters on each of these signals and holds a position in the S&P 500 index for 15 days. Figure 9.7 shows the ratio with lines to indicate the buy and sell signal levels.

Note that when these levels are violated, often there is usually a pretty quick rebound of the ratio. However, a few instances of market turbulence have resulted in extreme readings that were maintained for days and even, in the case of 2008, for months. The tendency for this indicator to remain overbought or oversold at times led to developing a signal based on a return to the normal range of prices for the ratio. Table 9.9 is a summary of the

TABLE 9.9 Summary of Ratio System Results

	Long System	Short System	Combined System
Total points	415.45	321.28	736.73
Maximum	75.14	81.25	81.25
Minimum	−28.36	−43.95	−43.95
Average	21.87	24.71	23.02
Signals	19	13	32
Winners	15	8	23
Percent win	78.95%	61.54%	71.88%

results from taking the GLD/VIX ratio crossover as a signal to buy or sell the S&P 500 index.

This system was tested from the beginning of 2005 to late 2010, covering 1,468 trading days. Only 32 signals were generated, so this is a case of very infrequent signals emanating from these rules. However, the results are fairly impressive for using this indicator as a stand-alone system.

Using this method of being long or short the market results in a total profit of 736 S&P 500 points, or 415 points from the long system and 321 from the short signals. Over the tested period, the S&P 500 index was down slightly, from 1,202 to 1,183 for a loss of 19 points, or basically flat. Even just using the long-only system would have added value.

On the long side, there were 19 signals with 15 of those trades resulting in a profit from holding the S&P 500 index over 15 trading days, or a win percentage of almost 79 percent. The short side had few signals and a slightly lower win rate. On the short side, there were 13 signals with 8 winners, for a winning percentage of just over 61 percent.

The average winners for both long and short came to about 20 S&P points, and the maximum loser for each was much lower than the points lost on the maximum losing trade. Again, this indicator has limited history, but it seems to have performed well signaling market reversals.

VIX OPTION PUT-CALL RATIO

Historically the most common use of option market data as some sort of market indicator has been the put-call ratio. This measure is a ratio of put volume to call volume, and the theory behind it is that an increase in put volume indicates an abundance of bearishness in the market. Too much bearishness in the market may be considered a contrarian indicator. This theory coincides with the thought behind some of the uses of the VIX index as an indicator. Basically, lower stock prices bring in put buying, this increase in put buying pushes implied volatility higher, and the result is a move higher in the VIX index.

There are flaws that go along with using option volume data as a predictive indicator for the overall market. A major one is the ability to create a bullish payout using all put options. In this case, put option volume would increase due to a bullish outlook. Selling call options to increase income in a portfolio due to the market or a stock appearing overbought to a trader is a situation where a neutral to slightly bearish outlook may prompt an increase in call volume. However, in general the put-call ratio has held up as a market indicator for some time.

TABLE 9.10 Put-Call Ratios Calculated and Published by the CBOE

Ratio	Description
Index put-call ratio	Ratio of all index option volume
Equity put-call ratio	Ratio of equity option volume
S&P 500 index put-call ratio	Ratio of S&P 500 index option volume
VIX put-call ratio	Ratio of VIX option volume
Total exchange put-call ratio	Ratio of all exchange option volume

The CBOE publishes a variety of put-call ratios going back as far back as 1995. Table 9.10 is a table of put-call ratios that are calculated by the CBOE along with their respective descriptions.

Due to the longevity of available and consistent data, the CBOE Equity Put-Call Ratio is the most commonly quoted version of a put-call ratio. Historical data going back to 1995 on some of these ratios are available for free from the CBOE at www.cboe.com/data/putcallratio.aspx.

Figure 9.8 is a typical put-call ratio chart depicting the ratio over a 10-month period in 2010. This chart is fairly normal, with the ratio oscillating around the 0.6 range. A reading of 0.6 would indicate that for every 10 call contracts traded there were 6 put contracts. Generally, call volume is higher than put volume. The exception to this occurs during periods of increased concern regarding the equity markets. When there is increased worry in the market regarding the direction of stocks, usually the result is higher than normal put volume relative to call volume.

A put-call ratio developed using option volume data from the VIX option marketplace is an interesting approach to this indicator. Activity in the VIX option market has increased tremendously over the past few years. A

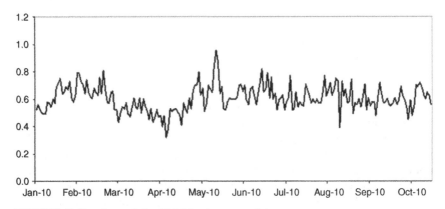

FIGURE 9.8 Chart of the CBOE Equity Put-Call Ratio

good portion of this trading is by institutions using VIX call options as a hedge against a bearish move in the equity market. The leverage provided by out of the money VIX call options can be tremendous in a bear market. Using VIX options as a portfolio hedge is discussed in the next chapter. Also, a study of the usefulness of out of the money VIX call options during the bear market of 2008 is discussed.

VIX call volume would be expected to increase when institutions are most concerned about bearishness in the equity market. Therefore, an indicator developed with VIX put and call volume would be viewed inversely to a traditional equity put-call ratio. That is, increased call volume would indicate market bearishness as opposed to an increase in equity put volume, which may be considered an indication of excessive bearishness.

Figure 9.9 is a chart of the VIX put-call ratio for January 2010 through October 2010. This is the same period covered by the previous chart of the equity put-call ratio. Note that there is a much wider range of readings for the VIX put-call ratio. Being based on a single product, especially one that experiences an abundance of very large institutional orders, results in this increase in the day-to-day volatility of this indicator. Specifically, the high for this ratio was 3.87 and the low was 0.02; a much wider range than was seen for the put-call ratio based on equity option volume. One interesting side note is that the average put-call ratio based on VIX option volume did result in 0.58, which is very close to the average for the equity option put-call ratio.

Another cause of some of the extreme moves in this specific put-call ratio results from low-volume days that can occur in the VIX option arena. Table 9.11 is a summary of VIX index option volume by year from 2007 to late 2010. Note the average volume has steadily increased and been pretty strong. However, there are days when the low end of the spectrum can

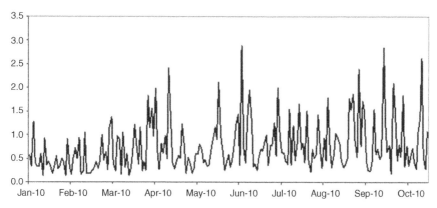

FIGURE 9.9 Chart of the VIX Index Put-Call Ratio

TABLE 9.11 Average Daily VIX Option Volume Statistics

	2007	2008	2009	2010
Maximum volume	361,120	426,661	717,330	605,235
Minimum volume	5,822	6,701	13,661	58,161
Average volume	104,668	102,560	132,732	240,237

skew these results. In order to adjust for this, when testing a trading system, a slight modification was applied to adjust for low-volume days.

The approach to using a VIX-related put-call ratio involves using the ratio to indicate that professionals anticipate bearishness in the marketplace. Increased VIX index call volume relative to VIX index put volume would be a sign that VIX option traders anticipate weakness in the overall stock market. With this specific use of VIX call options in mind, the displayed system will take only a short position on the S&P 500 based on a signal from the VIX put-call ratio. A long version is included, but the short system seems to have more validity than the long version. The long S&P 500 system also screens out days with volume below 75,000 contracts on the day and takes a long position in the S&P 500 for three days if the VIX put-call ratio closes above 1.00 on a day. This rule was added to eliminate those days when low trading volume would result in a signal that may be less than valid based on the fundamental concept.

As with all systems shown in this chapter, the rules behind this test are simple. If the VIX put-call ratio is under .33, indicating three times as much VIX call volume as VIX put volume, then a short position is taken in the S&P 500. This position would be held for three days from close to close. Table 9.12 is a summary of applying this system to short and long S&P 500 positions.

TABLE 9.12 Summary of System Using VIX Put-Call Ratio for Short Term S&P 500 Signals

Figure	Long Trades	Short Trades	Total Trades
Trades	229	100	329
Winners	112	59	171
Win %	48.91%	59.00%	51.98%
Total points	1015.96	377.47	1393.43
Average trade	4.44	3.77	4.24
Biggest winning trade	118.05	88.09	118.05
Biggest losing trade	−60.79	−56.92	−60.79

Note there are many more signals using the short system based on excessive VIX call volume relative to the signals created by more put than call volume. Also the short signal is based on three times the amount of calls traded than the number of puts, while the long version takes a position on days when the put volume just exceeds call volume.

Combining these systems would result in a gain of almost 1,400 S&P 500 points over 46 months. This gain in the S&P 500 from January 2007 to October 2010 is a stark contrast to a basically flat performance from the S&P 500 index over the same period.

Some concerns regarding this method would include the significant losses incurred from the biggest losing trades for both the long and short systems as well as the relatively low winning percentage of around 50 percent. However, this is just a single indicator that may be improved on through adding other analysis or even just using judgment when initiating trades.

Each of the methods for using the VIX as an indicator shows promise. The ideas in this chapter are meant to provide a basis for further work on the VIX as an indicator. Again, these methods of using the VIX or VIX trading vehicles to predict the direction of the stock market should be used in conjunction with other analysis or indicators. For example, combining a moving average or other indicator specific to the S&P 500 index with a VIX-related indicator is more successful than using a VIX-related indicator alone to develop an opinion on the overall market.

CHAPTER 10

Hedging with VIX Derivatives

The VIX futures and index option markets have experienced tremendous volume growth over the past few years. This has come as a result of institutions accepting volatility as an asset class. Both of these instruments are used as hedges against a drop in stock prices. This use of VIX derivatives comes into play due to the inverse relationship between market implied volatility and the direction of stocks. The performance of these trading vehicles during the bear market of late 2008 and early 2009 solidified their place as a legitimate method of portfolio diversification and hedging.

Although volatility-related trading vehicles continue to be introduced, the two most commonly used hedging vehicles are VIX index options and futures. The main focus of this chapter is how VIX index options and futures are used to hedge equity portfolios. In addition, this chapter covers how these products can be used in place of S&P 500 index options. Also, there is a study of how a consistent mix of VIX futures and long stock would have performed over the past few years. The end of this chapter touches on an academic study that looks at the use of VIX options and futures during a period of market weakness.

HEDGING WITH VIX OPTIONS

The first two tables in this chapter depict open interest for S&P 500 index options and VIX index options. The S&P 500 option open interest is heavily

TABLE 10.1 Dec S&P 500 Index Put Option Open
Interest, Late November 2010

Strike	Open Interest
800	133,159
825	32,240
850	83,403
875	43,693
900	191,613
925	68,617
950	163,341
975	93,561
1,000	207,753
1,025	110,481
1,050	125,175
1,075	110,834
1,100	236,583
1,125	120,129
1,150	**202,102**
1,175	**129,873**
1,200	**203,041**
1,225	18,743
1,250	25,772
1,275	1,683
1,300	48,269

weighted toward at the money contracts, while the VIX index options have
the greatest open interest at strikes that are out of the money.

Table 10.1 shows the open interest of S&P 500 index put options expiring in December 2010. This open interest was compiled in late November
2010 with the S&P 500 index closing at 1,170.

Two of the four put options that have open interest in excess of 200,000
contracts have strike prices very close to where the S&P 500 index is currently quoted. Contracts that have a strike very close to the underlying security price are referred to as being at the money. Higher open interest
around the at the money contracts is typical of most option series, whether
index, equity, or exchange-traded fund. Stated another way, the closer the
strike price to the price of an underlying, the higher the open interest would
be expected to be. In addition, the at the money option contracts are usually the most actively traded along with having the highest open interest.

The three strikes that are closest to the S&P 500 index level of 1,170
are highlighted in this table. There are levels of high open interest at
other lower strike prices. Quickly checking the previous nine months' price

history of the S&P 500 index resulted in a low of just over 1,000 and a high of around 1,200. Using that range of trading, any strike between 1,000 and 1,200 would be considered at the money at some time over the life of these option contracts.

Table 10.2 shows the open interest of VIX index call options expiring in December 2010 using data from the same date in late November of that year. The closing price for the VIX index on this date was 20.63 and the corresponding December VIX future contract had a closing price of 20.75. With a quick review of the table, an interesting observation can be made regarding the call option strikes that have the highest open interest.

The December 2010 30 Call has the highest open interest, followed closely by the 40 Call and the 27.50 Call. In fact, using the assumption that the VIX Dec 21 Call is the at the money option, there are eight further out of the money option contracts that have higher contract open interest than the at the money contract. This case of the open interest being highest at out of the money call strike prices is common and unique to VIX options.

The highest level for the December 2010 VIX future contract was 34.10. Therefore all strikes above 35.00 were never at the money contracts. The December VIX 40 Call with an open interest of almost 120,000 contracts was almost 6 points out of the money with the VIX futures at their peak. Considering this contract in another light, the call was almost 15 percent out of the money at the peak of the underlying contract. When this table was created, the 40 Call was almost 100 percent out of the money.

TABLE 10.2   Dec VIX Index Call Option Open Interest, Late November 2010

Strike	Open Interest	Strike	Open Interest
10.00	9,986	32.50	65,002
15.00	889	35.00	56,102
16.00	3,346	37.50	95,454
17.00	700	40.00	119,706
18.00	14,431	42.50	29,516
19.00	2,260	45.00	54,966
20.00	**24,959**	47.50	4,054
21.00	**35,115**	50.00	28,452
22.50	**61,854**	55.00	37,997
24.00	19,361	60.00	15,486
25.00	64,395	65.00	6,729
26.00	26,390	70.00	2,695
27.50	102,904	75.00	2,222
29.00	19,915	80.00	813
30.00	122,175		

TABLE 10.3 S&P 500 Index and VIX Performance from August to November 2008

	8/1/2008	11/20/2008	Change	% Change
S&P 500	1261.31	752.44	−508.87	−40%
VIX Index	22.57	80.86	+58.29	+258%
VIX Future	21.44	76.81	+55.37	+258%

The reason behind high open interest for VIX index option contracts that are 10 to 20 points out of the money emanates from how investors have started to use VIX options for hedging. Many institutions will buy out of the money VIX calls as a version of disaster insurance on the overall equity market. The expectation is that the VIX index and futures contracts will rally in a magnitude that is in excess of the movement to the downside that would occur in the S&P 500 index.

In times of market turbulence, the VIX index often rallies in a magnitude that is many times that of the drop of the S&P 500 index. An excellent example of this occurred during the market turbulence in 2008. Table 10.3 compares the performance of the VIX index and futures contracts to that of the S&P 500 index.

On November 20, 2008, the S&P 500 index closed at 752.44. This closing price represented a loss of about 40 percent from the closing price of 1,260.31 on August 1, 2008. Over the same period, both the VIX index and front month VIX futures markets gained over 250 percent. The expectation that a large equity market drop would be accompanied by a much larger rally in the VIX is behind the increased institutional use of out of the money VIX call options. By purchasing these calls, institutions may obtain cheap protection against a dramatic loss in the equity market. Based on the magnitude of the drawdown in stock prices, buying VIX calls may end up being a more attractive method of hedging relative to buying S&P 500 index put options.

In 2009 a study by Edward Szado of the University of Massachusetts analyzed the financial market activity in the last four months of 2008. A variety of model portfolios were combined with different weightings attributed to VIX derivatives. One conclusion of this study was how the use of VIX call options in this manner can provide superior hedging results to traditional hedging strategies. The specifics of this study will be discussed later in this chapter.

A couple of unique difficulties arise regarding using out of the money VIX call options to hedge an equity portfolio. What strike to choose would be an initial consideration with how many to purchase being a secondary concern.

Any option purchase or hedging strategy should begin with a price opinion on the underlying security. In this case, although VIX call options are being considered for purchase, the purchase is based on concern regarding the direction of the level of the S&P 500 index. An arbitrary 2.5 percent down move in the S&P 500 index on a single day will be the definition of a bearish day. Between 2007 and 2010 there have been 50 days where the S&P 500 index dropped more than 2.5 percent on a single day. Taking the days that the S&P 500 has dropped by 2.5 percent or more, the average move higher for the VIX index has been around 15 percent. The front month future contract has averaged a 9 percent move higher based on a drop of 2.5 percent or more in the S&P 500 index. Looking at even more bearish days of down 5 percent does not change the outcome, as the VIX index rallies on average 17.5 percent and the VIX futures increase on average about 11 percent. Although the index may be a more dramatic number, the future price has more significance as the option contracts are priced off this contract.

As a hypothetical exercise, on Friday, December 18, 2010, the S&P 500 index closed at 1,244, the VIX index closed at 16.11, and the January VIX future contract closed at 20.20. If there is concern regarding a 2.5 percent to 5 percent drop on Monday of the following week, the S&P 500 index put options from Table 10.4 might be considered to hedge an equity portfolio.

TABLE 10.4 December 31, 2010, SPX Put Option Quotes

Put Contract	Bid	Ask
SPX 1160	0.65	1.20
SPX 1165	0.75	1.30
SPX 1170	0.95	1.40
SPX 1175	1.00	1.50
SPX 1180	1.35	1.65
SPX 1185	1.40	1.85
SPX 1190	1.45	2.20
SPX 1195	1.65	2.50
SPX 1200	2.00	2.70
SPX 1205	2.35	3.30
SPX 1210	2.85	3.80
SPX 1215	3.50	4.50
SPX 1220	4.20	5.40
SPX 1225	5.30	6.40
SPX 1230	6.80	7.70
SPX 1235	7.90	9.50
SPX 1240	10.00	11.10
SPX 1245	11.80	13.50

To hedge a $500,000 S&P 500 index portfolio, approximately four at the money SPX 1,245 Put contracts would be purchased. The number of option contracts is determined by dividing the dollar amount of the portfolio by the current index level times 100. As an equation, it would look like this:

$$\$500{,}000/(\$100 \times 1{,}244) = 4.02(4\,\text{contracts})$$

The hedging transaction would be a cost of $5,400, determined by purchasing four contracts at 13.50 each ($1,350). This amount comes to approximately 1 percent of the value of the portfolio. However, if the plan is to hedge for only a day so the cost can be estimated through estimating the price, the contract may be sold the following day if the S&P 500 index closed unchanged. All else staying the same, the SPX 1,245 Put could be sold the following day at 11.25, resulting in a loss of $900 (13.50 – 11.25 × 4 × 100). This change in price is due to the width of the bid-ask spread along with the impact of the passage of one day of time value.

Table 10.5 applies the cost of hedging for a day to a variety of S&P 500 Put options. These dollar amounts may be considered the per contract one-day cost of hedging a portfolio against a drop in the S&P 500, but again the protection gained varies by strike. Table 10.6 shows the results of a 2.5 percent drop and resulting gain or loss by applying the full $5,400 to a variety of put option contracts. The result is a great number of contracts

TABLE 10.5 Cost of Hedging Based on One Day Hold

Put Contract	Cost	Bid Next Day	Cost	$ Cost
SPX 1160	1.20	0.45	−0.75	$300
SPX 1165	1.30	0.55	−0.75	$300
SPX 1170	1.40	0.60	−0.80	$320
SPX 1175	1.50	0.75	−0.75	$300
SPX 1180	1.65	0.85	−0.80	$320
SPX 1185	1.85	1.00	−0.85	$340
SPX 1190	2.20	1.20	−1.00	$300
SPX 1195	2.50	1.40	−1.10	$440
SPX 1200	2.70	1.60	−1.10	$440
SPX 1205	3.30	1.95	−1.35	$540
SPX 1210	3.80	2.40	−1.40	$560
SPX 1215	4.50	3.05	−1.45	$580
SPX 1220	5.40	3.80	−1.60	$640
SPX 1225	6.40	4.80	−1.60	$640
SPX 1230	7.70	6.10	−1.60	$640
SPX 1235	9.50	7.60	−1.90	$760
SPX 1240	11.10	9.40	−1.70	$680
SPX 1245	13.50	11.25	−2.25	$900

TABLE 10.6 Hedged S&P 500 Portfolio Performance with 2.5 Percent Drop in S&P 500 Index

Put Contract	Cost	Bid	Profit	% Profit	Puts	$ Profit	S&P Portfolio Loss	Net Gain/ Loss	% Port Gain/ Loss
SPX 1160	1.20	3.20	2.00	167	12	2,400	−12,500	−10,100	−2.02
SPX 1165	1.30	3.70	2.40	185	12	2,880	−12,500	−9,620	−1.92
SPX 1170	1.40	4.40	3.00	214	12	3,600	−12,500	−8,900	−1.78
SPX 1175	1.50	4.85	3.35	223	12	4,020	−12,500	−8,480	−1.70
SPX 1180	1.65	5.90	4.25	258	11	4,675	−12,500	−7,825	−1.57
SPX 1185	1.85	6.40	4.55	246	10	4,550	−12,500	−7,950	−1.59
SPX 1190	2.20	7.00	4.80	218	9	4,320	−12,500	−8,180	−1.64
SPX 1195	2.50	7.90	5.40	216	8	4,320	−12,500	−8,180	−1.64
SPX 1200	2.70	9.25	6.55	243	8	5,240	−12,500	−7,260	−1.45
SPX 1205	3.30	10.60	7.30	221	6	4,380	−12,500	−8,120	−1.62
SPX 1210	3.80	12.40	8.60	226	6	5,160	−12,500	−7,340	−1.47
SPX 1215	4.50	14.50	10.00	222	6	6,000	−12,500	−6,500	−1.30
SPX 1220	5.40	16.80	11.40	211	5	5,700	−12,500	−6,800	−1.36
SPX 1225	6.40	19.70	13.30	208	5	6,650	−12,500	−5,850	−1.17
SPX 1230	7.70	23.00	15.30	199	5	7,650	−12,500	−4,850	−0.97
SPX 1235	9.50	26.00	16.50	174	5	8,250	−12,500	−4,250	−0.85
SPX 1240	11.10	29.95	18.85	170	4	7,540	−12,500	−4,960	−0.99
SPX 1245	13.50	36.00	22.50	167	4	9,000	−12,500	−3,500	−0.70

at lower strike price. Even though more puts may be purchased at lower strike prices, there is not an improvement protection received based on this 2.5 percent estimated price move. The best protection actually comes from the 1,245 strike contract.

Table 10.7 shows the results of using the same number of option contracts, but looking at the portfolio results of a 5 percent drop in the stock market. With a more dramatic drop in the stock market, the 1,235 strike put is the best choice with the portfolio losing only 0.60 percent of value instead of losing 5 percent for the portfolio that was not hedged.

An alternative to hedging with S&P 500 put options would be to purchase January 2011 VIX calls. VIX call option choices appear in Table 10.8. For a quick comparison using the at the money VIX call options a couple of methods are available for a direct comparison with the cost of hedging for a single day using at the money SPX put options. First, the one-day dollar amount of protection using the at the money 1,245 strike put contracts was estimated at $900. Using this as the one-day cost of hedging could result in determining how many VIX call options may be purchased in place of

TABLE 10.7 Hedged S&P 500 Portfolio Performance with 5 Percent Drop in S&P 500 Index

Put Contract	Cost	Bid	Profit	% Profit	Puts	$ Profit	S&P Portfolio Loss	Net Gain/ Loss	% Port.
SPX 1160	1.20	9.70	8.50	708	12	10,200	−25,000	−14,800	−2.96
SPX 1165	1.30	11.05	9.75	750	12	11,700	−25,000	−13,300	−2.66
SPX 1170	1.40	12.80	11.40	814	12	13,680	−25,000	−11,320	−2.26
SPX 1175	1.50	14.10	12.60	840	12	15,120	−25,000	−9,880	−1.98
SPX 1180	1.65	16.45	14.80	897	11	16,280	−25,000	−8,720	−1.74
SPX 1185	1.85	18.00	16.15	873	10	16,150	−25,000	−8,850	−1.77
SPX 1190	2.20	19.85	17.65	802	9	15,885	−25,000	−9,115	−1.82
SPX 1195	2.50	22.25	19.75	790	8	15,800	−25,000	−9,200	−1.84
SPX 1200	2.70	25.15	22.45	831	8	17,960	−25,000	−7,040	−1.41
SPX 1205	3.30	28.20	24.90	755	6	14,940	−25,000	−10,060	−2.01
SPX 1210	3.80	31.70	27.90	734	6	16,740	−25,000	−8,260	−1.65
SPX 1215	4.50	35.50	31.00	689	6	18,600	−25,000	−6,400	−1.28
SPX 1220	5.40	39.50	34.10	631	5	17,050	−25,000	−7,950	−1.59
SPX 1225	6.40	43.85	37.45	585	5	18,725	−25,000	−6,275	−1.26
SPX 1230	7.70	48.45	40.75	529	5	20,375	−25,000	−4,625	−0.93
SPX 1235	9.50	53.50	44.00	463	5	22,000	−25,000	−3,000	−0.60
SPX 1240	11.10	57.75	46.65	420	4	18,660	−25,000	−6,340	−1.27
SPX 1245	13.50	62.70	49.20	364	4	19,680	−25,000	−5,320	−1.06

buying S&P 500 put contracts. A one-day passage of time would lower the bid price of the VIX Jan 20.00 Call to 1.95. Using $900 as the willing cost of the hedge along with an expected loss of 0.15 over the course of the passage of a day results in the formula:

$$\$900/(\$100 \times 0.15) = 60 \, \text{contracts}$$

TABLE 10.8 January VIX Call Option Quotes

VIX Call	Bid	Ask
Jan 20.00	2.00	2.10
Jan 21.00	1.60	1.80
Jan 22.50	1.30	1.40
Jan 24.00	1.00	1.10
Jan 25.00	0.90	0.95
Jan 26.00	0.75	0.85
Jan 27.50	0.60	0.70
Jan 30.00	0.50	0.55
Jan 32.50	0.35	0.40
Jan 35.00	0.25	0.30

TABLE 10.9 Cost of Hedging with Various VIX Calls Based on One-Day Hold

VIX Call	Ask	Next Day Bid	Cost	% Cost	Contracts
Jan 20.00	2.10	1.95	−0.15	−7	60
Jan 21.00	1.70	1.55	−0.15	−9	60
Jan 22.50	1.40	1.25	−0.15	−11	60
Jan 24.00	1.10	0.95	−0.15	−14	60
Jan 25.00	1.00	0.85	−0.15	−15	60
Jan 26.00	0.85	0.70	−0.15	−18	60
Jan 27.50	0.70	0.55	−0.15	−21	60
Jan 30.00	0.55	0.45	−0.10	−18	90
Jan 32.50	0.40	0.30	−0.10	−25	90
Jan 35.00	0.30	0.20	−0.10	−33	90

The result is if $900 is the cost of hedging, 60 of the VIX Jan 20.00 Call options could be purchased with the same expectation for a loss.

Depending on the contract and cost associated with the spread and the passage of a day, either 60 or 90 VIX Calls may be purchased as a hedge against a drop in the S&P 500. These potential weightings appear in Table 10.9.

The results for using a variety of long call positions appear in Table 10.10. The actual result is pretty similar protection that is offered by S&P 500 index option contracts. A portfolio loss of just over 1 percent is realized using the Jan 20.00 Calls for a single-day hold.

When traders or portfolio managers are concerned about potential portfolio losses, but not willing to pay the option premium for protection, there is a viable alternative. This alternative is known as a col-

TABLE 10.10 Outcome of 10 Percent Rise in VIX

VIX Call	Cost	Bid	Profit	% Profit	Calls	$ Profit	S&P Portfolio Loss	Net Gain/ Loss	% Port
Jan 20.00	2.10	3.25	1.15	55	60	6900	−12,500	−5,600	−1.12
Jan 21.00	1.70	2.65	0.95	56	60	5700	−12,500	−6,800	−1.36
Jan 22.50	1.40	2.15	0.75	54	60	4500	−12,500	−8,000	−1.60
Jan 24.00	1.10	1.70	0.60	55	60	3600	−12,500	−8,900	−1.78
Jan 25.00	1.00	1.52	0.52	52	60	3120	−12,500	−9,380	−1.88
Jan 26.00	0.85	1.28	0.43	51	60	2580	−12,500	−9,920	−1.98
Jan 27.50	0.70	1.05	0.35	50	60	2100	−12,500	−10,400	−2.08
Jan 30.00	0.55	0.85	0.30	55	90	2700	−12,500	−9,800	−1.96
Jan 32.50	0.40	0.60	0.20	50	90	1800	−12,500	−10,700	−2.14
Jan 35.00	0.30	0.40	0.10	33	90	900	−12,500	−11,600	−2.32

lar. A traditional collar consists of buying a put for protection and funding the cost of this protection by selling a call option. The result would be protection against a downside move, but it would sacrifice profits if there were a bullish move out of the underlying.

For example, 100 shares of XYZ stock are owned at 37.50. With concern regarding a bearish move out of XYZ in the next 30 days, purchasing a put option is considered. A 35 strike put is trading at 2.00, which may be considered a bit expensive by the trader. However, a 30-day 40 strike call is also trading at 2.00. To gain protection, a trader may sell the 40 strike call and purchase the 35 strike put for no cost. No cost is the result of taking in 2.00 on the call and paying 2.00 for the put. For the next 30 days the trader now has protection below 35.00 for XYZ but also has sacrificed upside over 40.00 on XYZ.

Using VIX options as a collar would involve selling a put to fund a call. If the collar is initiated to protect against a downside move in the overall stock market, then the position should be set up to benefit from a rise in the VIX. The long call should increase in value, while the short put should lose value in a case of a rising VIX based on a drop in the market.

On November 9, 2010, the November VIX futures contract was trading at 18.90 and the spot VIX index was at 19.08. If there were concern over a drop in the S&P 500 over the next week and a feeling that the market would not rise dramatically over the same period, a collar may be considered using VIX options. Some of the November VIX option quotes appear in Table 10.11.

With the S&P 500 index at 1,213.40, a portfolio manager is concerned about a drop in the index over the next week. He checks the markets and sees an opportunity to place a favorable hedge using VIX options. A collar that would expire in seven days could be initiated by purchasing a November 20.00 Call at 0.60 and selling the November 19.00 Put for 0.85. The result is actually a credit of 0.25. As a bonus for this position, as the VIX index is currently trading at 19.08, if the VIX is unchanged at expiration this trade would actually yield a small profit. In fact, at any price above 18.75 this

TABLE 10.11 VIX November Option Quotes, November 9, 2010

Call	Bid	Ask	Put	Bid	Ask
Nov 18.00	1.25	1.35	Nov 18.00	0.35	0.45
Nov 19.00	0.75	0.85	Nov 19.00	0.85	1.00
Nov 20.00	0.50	0.60	Nov 20.00	1.55	1.70
Nov 21.00	0.35	0.40	Nov 21.00	2.40	2.55
Nov 22.50	0.20	0.25	Nov 22.50	3.70	4.00

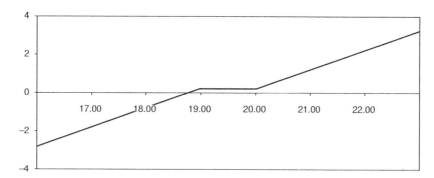

FIGURE 10.1 VIX Collar Payout at November Expiration

collar there would be a profititable trade. This is shown in the payout diagram in Figure 10.1.

Remember, this position is initiated in conjunction with long exposure to the S&P 500. Below 18.75 on the VIX, there would be losses incurred for the option spread, but there should be S&P 500 gains associated with those losses.

November VIX expiration came in at 22.21, so the portfolio manager was correct in his short-term outlook for the overall market. The profit on this trade would be 2.46, or $246 per contract. At the same time, the S&P 500 came under pressure, dropping about 3 percent to 1,178.34.

The hedging decision would start with an outlook for the overall stock market. After establishing this outlook, the cost of VIX calls relative to S&P 500 index put options hedging would need to be analyzed. There may be times when VIX calls are a favorable method for hedging market exposure, especially in situations where a dramatic drop in the overall market is feared.

HEDGING WITH VIX FUTURES

VIX futures may also benefit from periods of equity market bearishness and a subsequent rally in volatility. However, a consistent hedging program with front month VIX futures contracts would be costly and the result would be a benefit in bearish market environments, underperformance in bullish markets, and an overall underperformance versus a pure long portfolio of stocks. This underperformance would be a result of how VIX futures contract prices gravitate to the index over time. Using the front two month VIX futures as opposed to just the front month contract will avoid this constant gravitation to the index by the front month.

TABLE 10.12 Monthly S&P 500 Index Returns

	2007	2008	2009	2010
Jan	1.41%	−6.12%	−8.57%	−3.70%
Feb	−2.18%	−3.48%	−10.99%	2.85%
Mar	1.00%	−0.60%	8.54%	5.88%
Apr	4.33%	4.75%	9.39%	1.48%
May	3.25%	1.07%	5.31%	−8.20%
Jun	−1.78%	−8.60%	0.02%	−5.39%
Jul	−3.20%	−0.99%	7.41%	6.88%
Aug	1.29%	1.22%	3.36%	−4.74%
Sep	3.58%	−9.08%	3.57%	8.76%
Oct	1.48%	−16.94%	−1.98%	3.69%
Nov	−4.40%	−7.48%	5.74%	−0.23%
Dec	−0.86%	0.78%	1.78%	6.53%
Annual	**3.53%**	**−38.49%**	**23.45%**	**13.27%**

Table 10.12 shows the return based on holding a portfolio that matches the performance of the S&P 500 index monthly from 2007 to 2010. This will be representative of a buy-and-hold portfolio. The next table shows the performance of a portfolio with weightings in the front two month futures contracts. This method of smoothing the futures data was discussed in Chapter 9.

Table 10.13 is a return calculation based on holding a continuously rebalanced portfolio representing the next two expiring VIX futures contracts. This return is based on there being no rebalancing costs associated with this portfolio. To replicate this performance, trading would occur every day. Note the strong performance of this strategy in 2007 and 2008 and then the resulting dropoff over the latter two years.

Table 10.14 assumes a portfolio with 90 percent exposure to the S&P 500 combined with 10 percent exposure to the VIX futures portfolio. Note the outperformance in 2007 and 2008 with underperformance in 2009 and 2010. This relative performance can be attributed to an uptrend in volatility through 2007 and 2008 and basically a downtrending to flat volatility market in 2009 and 2010.

For a final and possibly better comparison, the next two tables display the result of investing $10,000 in either the balanced portfolio or purely in an S&P 500 index portfolio. Table 10.15 shows the result of $10,000 invested in the S&P 500 and compounded monthly.

Ten thousand dollars invested in the S&P 500 at the end of 2006 and held through the end of 2010 would result in a portfolio worth $8,867. This

TABLE 10.13 Monthly VIX Futures Portfolio Returns

	2007	2008	2009	2010
Jan	−5.73%	5.89%	0.51%	0.54%
Feb	10.89%	3.54%	2.70%	−9.42%
Mar	6.49%	−0.19%	0.21%	−10.34%
Apr	−4.45%	−16.55%	−16.19%	10.74%
May	2.24%	−3.42%	−15.53%	37.31%
Jun	14.81%	13.36%	−7.44%	9.59%
Jul	28.05%	−4.51%	0.58%	−18.40%
Aug	10.86%	−0.84%	4.78%	10.17%
Sep	−14.61%	27.25%	−9.74%	−10.29%
Oct	1.90%	63.87%	0.83%	−13.94%
Nov	21.81%	8.11%	−4.24%	6.05%
Dec	−1.40%	−16.64%	−5.69%	−22.50%
Annual	**85.20%**	**77.90%**	**−41.29%**	**−22.81%**

is based on the index return and not total returns that may be earned if dividends were also received.

The result from the combined portfolio with exposure to VIX has superior results to the S&P 500 portfolio. Table 10.16 shows the result of 90 percent of a portfolio invested in the S&P 500 and 10 percent of a portfolio with exposure to the balanced VIX future strategy.

As of the end of 2010, regular exposure to VIX futures does result in superior performance to the buy-and-hold S&P 500 index portfolio. Ten

TABLE 10.14 Monthly 90 Percent S&P 500 + 10 Percent VIX Portfolio Performance

	2007	2008	2009	2010
Jan	0.69%	−4.92%	−7.66%	−3.27%
Feb	−0.88%	−2.77%	−9.62%	1.62%
Mar	1.55%	−0.56%	7.71%	4.26%
Apr	3.45%	2.62%	6.83%	2.40%
May	3.15%	0.62%	3.22%	−3.65%
Jun	−0.12%	−6.40%	−0.73%	−3.89%
Jul	−0.07%	−1.34%	6.73%	4.35%
Aug	2.24%	1.01%	3.50%	−3.25%
Sep	1.76%	−5.45%	2.24%	6.85%
Oct	1.52%	−8.86%	−1.70%	1.92%
Nov	−1.78%	−5.93%	4.74%	0.40%
Dec	−0.92%	−0.96%	1.03%	3.63%
Annual	**11.70%**	**−26.85%**	**16.98%**	**11.16%**

TABLE 10.15   Performance of $10,000 Invested in the S&P 500 Index
Compounded Monthly

	2007	2008	2009	2010
Jan	$10,141	$9,720	$5,823	$7,572
Feb	$9,919	$9,382	$5,183	$7,787
Mar	$10,018	$9,326	$5,626	$8,245
Apr	$10,452	$9,769	$6,154	$8,367
May	$10,792	$9,874	$6,481	$7,681
Jun	$10,600	$9,025	$6,482	$7,267
Jul	$10,261	$8,936	$6,962	$7,767
Aug	$10,393	$9,045	$7,196	$7,399
Sep	$10,765	$8,224	$7,453	$8,046
Oct	$10,924	$6,830	$7,306	$8,343
Nov	$10,443	$6,319	$7,725	$8,324
Dec	$10,353	$6,369	$7,862	$8,867

thousand dollars in the balanced portfolio would have held up better than
the S&P 500, and at the end of 2010 it would have been worth $10,139, for
a result of just above breakeven.

As the VIX and VIX futures have gone through periods of high and low
levels, an approach that dynamically hedges based on some sort of indicator or market analysis may result in stronger outperformance. This outperformance may be achieved through increasing and decreasing exposure to
volatility based on some systematic approach.

TABLE 10.16   Performance of $10,000 with 90 Percent Exposure to the S&P 500
Index and 10 Percent in VIX Futures Compounded Monthly

	2007	2008	2009	2010
Jan	$10,069	$10,551	$7,285	$8,822
Feb	$9,981	$10,258	$6,584	$8,966
Mar	$10,135	$10,201	$7,091	$9,347
Apr	$10,485	$10,469	$7,576	$9,572
May	$10,816	$10,533	$7,820	$9,223
Jun	$10,802	$9,859	$7,764	$8,864
Jul	$10,794	$9,727	$8,286	$9,250
Aug	$11,037	$9,826	$8,576	$8,949
Sep	$11,231	$9,291	$8,768	$9,562
Oct	$11,402	$8,467	$8,619	$9,746
Nov	$11,199	$7,966	$9,028	$9,784
Dec	$11,096	$7,889	$9,121	$10,139

UNIVERSITY OF MASSACHUSETTS STUDY

After the market turmoil of 2008, a study was conducted at the University of Massachusetts–Amherst, to determine the potential benefits of VIX futures and options as hedging vehicles. The study, "VIX Futures and Options—A Case Study of Portfolio Diversification During the 2008 Financial Crisis," appeared in the *Journal of Alternative Investments*. (The full report and a two-page summary are available for download from the CBOE at www.cboe.com/Institutional/reports.aspx.)

The key question was whether these two VIX-related derivatives would have served as useful diversification tools during the financial crisis of 2008. Specifically, returns based on performance of assets from August 1, 2008, to December 31, 2008, were studied. Several traditionally constructed portfolios were analyzed with a variety of VIX derivative weightings added to the portfolio. The types of portfolios studied were 100 percent long-only equity portfolio, mixed portfolio with 60 percent stocks and 40 percent bonds, and fully diversified portfolio with multiple asset classes. VIX weightings that were added to these standard portfolios included a long 2.5 percent VIX futures weighting, a 10 percent long VIX futures weighting, 1 percent long at the money VIX calls, 3 percent long at the money VIX calls, 1 percent long out of the money VIX calls, and 3 percent long out of the money VIX calls. Out of the money calls were strikes that were 25 percent higher than the VIX index.

One interesting outcome involved the returns for the fully diversified portfolio when weightings of out of the money VIX call options were included. From August 1, 2008, to December 31, 2008, the fully diversified model portfolio lost 19.68 percent in value. Contributing 1 percent out of the money VIX calls to the portfolio resulted in a portfolio return of 17.70 percent. A 3 percent weighting of out of the money VIX calls resulted in a portfolio return of 97.18 percent. These results show the dramatic benefits of the leverage gained from out of the money VIX calls. This leverage resulted from the dramatic magnitude of the inverse relationship between the VIX index and the S&P 500 combined with the normal leverage that comes with using out of the money options.

Two findings were determined by the study. First, in a period of dramatic market losses, such as this four-month period in 2008, all financial assets tend to lose value, so a portfolio that is considered diversified may not hold up as well as anticipated. The second finding involves the use of volatility as a diversification tool. The result is that during a period of a market downturn, VIX diversification results in protection. However, over the long term, exposure to the VIX for diversification purposes may result in underperformance.

The growth of VIX option and futures contracts can be directly attributed to the use of these instruments to hedge an equity portfolio. A consistent program of hedging an equity portfolio with VIX instruments can result in underperformance of a portfolio. However, there are often instances when using VIX options or futures to hedge an equity portfolio would result in cheaper protection that would result in strong performance in the case of a dramatic loss in the equity market.

CHAPTER 11

Speculating with VIX Derivatives

A s discussed in Chapter 10, the ability to use VIX options and futures for hedging purposes has greatly contributed to strong volume growth for both instruments. The hedging and speculating function that these instruments serve is only one piece to the puzzle. The VIX pit, where several volatility-related derivatives are traded, is now the second largest pit at the CBOE. Multiple market-making firms involved in trading VIX futures and options are continuously posting bids and offers for both the futures and index options. Due to the large number of market makers, speculators have the ability to easily move in and out of positions. With this comfort, speculators use VIX instruments based on an outlook for volatility or the overall stock market. A successful market requires speculators to provide liquidity to allow participants to easily enter and exit positions. VIX futures, options, and exchange-traded notes have definitely attracted these participants.

A long or short opinion regarding the direction of the VIX index will mostly be based on an opinion tied to the direction of the stock market as a whole. However, there is an anticipatory component to these VIX derivative products. Due to this aspect to pricing, more than just what occurs in the level of the S&P 500 index may influence prices of VIX futures, options, and exchange-traded notes.

This chapter will address directionally based trading strategies using these three classes of VIX derivatives individually. Later chapters will dive into spread strategies that use multiple instruments at the same time.

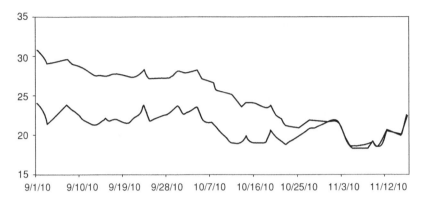

FIGURE 11.1 November 2010 VIX Futures and VIX Index Prices 9/1/2010–11/16/2010

VIX FUTURES TRADING

The first derivative product developed to be based on a volatility oriented index was the VIX futures contract. These instruments offer a direct method of speculating on higher or lower implied volatility. Also, these futures may be used opportunistically, based on an overall market opinion. Specifically, VIX futures anticipate the direction of the VIX index and are cash settled based on a calculation of the VIX index. As time passes, the VIX futures contract will gravitate toward the level of the VIX index. Figure 11.1 is a chart of the November 2010 VIX futures contract and the VIX index.

The higher line on this chart represents the November VIX futures contract, while the lower line is the VIX index. In early September the futures were trading at a nice premium to the index and were also the third month in order of expiration behind September and October. As time passed and the November contract moved from being the third month to the front month, the contract's price approached the index. Over the final two weeks before expiration, the November contract started to closely follow the index.

Before placing any VIX futures trade, a trader should be aware of a few factors. First, as VIX futures do have an expiration date, a trader should be aware of when the contract expires. Second, where the index is relative to the future contract should be a consideration. Finally, where the future is relative to other contracts should be analyzed.

The first step, being aware of expiration of a VIX futures contract, makes common sense, but there is an aspect to VIX expiration that may

TABLE 11.1 Standard Option and VIX Future/Option Expiration Dates in 2011

	Standard Option Expiration	VIX Expiration
January	January 21	January 19
February	February 18	February 16
March	March 18	March 16
April	**April 15**	**April 20**
May	May 20	May 18
June	June 17	June 15
July	**July 15**	**July 20**
August	August 19	August 17
September	**September 16**	**September 21**
October	October 21	October 19
November	November 18	November 16
December	**December 21**	**December 16**

result in a surprise. When trading the front month future, a trader should always be aware of the contract expiration date. Unlike option contracts that expire on a Friday, VIX futures and options expire on a Wednesday. The last day of trading is Tuesday for Wednesday morning settlement.

However, the Wednesday that this occurs may vary from month to month. The specific Wednesday is based on standard option expiration the following month, so at times this may be that month's option expiration week and it also may be the following week. Table 11.1 lists the expiration dates in 2011 for standard option contracts and expiration for VIX futures and option contracts.

In 2011 there are eight months where the futures contracts expire in the same week as standard option expiration. During the other four weeks, VIX expiration is the week following standard option expiration. This occurs due to the expiration of VIX futures and options is based on the following standard expiration, not the current month's expiration. Since it varies at times, the contract expiration date should be double checked, especially for shorter-term trades. A calendar that lists standard option expiration along with VIX expiration dates is available at www.cboe.com under the trading tools table.

A key component for shorter-term trades may often be where the index is trading relative to the future contract. If a trader has a short-term expectation of a rise in S&P 500 implied volatility, but VIX futures are already trading at a premium to the index, then a long position may not be advisable. Also, if there is an expectation that S&P 500 index option implied volatility will drop in the near future, a short position in the VIX futures may not be feasible based on the price of the future relative to the price of the index. However, if the futures are at a premium, then this may make trading this outlook even more attractive.

For example, in 2008 the front month VIX futures were trading at a discount to the VIX index almost 50 percent of trading days. If there was an expectation that the index were going to drop, then a short position in the futures may have been considered. Consider the following pricing from October 17, 2008:

VIX index—70.33
November 2008 VIX future—46.85

With the VIX trading at an unprecedented level over 70, a trader considers a short position in VIX futures. He believes by the end of October that the VIX index should be trading at a much lower level than this. In order to place a trade on this opinion, he sells a November 2008 VIX contract on the close. The November 2008 is the front month contract and the pricing is much lower than in the index at 46.85, so he needs a pretty dramatic drop in the VIX index to make a profit on this trade.

On October 31, the index and futures closed with the following prices:

VIX index—59.89 (down 10.44)
November 2008 VIX future—54.50 (up 7.65)

Even though his outlook for the VIX index was correct, the trade was still a losing transaction. This is an extreme case of the future contract climbing while the index lost value, but a good illustration of what may occur on a smaller scale.

Finally, a trader may want to consider where VIX futures contracts are trading relative to each other. Often, a front month contract may be trading at a discount to the index while the second month may be at a premium. In this situation a long position may be best served using the near term contract and a short position may be best traded with the second month contract.

As an example, consider the prices for the VIX index, November 2010 futures, and December futures contract on November 2, 2010.

VIX index—21.57
November 2010 VIX future—21.00
December 2010 VIX future—23.75

Consider these prices along with a one-day bearish outlook for the VIX. The November future contract is trading 0.57 below the index, while the

December contract is at a premium of 2.75. If a short position to be held to the next day's closing were considered, the December contract would be the preferable instrument. November 3 closing prices and changes for all three instruments were:

VIX index—19.56 (down 1.01)
November 2010 VIX future—19.80 (down 1.20)
December 2010 VIX future—22.35 (down 1.40)

Note that the December future contract lost 0.20 point more than the November contract. A single short position in the December contract would have gained $200 more than the short position in a November contract.

When considering a VIX future trade based solely on the direction of the index, there may be as many as three steps taken before putting the trade on. First, there should be an opinion on the future direction of the VIX index. Second, the time outlook for the trade combined with the time until expiration for the VIX future contract. Finally, the proximity of the VIX future contract to the index as well as other VIX futures contracts may be considered.

VIX OPTION TRADING

Buying a VIX index call to benefit from a rise in the VIX or buying a VIX index put when there is an expectation that there will be a drop in the VIX appears to be two straightforward trades. However, like trading the VIX futures contracts based on an opinion of the outlook for the VIX, option trades also should be approached with knowledge of the unique nature of VIX options relative to other option contracts.

When a trader first approaches VIX index options, there is often confusion associated with interpreting the pricing of these options. As discussed in Chapter 4 when valuing a VIX option contract, the best underlying instrument to use when valuing a VIX option contract is the VIX future with the same expiration date. Even though these contracts are valued using the underlying futures, they are settled in cash based on the VIX index. So, even though the contract is being valued with the future contract as the underlying, there should be an awareness of where the index is trading as well.

In late November 2010 the VIX future contract expiring in January 2011 closed at 23.25 while the VIX index closed at 19.50. Table 11.2 is a summary of January 2011 put quotes. Two more columns are added to this

TABLE 11.2 January 2011 Put Option Quotes

Option	Bid	Ask	ITM @ 19.50	Profit/Loss @ 19.50	Break Even
Jan 20.00 Put	1.00	1.10	0.50	−0.60	18.90
Jan 21.00 Put	1.35	1.50	1.50	0.00	19.50
Jan 22.50 Put	2.15	2.25	3.00	0.75	20.25
Jan 24.00 Put	3.10	3.20	4.50	1.30	20.80
Jan 25.00 Put	3.70	3.90	5.50	1.60	21.10
Jan 26.00 Put	4.50	4.70	6.50	1.80	21.30
Jan 27.50 Put	5.70	5.80	8.00	2.20	21.70
Jan 30.00 Put	7.70	8.00	10.50	2.50	22.00

quote line. The next column indicates the in the money value of the option contract based on the VIX index price of 19.50. The second-to-last column, Profit/Loss @ 19.50, indicates the gain or loss based on buying the put option, holding the contract to settlement, and the resulting gain or loss on that trade. Also, this breakeven level just happens to be where the VIX index is trading on this date.

Finally, the last column, labeled Break Even, shows levels at January VIX expiration where a long position in each of these put options would result in a breakeven trade. At all strikes higher than the Jan 21.00 Put, the breakeven level is higher than the VIX index price. This means that even if the VIX index is unchanged between initiating the trade and expiration that there may still be a profit from purchasing these contracts. In fact, even though a bearish outlook would be in place in order to purchase a put, the index could rise slightly and there might still be a profit at expiration.

On the day these January contract prices were recorded, 56 days remained to January VIX expiration. The interesting aspect regarding potentially purchasing the majority of the put contracts on this table is that a profit may be realized if the VIX index is unchanged over the next 56 days. In fact, for many of the put contracts on the table, a profit may be realized even if the VIX index moves higher. Stated another way, the trader could be wrong on the direction of the VIX index and still make a profit.

This aspect of trading VIX options is counterintuitive relative to traditional long-option positions. The majority of option contracts have a time value component to the pricing of the option. If the price of the underlying security does not move over the life of the option, there would be a loss equal to the time value priced into the option when it was purchased. It is possible to think of the VIX put options in Table 11.3 as having negative time value based on the index as the underlying. Traders are pricing the options based on the futures, but over time the futures pricing will approach

TABLE 11.3 Key Levels for Long VIX January 25.00 Put

Key Levels	Price/Level
Maximum profit	21.10
Maximum profit VIX settlement	0.00
Maximum loss	3.90
Maximum loss VIX settlement	25.00
Break even	21.10

the VIX index. This "gravitation" to the index by the futures contract would be a benefit to the option holder.

For example, if the Jan 25.00 Put is purchased for the ask price of 3.90, with the intention of holding the contract to expiration, a profit of 1.60 would be realized. The key levels for this trade appear in Table 11.3.

The maximum potential profit from purchasing this put option is 21.10, based on the VIX index at 0.00 at expiration. This is a theoretical level based on the VIX index reacting 0.00. The lowest VIX index level over the past 20 years has been slightly under 10.00. The maximum potential loss from buying this option is limited to the premium paid for the contract of 3.90, and this would occur if the VIX settlement price is at the strike price of 25.00 at expiration.

Possibly the most interesting key level on this table is the breakeven price of 21.10. With the VIX index at 19.50 when this trade was initiated, this also represents how much the VIX may rise before this trade goes from being a profit to being a loss. There is a 1.60 of cushion between the current VIX index level and the price at expiration. Figure 11.2 is a payout diagram of this trade at expiration.

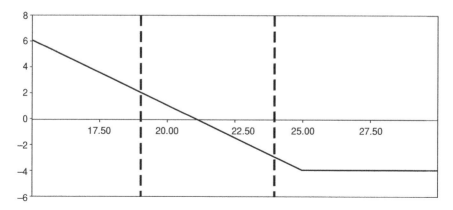

FIGURE 11.2 Payout Diagram for Long VIX January 25.00 Put

TABLE 11.4 January 2011 Call Option Quotes

Option	Bid	Ask	Break Even	BE > 19.50	BE > 23.25
Jan 10.00 Call	12.90	13.70	23.70	4.20	0.45
Jan 15.00 Call	8.10	8.60	23.60	4.10	0.35
Jan 17.00 Call	6.40	6.80	23.80	4.30	0.55
Jan 18.00 Call	5.60	5.90	23.90	4.40	0.65
Jan 19.00 Call	4.90	5.10	24.10	4.60	0.85
Jan 20.00 Call	4.30	4.40	24.40	4.90	1.15
Jan 21.00 Call	3.70	3.90	24.90	5.40	1.65
Jan 22.50 Call	3.00	3.10	25.60	6.10	2.35
Jan 24.00 Call	2.35	2.50	26.50	7.00	3.25
Jan 25.00 Call	2.10	2.20	27.20	7.70	3.95
Jan 26.00 Call	1.80	1.95	27.95	8.45	4.70
Jan 27.50 Call	1.50	1.60	29.10	9.60	5.85
Jan 30.00 Call	1.20	1.25	31.25	11.75	8.00

This payout diagram is typical for a long put. A couple of lines have been added to indicate VIX price levels when the trade was initiated. The dashed line on the left indicates the level of the VIX index (19.50), while the vertical dashed line on the right indicates the price of the January 2011 VIX Future contract (23.25). Note that the VIX index line is placed on the diagram to illustrate the level where there would be a profit realized at expiration through a long position in this January 25.00 Put.

The price relationship between VIX options and the underlying VIX index works to the benefit of a trader who has a bearish outlook for market volatility. What about the trader who is bullish on volatility when the VIX futures are trading at a premium to the VIX index?

When bullish and considering an option trade to benefit from this, buying a call is often one of the first strategies that are explored. As with a VIX put trade, the pricing of the corresponding VIX future contract can have an impact on the chosen strategy. Table 11.4 is a summary of January 2011 call options, their quotes, and a couple of additional columns for analysis.

The additional columns vary from the added columns on the table related to the put option example. There are columns indicating the breakeven level for each contract if held to expiration and the required price increase needed from the spot VIX index to reach this breakeven level. Also, mostly for illustration purposes, the amount the VIX future contract is below the breakeven level is shown. For the deep in the money VIX Jan 10.00, there is only 0.45 difference between break even and the future price while there is 4.20 between break even and the index.

On this date the index is at a discount of almost 4 points to the January VIX future. Since the pricing of the options is based on those futures, this results in breakeven levels significantly higher than the VIX index. This also may result in the cost of call options being prohibitively expensive.

VALUING OPTION CONTRACTS WITHOUT FUTURES QUOTES

Often many option traders do not have access to VIX futures quotes and have a difficult time properly valuing VIX option contracts. There is a solution to this issue using VIX option pricing. This is not a perfect solution, but it is a method of estimating the VIX futures prices based on option prices.

Using the midpoint of the deepest in the money call option and deepest in the money put, the corresponding futures price may be estimated. The following steps demonstrate this using the January 2011 quotes.

Step 1

Determine the midpoint of the deepest in the money call and put option contracts. The midpoint of the quote of the deepest in the money VIX January 2011 10 Call is determined by adding the bid and offer together and dividing by 2.

$$(13.70 + 12.90)/2 = 13.40$$

The midpoint of the quote of the deepest in the money VIX January 2011 50 Put is also determined by adding the bid and offer together and dividing by 2.

$$(26.40 + 27.40)/2 = 26.90$$

Step 2

Add the call midpoint to the call strike price and subtract the put midpoint from the put strike.

Call Calculation = Call Strike + Midpoint
Call Calculation = 10.00 + 13.40 = 23.40
Put Calculation = Put Strike = Midpoint
Put Calculation = 50.00 − 26.90 = 23.10

Step 3

Sum the two results from Step 2 and divide by 2.

$$(23.40 + 23.10)/2 = 23.25$$

Result

23.25 is a rough estimate of the January 2011 VIX Future price.

TABLE 11.5 VIX 2011 January Calls

Option	Cost	Break Even	Profit at 27.50	% Return at 27.50
Jan 10.00 Call	13.70	23.70	3.80	28%
Jan 15.00 Call	8.60	23.60	3.90	45%
Jan 17.00 Call	6.80	23.80	3.70	54%
Jan 18.00 Call	5.90	23.90	3.60	61%
Jan 19.00 Call	5.10	24.10	3.40	67%
Jan 20.00 Call	4.40	24.40	3.10	70%
Jan 21.00 Call	3.90	24.90	2.60	67%
Jan 22.50 Call	3.10	25.60	1.90	61%
Jan 24.00 Call	2.50	26.50	1.00	40%
Jan 25.00 Call	2.20	27.20	0.30	14%
Jan 26.00 Call	1.95	27.95	−0.45	−23%
Jan 27.50 Call	1.60	29.10	−1.60	−100%
Jan 30.00 Call	1.25	31.25	−3.75	−300%

A very bullish outlook for volatility would need to be in place in order to consider purchasing one of these January 2011 VIX call options. With a target of 27.50, a long position in most of these options would be a viable trading decision. Table 11.5 shows the cost, break even, profit or loss at the target, and the percent return for each option based on the target of 27.50.

After analyzing the information in the table, the January 20 Call appears to be the best choice to benefit from a 27.50 target for the VIX. Purchasing this call for 4.40 would result in a profit of 3.10 if January VIX settlement is 27.50. This would result in a return of 70 percent based on the 4.40 cost and the contract being worth 7.50 at expiration. Break even for this call purchase would be 24.40, almost 5 points above the VIX index level of 19.50. Finally, the maximum loss for this trade is the 4.40 premium paid for the option which would occur at 20.00 or lower. Note that this places the index at 19.50 in the maximum loss range when the trade is initiated. All key levels for this call purchase are summarized in Table 11.6.

TABLE 11.6 Key Levels for Long VIX January 20.00 Call

Key Level	Price/Amount
Maximum profit	Unlimited
Maximum profit VIX settlement	Unlimited
Maximum loss	4.40
Maximum loss VIX settlement	20.00
Break even	24.40

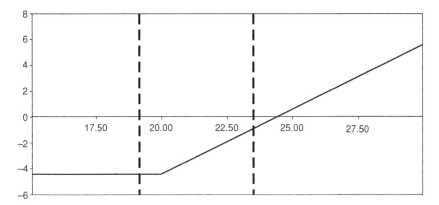

FIGURE 11.3 Payout Diagram for Long VIX January 20.00 Call

Figure 11.3 is a payout diagram depicting a long position for the VIX Jan 20 Call. Both the VIX index and the January VIX future contract prices are highlighted on this payout diagram as they were on the previous example.

A trade that may be a good alternative in this case would be a vertical spread. This would involve purchasing a call option and selling another call with a higher strike price. Through selling another call, some of the cost of the long option will be offset. If considering equity option contracts, when a long position is costly due to high implied volatility, a good alternative to a pure long option position is a vertical spread. This holds true in this case also.

Table 11.7 is a quick summary combining a variety of short positions in VIX Jan Call options with a long position in the VIX Jan 20 Call.

TABLE 11.7 Long VIX January 20.00 Call Combined with a Variety of Short Call Options

Short Option	Option Premium	Vertical Cost	Profit @ 27.50	% Profit	Maximum Profit Price	Break Even
Jan 21.00 Call	3.70	0.70	0.30	43%	21.00	20.70
Jan 22.50 Call	3.00	1.40	0.90	64%	22.50	21.40
Jan 24.00 Call	2.50	1.90	2.10	111%	24.00	21.90
Jan 25.00 Call	2.10	2.30	2.70	117%	25.00	22.30
Jan 26.00 Call	1.80	2.60	3.40	131%	26.00	22.60
Jan 27.50 Call	1.50	2.90	4.60	159%	27.50	22.90

TABLE 11.8 Long VIX Jan 20.00 Call versus VIX Jan 20.00/27.50 Bull Call Spread

	Long Jan 20.00 Call Profit / Loss	Long Jan 20.00 Call % Profit	20.00/27.50 Call Spread Profit / Loss	20.00/27.50 Call Spread % Profit
20.00	−4.40	−100%	−2.90	−100%
22.50	−1.90	−43%	−0.40	−14%
25.00	0.60	14%	2.10	72%
27.50	3.10	70%	4.60	159%
30.00	5.60	127%	4.60	159%
32.50	8.10	184%	4.60	159%

A short call option combined with a long VIX Jan 20 Call position can result in an improved payout. The payout improves, based on a target price of 27.50, when all strikes from 24.00 to 27.50 are added as a short position. The final decision on which option contract to sell to initiate this vertical spread would be based on a combination of the most attractive breakeven price: the price level where each spread reaches maximum profit and the percent profit achieved at these levels.

If there is a high level of confidence in the target of 27.50, then the best choice would be a vertical spread combining a long VIX Jan 20.00 Call and short VIX Jan 27.50 Call. With the VIX at 27.50 on January settlement, a 2.90 investment would result in a 4.60 profit. This is over twice the return realized through purchasing the January 20 Call and a good alternative to this single long position. A quick comparison of this long call and the bullish vertical spread appear in Table 11.8.

With a January VIX settlement price of 20.00, both strategies result in a 100 percent losing trade. As the settlement price rises from there, the call spread has a superior payout on a use of capital basis. This advantage actually extends above the higher strike price of 27.50 to a level above 30.00. Note the profit for the call spread is capped out at 27.50 as the short position in the VIX 27.50 call offsets the value gained from the long position in the 20.00 call.

A vertical spread is often a good alternative to a long call or put position. When considering a vertical spread relative to a stock or index, it normally is a superior choice when the long option appears to be a prohibitively expensive trade based on the premium associated with the option. A method of offsetting this high premium is to sell another option. This also holds true for VIX options when the future contract price results in a prohibitively expensive long option. Vertical spreads and their potential advantages with respect to VIX Index options is discussed more extensively in Chapter 15.

VIX ETN TRADING

There are three VIX exchange-traded notes (ETNs) that have sufficient liquidity to actively trade to capitalize on opinions related to the direction of volatility. Two of these are long-volatility ETNs with the VXX focusing on short-term volatility and the VXZ, which focuses on midterm implied volatility. In addition, the XXV is an inverse ETN that replicates a short position in short-term volatility. These three ETNs were introduced in Chapter 6.

A VIX ETN trade is a straightforward prospect. They trade like stocks and exchange-traded funds, and a long or short position in the VXX or VXZ may be taken. This position would be based on what the outlook is for market volatility. An advantage these two ETNs have on options and futures is that they may be held for longer periods since there is no expiration date. However, at times the direction of implied volatility and these instruments does not move in sync.

VXX Relative to the VIX Index

Also, the performance of the VXX relative to the VIX was discussed in Chapter 6. As a review, the VXX is structured to maintain a long position in the next two expiring VIX futures contracts. Due to the overwhelming popularity of the VXX, this has led to some performance issues related to the daily restructuring of this ETN. Table 11.9 shows the monthly performance of the VIX index, front month VIX future, and VXX since the inception of the VXX.

There is limited price history for the VXX with 21 months' performance to use to compare the VXX to the spot VIX index or a weighted near-term future contract. As of the end of October 2010, the VXX ETN had underperformed the spot VIX index 8 of 21 months. What is more dramatic is the overall performance of the VXX related to the VIX index. From January 31, 2009, to October 29, 2010, the VXX was down about 87 percent compared to a drop in the VIX index of around 52 percent.

On a short-term basis, many day traders are finding the VXX a useful intraday trading vehicle relative to volatility. Trading volume for the VXX is consistently in the tens of millions of shares. Also on a short-term basis, the VXX can provide a good mirror of the VIX index for a single-day trade. Table 11.10 is a summary of the direction of the VIX index relative to the one-day change in the VXX.

Over the 21-month period covered by the data in the table, there have been 441 trading days. There was never an occurrence where the VIX was unchanged. There were 188 instances of the VIX closing higher, and

TABLE 11.9 Monthly Performance of the VIX Index, VIX Futures, and VXX ETN

	VIX Index	VIX Future	VXX
Feb 2009	3.37%	2.70%	3.91%
Mar 2009	−4.77%	0.21%	4.18%
Apr 2009	−17.31%	−16.19%	−17.18%
May 2009	−20.77%	−15.53%	−16.88%
Jun 2009	−8.89%	−7.44%	−12.60%
Jul 2009	−1.63%	0.58%	−9.01%
Aug 2009	0.35%	4.78%	−4.52%
Sep 2009	−1.54%	−9.74%	−15.51%
Oct 2009	19.84%	0.83%	−3.54%
Nov 2009	−20.14%	−4.24%	−16.47%
Dec 2009	−11.55%	−5.69%	−15.42%
Jan 2010	13.56%	0.54%	−7.13%
Feb 2010	−20.80%	−9.42%	−16.91%
Mar 2010	−9.79%	−10.34%	−20.08%
Apr 2010	25.36%	10.74%	0.95%
May 2010	45.44%	37.31%	34.75%
Jun 2010	7.70%	9.59%	9.17%
Jul 2010	−31.96%	−18.40%	−27.66%
Aug 2010	10.85%	10.17%	−2.70%
Sep 2010	−9.02%	−10.29%	−21.27%
Oct 2010	−10.55%	−13.94%	−24.23%

76 percent of the time the VXX followed suit. On 253 days the VIX index was lower, and the VXX was down 88 percent of the instances or on 222 trading days. On a cumulative basis, the VXX followed the one-day direction of the VIX index 83 percent of trading days.

Over a five-day holding basis, the numbers start to skew a little. Table 11.11 shows the number of instances the VIX index was higher and lower over a rolling five-day period and the related performance of the VXX. Note that the long side starts to slip a bit, with 69 percent of instances seeing both the VIX index and the VXX higher. On the short side, there is

TABLE 11.10 Percent Coincidence between Direction of VIX Index and VXX over One Day, 2/1/2009–10/31/2010

	VIX Index	VXX	Percent Same
Higher close	188	143	76%
Lower close	253	222	88%
Combined	441	365	83%

TABLE 11.11 Percent Coincidence between Direction of Five-Day Performance of VIX Index and VXX, 2/1/2009–10/31/2010

	VIX Index	VXX	Percent Same
Higher close	184	127	69%
Lower close	254	234	92%
Combined	438	361	82%

some improvement with the VXX moving lower 92 percent of instances where the VIX index was lower over a five-day period.

As a final look at the VXX for trading purposes, how the VXX did relative to the VIX on an intraday basis was studied. Taking the opening level of the VIX relative to the closing price of the VIX and comparing it to the VXX open and close yielded interesting results. Table 11.12 shows the results.

There were three instances where the VIX was unchanged on the day, so the total in this table is not the same as the 441 trading days from the one-day hold example. There were 167 higher closes, with the VXX following suit 127 times for a 76 percent coincidence between the two. On lower VIX days, 83 percent of days that the VIX was lower also resulted in a lower VXX on the day.

Finally, an overnight trade was considered for comparison purposes. In this case, the VXX would be purchased with the expectation that the VIX would be higher on the open the following day or be sold short with the expectation of a lower VIX open. Table 11.13 shows how often the VXX opened lower when there was a lower opening price for the VIX index along with what the VXX did when the VIX was higher overnight.

A little over three-quarters of the time when the VIX moves higher or lower the VXX would follow. Note that there are only 353 days on which the VIX was at a different level on the open versus the previous day's close, so the number of tested dates differs greatly from the previous three tables.

Over a short term, such as a day trade, overnight hold, or one-day to five-day hold, the VXX may be a good instrument for taking a position on the direction of the VIX. However, due to the consistent underperformance of the VXX related to the VIX index, the VXX may be a good vehicle for

TABLE 11.12 Percent Coincidence between Intraday Direction of VIX Index and VXX, 2/1/2009–10/31/2010

	VIX Index	VXX	Percent Same
Higher close	167	127	76%
Lower close	271	225	83%
Combined	438	352	80%

TABLE 11.13 Percent Coincidence between Overnight Direction of VIX Index and VXX, 2/1/2009–10/31/2010

	VIX Index	VXX	Percent Same
Higher overnight change	203	150	74%
Lower overnight change	150	121	81%
Combined	353	271	77%

taking a short position in volatility for a longer-term trade. Also, when the VIX futures are at a discount to the VIX index, the VXX may be a preferred instrument to implement a short position based on a lower outlook for the VIX index.

VXZ Relative to the VIX Index

The VXZ was introduced a few weeks after the VXX. This ETN has performed a little differently relative to the VIX than the VXX. A monthly summary of this performance appears in Table 11.14.

TABLE 11.14 Monthly Performance of the VIX Index, VIX Futures, and VXZ ETN

	VIX Index	VIX Future	VXZ
Mar-09	−4.77%	0.21%	3.66%
Apr-09	−17.31%	−16.19%	−7.33%
May-09	−20.77%	−15.53%	−14.11%
Jun-09	−8.89%	−7.44%	−3.77%
Jul-09	−1.63%	0.58%	−1.15%
Aug-09	0.35%	4.78%	3.41%
Sep-09	−1.54%	−9.74%	−3.42%
Oct-09	19.84%	0.83%	−2.31%
Nov-09	−20.14%	−4.24%	−0.11%
Dec-09	−11.55%	−5.69%	−7.67%
Jan-10	13.56%	0.54%	−3.94%
Feb-10	−20.80%	−9.42%	−4.96%
Mar-10	−9.79%	−10.34%	−3.75%
Apr-10	25.36%	10.74%	6.87%
May-10	45.44%	37.31%	22.99%
Jun-10	7.70%	9.59%	10.67%
Jul-10	−31.96%	−18.40%	−12.97%
Aug-10	10.85%	10.17%	7.97%
Sep-10	−9.02%	−10.29%	−6.09%
Oct-10	−10.55%	−13.94%	−14.04%

TABLE 11.15 Percent Coincidence between Direction of VIX Index and VXZ over One Day, 2/23/2009–10/31/2010

	VIX Index	VXZ	Percent Same
Higher close	181	138	76%
Lower close	246	192	78%
Combined	427	330	77%

Since the opening price of the VXZ on February 20, 2009, of 108.17, the ETN has lost 33.66 points. On a percentage basis, the VXZ had lost 31 percent through October 29, 2010. Over this same period the VXX has gone from 111.89 to 13.10 losing 98.79 points or 88 percent. The VIX index has gone from 47.08 to 21.20 over this same period for a loss of 55 percent. It is expected that both the VXX and VXZ would have lost value over this period.

The VXZ focuses on longer-term volatility, but over a short term it mirrors the performance of the VIX on a directional basis. The same periods that were explored for the VXX relative to the VIX were also explored, using the VXZ to compare to the VIX. Table 11.15 shows a one-day hold for the VXZ relative to the VIX.

The VXZ started trading at February 20, 2009, so the studies of the VXZ versus the VIX encompass fewer trading days than the VXX tests. The VXZ held over a single-day results in a pretty consistent correlation when comparing higher and lower price changes to the VIX index. The result was 76 percent coincidence when there was a higher VIX close and 78 percent with a lower VIX close.

The next table shows the same test using a five-day period. The results in Table 11.16 do vary from what was seen when comparing the VXX and the VIX. Specifically, note the similarity in direction between the VIX index and VXZ when there is a higher close over a five-day period.

There were 177 days where the VIX index closed higher than the closing price five days earlier over this 20-month period. On almost 80 percent of those times, the VXZ also rose over five days. This differs greatly relative

TABLE 11.16 Percent Coincidence between Direction of VIX Index and VXZ over Five Days, 2/23/2009–10/31/2010

	VIX Index	VXZ	Percent Same
Higher close	177	140	79%
Lower close	247	203	82%
Combined	424	343	81%

TABLE 11.17 Percent Coincidence between Intraday Direction of VIX Index and VXZ, 2/23/2009–10/31/2010

	VIX Index	VXZ	Percent Same
Higher close	162	122	75%
Lower close	262	204	78%
Combined	424	326	77%

to the 69 percent difference between five-day periods where the VIX was higher and the VXX followed suit.

The correlation of up and down periods over less than a day remains consistent when comparing the VXZ and VIX index on an intraday and overnight basis. Table 11.17 shows the VXZ direction versus the VIX index on days when the index closes higher and lower.

The VXZ direction based on where the VIX closes relative to the opening price is not quite as close as that of the VXX. The VXX matched the VIX index on intraday direction about 80 percent of the time, while the VXZ has a little lower coincidence at 77 percent. Finally, the overnight price change between the VIX and VXZ is compared in Table 11.18.

The overnight price change is based on the closing price to the following day opening price. This result was surprisingly low at 69 percent coincidence between the VXZ and the VIX. Also, this result was much lower than 77 percent directional similarity between the VXX and VIX.

The VXZ has outperformed the VIX index since inception through the end of October 2010. Part of this disconnect should be attributed to the focus of the VXZ. As the VXZ is replicating performance of a balanced portfolio of third- through seventh-month VIX futures, there would be an expectation that the VIX index and VXZ would not have similar performance.

COMPARING VIX TRADING INSTRUMENTS

These two exchange-traded notes are the first of many equity-like products that allow traders and investors to take a position related to the VIX.

TABLE 11.18 Percent Coincidence between Overnight Direction of VIX Index and VXZ, 2/23/2009–10/31/2010

	VIX Index	VXZ	Percent Same
Higher close	196	135	69%
Lower close	147	103	70%
Combined	343	238	69%

Before considering any of these products, be sure to explore what their performance goal is and how well the price history has matched up to the performance they are trying to emulate.

When a trader has an outlook for the overall market or specifically for the direction of volatility as measured by the VIX index, there are many alternatives. Futures, options, and exchange-traded notes offer different benefits. At certain times the futures contracts may be the best instrument for a trading position, and under other circumstances an option position may be the best trade.

As the number of market participants trading volatility expands, so will the number of instruments that may be used to trade a specific outlook. A variety of exchange-traded notes applying different strategies to trading the VIX are being introduced or are on the drawing board.

CHAPTER 12

Calendar Spreads with VIX Futures

A popular strategy with individual traders involves trading the spread between two VIX futures contracts that have different expirations. These spreads are commonly referred to as calendar spreads. The goal of a calendar spread is for the long position to outperform the short position or for the spread between the long and short to widen. Although consisting of two positions, these trades should be thought of as a single trade, and the profit or loss of both legs of this spread should be combined when analyzing the outcome.

Calendar spreads using futures contracts are common and have been around as long there have been commodity markets. For decades, traders have been selling one soybean contract and purchasing another in an attempt to benefit from the price changes between the two. Often there are seasonal patterns that traders attempt to capitalize on each year. This holds true for a variety of financial markets, too. Spreading VIX futures contracts versus each other is another strategy in a long line of calendar-spread strategies.

In the past, there have been seasonal trends of higher and lower volatility in the stock market. However, due to how new VIX futures trading is to the marketplace, there is really only about four years of valid data for testing seasonal theories. As more price history is accumulated, it is possible that seasonal tendencies may emerge. However, during what may be considered a normal market environment, there has been a fairly consistent pattern with respect to the movement of VIX futures over the life of a contract.

Like directional positions using VIX derivatives, buying one VIX futures contract and selling another contract and the price behavior between contracts is specific to the VIX. As with a single bullish or bearish position with VIX futures, this sort of trade also has some risks associated with it that are specific to the price behavior of VIX futures contracts. An awareness of the price association between VIX futures contracts with different expirations is essential before attempting one of these spread trades.

COMPARING VIX FUTURES PRICES

If plotted against each other, the prices of VIX futures often appear in the shape of a normal yield curve. Bond traders often approach trading bonds based on the shape of the yield curve. VIX traders may use a similar approach to trading VIX contracts. In fact, more often than not, charting closing VIX futures prices against each other has resulted in a pattern that has mimicked a normal yield curve. Table 12.1 shows the closing prices for the eight available VIX futures in addition to the closing price for the spot VIX index on January 8, 2010.

With one exception starting with the VIX index, moving down the table, the prices increase from one period to the next. The exception on this table relates to May and June where the June contract closed one tick (0.05) lower than the May contract. Also, note that the slope of this increase begins to level off with the contracts that expire further in the future. A graphical depiction of this appears in Figure 12.1.

This upward-sloping then leveling-off curve is a typical shape of VIX futures prices. That is, in a market environment that is not experiencing too much volatility the VIX curve often slopes upward and levels off a few

TABLE 12.1 Closing VIX Index and VIX Futures Prices, January 8, 2010

Contract	Close
VIX Index	18.13
Jan 2010	19.90
Feb 2010	22.55
Mar 2010	23.40
Apr 2010	24.40
May 2010	24.65
Jun 2010	24.60
Jul 2010	24.75
Aug 2010	24.90

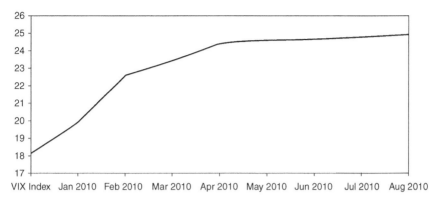

FIGURE 12.1 Closing VIX Index and VIX Futures Prices, January 8, 2010

months into the future. With more time until expiration, there is always the potential for some sort of market event that could result in a spike in volatility. This results in higher VIX futures prices for contracts that expire further in the future. Another way to visualize this is that the more time to expiration, the more likely a large move may occur in the equity market. The result is higher implied volatility for option contracts with more time to expiration. To get a perspective on the VIX curve in different market environments, the S&P 500 price action leading up to certain dates will be analyzed. The first example uses the three-month chart of the S&P 500 index, which appears in Figure 12.2. Note that from mid-November until the day the data were captured there was a steady uptrend in the S&P 500 index. This steady uptrend with an absence of days with large price moves,

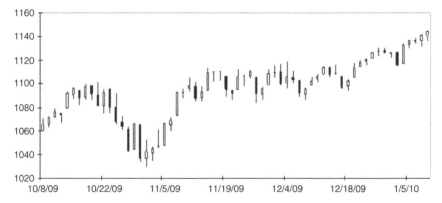

FIGURE 12.2 S&P 500 Index Prices for Three Months Leading up to January 8, 2010

TABLE 12.2 Closing VIX Index and VIX Futures
Prices, October 30, 2009

Contract	Close
VIX Index	30.69
Nov 2009	27.85
Dec 2009	27.70
Jan 2010	27.95
Feb 2010	28.25
Mar 2010	28.25
Apr 2010	28.40
May 2010	28.15
Jun 2010	28.20

higher or lower, often results in a VIX curve that resembles the previous "normal" example.

On the price chart in the previous figure, there is some market weakness in late October. The bottom of this bearish move is established on October 30, 2009. Since there is a bearish move into this date, it is interesting to see what sort of price action was occurring in the VIX futures markets. Table 12.2 shows the VIX index and futures closing prices for that date.

The data in the table show the spot VIX index closing at a much higher level than all the actively traded VIX futures contracts. Taking the closest expiring contract, November 2009, into account, this means traders expect the VIX index to move lower by November expiration. This prediction would have been made with only 12 trading days remaining until November VIX expiration. Remember, VIX futures are based on where the marketplace believes the VIX index will be on expiration. In this case, the November futures price reflects an anticipation that the VIX index is going to be lower at expiration. In fact, this turned out to be an accurate forecast of the direction of the VIX, as November 2009 settlement was 22.54.

Figure 12.3 shows the curve of the VIX index and actively traded VIX futures contracts on October 30, 2009. The index is above 30, while all the futures contracts are trading in the 27 to 28 range. The S&P 500 was down around 5.5 percent in a two-week period leading up to October 30. Due to the stock market being under pressure, the result was an increase in volatility based on S&P 500 index options and a higher level for the spot VIX index. However, the VIX futures did not move up as dramatically as the VIX index.

A time period that may be considered anything but normal for equity markets would be the final few months of 2008 into the beginning of 2009.

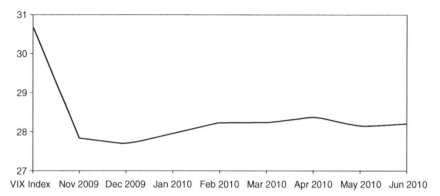

VIX Index Nov 2009 Dec 2009 Jan 2010 Feb 2010 Mar 2010 Apr 2010 May 2010 Jun 2010

FIGURE 12.3 Closing VIX Index and VIX Futures Prices, October 30, 2009

Table 12.3 shows the VIX curve after the S&P 500 had gone from over 1,300 to under 1,000 in the course of about 10 weeks. This was an equity market loss of about 23 percent as measured by the S&P 500 index. Although this is a dramatic drop, it was not the end of the bear move.

Note the consistent difference between the closing values in the table as calendar passes. Figure 12.4 shows exactly how dramatic the curve had gotten. The range of values runs from the upper 50s to high 20s as expiration is further in the future. With such a big move in such a short period of calendar, the market was expecting lower volatility to return in the next few weeks or months.

Figure 12.5 shows the equity market price action leading up to this inverted VIX curve from October 2008. The market started to react to an avalanche of bad news that stemmed from the mortgage crisis. The October

TABLE 12.3 Closing VIX Index and VIX Futures Prices, October 8, 2008

Contract	Close
VIX Index	57.53
Oct 2008	45.56
Nov 2008	35.39
Dec 2008	31.21
Jan 2009	30.20
Feb 2009	28.96
Mar 2009	28.02
Apr 2009	27.73
May 2009	27.60

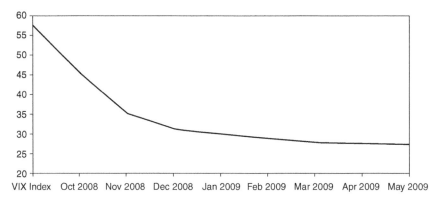

FIGURE 12.4   Closing VIX Index and VIX Futures Prices, October 8, 2008

futures contracts are at a dramatic discount to the index with only nine trading days left until expiration.

The previous examples show a flat (excluding the index), normal, and inverted VIX curve. Depending on the structure of the curve and the anticipation of how it will look in the future, a trader may put on a calendar spread. The anticipation that a normal market environment will return may result in one strategy, while starting out in a market with normal to low volatility may result in using a different strategy. Using closing VIX futures and VIX index prices going back to the beginning of 2007, it is possible to analyze the history of the VIX curve. Using this data, a measure of how often the curve developed using VIX futures fits the mold of a curve depicting a normal market environment can be studied.

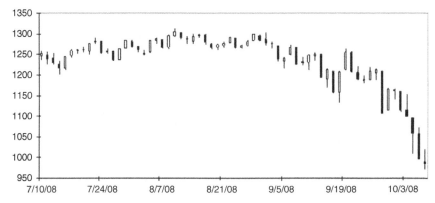

FIGURE 12.5   S&P 500 Index Price Action for Three Months Leading Up to October 8, 2008

THE MECHANICS OF A CALENDAR SPREAD

A calendar spread using futures contracts involves buying one contract and selling another on the same underlying instrument. The difference between the two instruments is the expiration date. For physical commodities, the pricing of contracts with different expirations may relate to the cost of storing a product for later delivery. The spread between physical commodity contracts may also reflect current demand versus expected demand. The latter may be a better explanation as to the relationship of different VIX futures prices to each other.

The pricing of VIX futures contracts is generally based on the expected movement of the VIX index until expiration of the contract. The longer the time to expiration, the more likely a spike in implied volatility will show up in the stock market. As the time to expiration approaches, VIX futures contract prices will move closer to and then converge with the VIX index. VIX futures contracts are cash settled based on a modified VIX index calculation, so the difference between the VIX futures contracts and the VIX index is very narrow on the last couple days that a VIX future contract is traded. Figure 12.6 is an example of this convergence of prices using the December 2009 VIX future versus the VIX index.

The dashed line on this chart represents the December 2009 VIX future contract while the solid line is the spot VIX index. At times, the future is at a discount and also a premium to the index. As expiration approaches, the spread between the two narrows. Finally over the final couple of weeks, the future practically overlaps with the index. This convergence is one of the keys to keep in mind about calendar spreads.

For an example of a calendar spread using VIX futures, see the prices in Table 12.4. The table displays spot VIX, April 2010 VIX, and May 2010 VIX

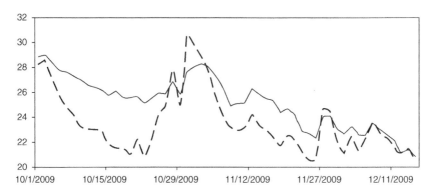

FIGURE 12.6 December 2009 VIX Future and VIX Index

TABLE 12.4 VIX Index, April 2010 VIX Futures, and May 2010 VIX Futures Prices

	VIX Index	Apr VIX	May VIX	May–Apr
3/15/2010	18.00	21.50	22.85	1.35
3/16/2010	17.69	20.90	22.30	1.40
3/17/2010	16.91	20.10	21.75	1.65
3/18/2010	16.62	19.80	21.45	1.65
3/19/2010	16.97	20.20	21.70	1.50
3/22/2010	16.87	19.90	21.65	1.75
3/23/2010	16.35	19.45	21.35	1.90
3/24/2010	17.55	19.90	21.65	1.75
3/25/2010	18.40	20.10	21.95	1.85
3/26/2010	17.77	19.90	21.70	1.80
3/29/2010	17.59	19.50	21.25	1.75
3/30/2010	17.13	19.10	21.00	1.90
3/31/2010	17.59	18.95	21.00	2.05

futures settlement prices for the second half of March 2010. The March contract expires during this period, so the April contract becomes the closest month to expiration during the calendar covered on this table.

The VIX index is at a discount to the April contract, and as time passes the April contract pricing should approach that of the index. Believing that the index should stay at current levels or move lower, the decision is made to take a short position the April contract. Also, combining this with the thinking that the May VIX future will not decline as rapidly as the April contract, a May VIX future is purchased. The result is a calendar spread that is short one April VIX future and long one May VIX future. The specific trades:

Sell short 1 April VIX future @ 21.50
Buy long 1 May VIX future @ 22.85
Net spread = 1.35

Each point for a VIX future contract represents $1,000, so this spread could be considered worth +$1,350. The positive sign for this spread value is necessary as the spread could have a negative sign if the April contract were to trade at a premium to the May contract. Following the spread from day to day, a slow steady profit is made. On March 31 the decision is made to exit the position. The transactions involved are:

Buy to cover 1 April VIX future @ 18.95
Sell long 1 May VIX future @ 21.00
Net spread = 2.05

Individually the April contract was sold at 21.50 and bought back at 18.95. The result is a profit of 2.55 or $2,550 on this part of the spread. For the other leg of the spread, the May contract was purchased at 22.85 and sold for 21.00. The result of the May contract trades was a loss of 1.85 or $1,850. As a net trade this results in a profit of $700.

As this was a spread trade, the two positions that comprise the spread should be considered as a single position. That is, the loss on the May contract should not be a disappointment as it is just one leg of a two-legged spread trade. When executing any spread trade, not just one using VIX futures, always think of the legs of the trade collectively as a single position.

For the duration of this table, the VIX index is at a discount to the April VIX futures contract. As time passes, the April contract approaches the index more quickly than the May contract. This was the goal for this trade and a small profit was the result. The profit was realized through the short position in the April futures, but it was offset some by the money-losing long position in the May future contract.

For another look at this strategy the last half of April 2010 was analyzed. Table 12.5 shows the May 2010 and June 2010 VIX contract prices along with the spot VIX close.

Note that the VIX index is again at a descent discount to the near-term future, which in this case is the May expiration. June is at a premium to May, but not to an extreme point, so the May contract is sold and June is purchased, as in the previous example.

Sell short 1 May VIX future @ 19.30
Buy long 1 June VIX future @ 20.95
Net spread = 1.65

TABLE 12.5 VIX Index, April 2010 VIX Futures, and May 2010 VIX Futures Prices

	VIX Index	May VIX	Jun VIX	Jun–May
4/15/2010	15.89	19.30	20.95	1.65
4/16/2010	18.36	19.95	21.45	1.50
4/19/2010	17.34	19.50	21.00	1.50
4/20/2010	15.73	18.60	20.45	1.85
4/21/2010	16.32	18.70	20.75	2.05
4/22/2010	16.47	18.65	20.75	2.10
4/23/2010	16.62	18.50	20.75	2.25
4/26/2010	17.47	18.75	20.95	2.20
4/27/2010	22.81	21.05	22.40	1.35
4/28/2010	21.08	20.80	22.20	1.40
4/29/2010	18.44	19.65	21.65	2.00
4/30/2010	22.05	21.60	23.00	1.40

As in the previous example, the spread may be thought of as having a value of +1.65 points or +$1,650. The spread should be thought of as an individual trade, so looking at it in this manner allows a trader the ability to not worry about a single leg of the spread. As the calendar passes, the VIX index starts to rally, moving from 15.89 to 22.05 over the last half of April.

As a result of a higher VIX index, the May VIX future contract increases in value. In fact, as the end of the month approaches, the VIX index closes some days at a premium to the May VIX future contract. As the trade seems to be coming apart with the VIX index moving higher and the near-term May futures follow the index's lead, a decision may be made to exit the trade. April 30 is an arbitrary exit, but a fortunate one.

Buy to cover 1 May VIX future @ 21.60
Sell long 1 Jun VIX future @ 23.00
Net spread = 1.40

Looking at the legs individually to determine the profit or loss of this trade, the May contract is covered at 21.60 for a net loss of 2.30 or $2,300. On the long side, the June contract was purchased at 20.95 and then sold at 23.00 for a profit of 2.05 or $2,050. The net result of this spread is loss of $250 on this calendar spread.

As a side note, if the spread had been held for a few more days, the result could have been much worse. The "flash crash" of May 6 occurred before May expiration. On May 6 the May VIX future closed at 29.20 and the June VIX future closed at 29.10. Using these closing prices, the net loss for the calendar spread would have been 1.65 or $1,650. This $1,650 loss is determined through a loss of $9,900 on the short May future and a gain of $8,750 on the long June future.

Although there is a spike in implied volatility and higher VIX futures prices, the result is not nearly as much of a loss that may have been incurred if a single short position had been taken in the May future. With a pure short initiated to take advantage of the convergence of the May contract with the index, the trading loss would have been just under 10 points, or 9.90 points based on the closing prices. A May contract would have been sold at 19.30 and bought back at 29.20. Using a calendar spread and having the hedge in place of a long June contract greatly lowers the risk associated with a spike in implied volatility.

PATTERNS IN THE DATA

Before moving forward, a disclaimer about this section is in order. The following information is for demonstration purposes only and not to be taken as a recommendation or a system that should be traded. The back

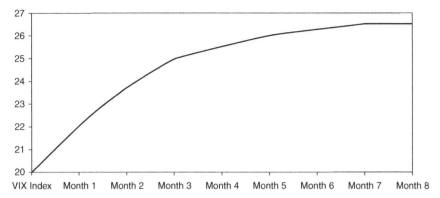

FIGURE 12.7 Typical VIX Index and Futures Pricing Curve

testing that went into this is rudimentary, and the results may not repeat themselves. However, it is interesting to note that VIX futures have a relationship that seems to play out more often than not. Using this pattern combined with more analysis and greater risk controls may yield a method of trading VIX futures in a calendar spread that may be a viable approach.

Figure 12.7 is picture of what the VIX curve often looks like. This is a hypothetical example, and the numbers were created just to show what typically may occur with the curve. Note that the slope steepens as contracts approach expiration. Considering this fairly consistent pattern, a test to quantify this was developed.

Always remember when considering any VIX futures trade that the contract will theoretically settle in the VIX index. The settlement is stated as being theoretical due to the special index calculation to determine the AM settlement price. However, as the expiration date for a VIX futures contract approaches, the VIX future price should gravitate toward the price of the index. If the VIX index is higher than the future contract, the contract may tend to move higher, and if the index is quoted at a lower price than the future, the future contract price should be pulled lower toward the index price. If a refresher is needed, the settlement process for the VIX futures was discussed extensively in Chapter 3.

Using Figure 12.7, focus on Month 4 and Month 5. The difference between the two months is slight. However, in the future, specifically four months in the future, the difference will be greater if the shape of this curve remains consistent. If the feeling is that in the future what is now Month 4 will be at a much greater discount to what is currently Month 5, then a calendar spread may be initiated. Specifically, a VIX futures contract that expires in Month 4 will be sold short and a VIX futures contract that expires in Month 5 will be purchased. In four months, when Month 4 is very

TABLE 12.6 October and September VIX Prices

Date	Oct Price	Sep Price	Spread
5/14/2010	29.10	29.15	−0.05
6/11/2010	31.80	31.70	0.10
7/16/2010	33.75	32.80	0.95
8/13/2010	31.90	30.70	1.20
9/10/2010	27.00	23.05	3.95

close to expiration, the price of the contract will be very near that of the index while the Month 5 contract will be at a premium to Month 4.

Using readily available free data from the CBOE's web site, this theory was tracked going back to early 2007. The beginning date was chosen based on past market liquidity, contracts listed, and available data. The first pair tracked was long the March 2007 contract and short the February 2007 contract. The final pair in this study consisted of long the October 2010 contract and a short position in the September 2010 contract.

The entry and exit dates consist of the Friday before the expiration of each futures contract. At that time the following expiration becomes Month 1, and even though there are a couple of days left before expiration of the nearest-term month, this contract is exited. Holding into expiration has issues that are best avoided by using this method of rolling to the front month. Also, using the Friday before expiration results in rigid rules for the beginning and ending of a test period.

For instance, testing the purchase of an October 2010 VIX contract and the sale of a September 2010 VIX futures contract uses the dates in Table 12.6 for execution, monitoring, and exit.

May 14 is the Friday before the May VIX futures expiration. Each date following May 14 is the Friday before that month's VIX future contract expiration date. Each of these dates is used to track the difference between the October VIX and September VIX futures contracts. Settlement on May 14 results in the October VIX being a little lower than the September VIX contract. The spread is determined by subtracting the nearer month from the further month. In this case the spread is −0.05 or −$50.

A month later on the Friday before June VIX expiration, the spread is still narrow. The settlement prices show October VIX at a 0.10 premium to the September VIX settlement price. However, the following three months show the spread widening, with the October VIX contract beginning to trade at a premium to the September VIX. September 10 is the Friday prior to September VIX expiration. On this day, the tracking ends with the spread widening a full 4.00 points from May 14 through September 10.

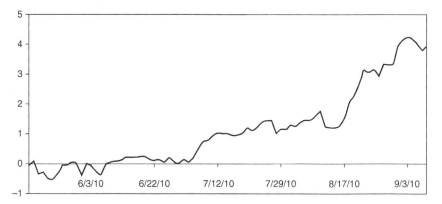

FIGURE 12.8 Long October VIX/Short September VIX Spread—5/14/2010 to 9/10/2010

Figure 12.8 shows the spread widening over the life of the monitored spread between the October 2010 VIX future and the September 2010 VIX future. This was an exceptional case of being able to sell the near month and buy the further month future contract. This is not always the case, but looking at 46 potential spreads from early 2007 to late 2010 shows that 78 percent of the time the further contract outperforms the nearer contract. In other words, 35 of the 46 tested periods resulted in the spread moving positively over the life of a spread trade.

There are cases in which trading VIX futures against each other in this manner would have the opposite outcome. In fact, 10 of the 46 tested periods resulted in the further contract underperforming the near-term contract. Table 12.7 shows the settlement prices for these contracts on the relevant Fridays before monthly VIX settlement. Table 12.7 also shows the results of consistently applying these rules to trading VIX futures contracts.

As in any consistently applied trading system, trading pairs of VIX futures contracts against each other in this manner does not always result in a favorable outcome. In fact, following these rules would have resulted in some very poor trades. An example of an unfavorable outcome can be seen with the pair of long November 2008 and short October 2008.

The pair of long the November 2008 VIX future and short the October 2008 one would have been entered on July 11, 2008. The year 2008 involved a dramatic amount of market volatility, and this also resulted in unusual VIX index and VIX futures pricing. July 2008 may be considered the quiet before the storm. Note on the table covering all trades the long November 2008, short October 2008 trade.

Assuming the October 2008 future would be at a discount to the November 2008 contract three months down the road, the October 2008

TABLE 12.7 Results of Trading VIX Futures Calendar Spreads

Entry Date	Exit Date	Short Future	Entry	Exit	P/L	Long Future	Entry	Exit	P/L	Trade P/L
11/10/06	2/9/07	Feb 07	13.16	11.23	1.93	Mar 07	13.75	12.20	−1.55	0.38
12/15/06	3/16/07	Mar 07	14.02	15.99	−1.97	Apr 07	14.26	15.79	1.53	−0.44
1/12/07	4/13/07	Apr 07	13.82	12.39	1.43	May 07	14.45	13.57	−0.88	0.55
2/9/07	5/11/07	May 07	13.74	12.77	0.97	Jun 07	14.14	13.94	−0.20	0.77
3/16/07	6/15/07	Jun 07	14.95	13.64	1.31	Jul 07	14.73	14.43	−0.30	1.01
4/13/07	7/13/07	Jul 07	14.13	15.45	−1.32	Aug 07	14.28	16.50	2.22	0.90
5/11/07	8/17/07	Aug 07	14.46	30.07	−15.61	Sep 07	14.59	26.47	11.88	−3.73
6/15/07	9/14/07	Sep 07	14.91	24.80	−9.89	Oct 07	15.00	23.78	8.78	−1.11
7/13/07	10/12/07	Oct 07	16.70	17.95	−1.25	Nov 07	16.77	19.45	2.68	1.43
8/17/07	11/16/07	Nov 07	22.60	26.04	−3.44	Dec 07	22.64	26.45	3.81	0.37
9/14/07	12/14/07	Dec 07	21.49	22.64	−1.15	Jan 08	21.35	24.66	3.31	2.16
10/12/07	1/11/08	Jan 08	19.55	24.96	−5.41	Feb 08	19.76	26.15	6.39	0.98
11/16/07	2/15/08	Feb 08	25.98	26.07	−0.09	Mar 08	25.77	25.93	0.16	0.07
12/14/07	3/14/08	Mar 08	24.36	29.03	−4.67	Apr 08	24.47	28.52	4.05	−0.62
1/11/08	4/11/08	Apr 08	25.92	23.91	2.01	May 08	25.50	24.98	−0.52	1.49
2/15/08	5/16/08	May 08	25.50	17.15	8.35	Jun 08	25.36	20.14	−5.22	3.13
3/14/08	6/13/08	Jun 08	27.24	21.62	5.62	Jul 08	26.96	23.00	−3.96	1.66
4/11/08	7/11/08	Jul 08	25.14	27.15	−2.01	Aug 08	24.72	25.25	0.53	−1.48
5/16/08	8/15/08	Aug 08	21.69	20.18	1.51	Sep 08	21.95	21.92	−0.03	1.48
6/13/08	9/12/08	Sep 08	23.89	24.68	−0.79	Oct 08	23.78	24.57	0.79	0.00
7/11/08	10/17/08	Oct 08	24.78	63.25	−38.47	Nov 08	24.44	47.04	22.60	−15.87
8/15/08	11/14/08	Nov 08	22.71	62.90	−40.19	Dec 08	22.47	53.51	31.04	−9.15
9/12/08	12/12/08	Dec 08	23.97	54.58	−30.61	Jan 09	24.37	54.46	30.09	−0.52

10/17/08	1/16/09	Jan 09	36.08	49.65	−13.57	Feb 09	34.75	48.53	13.78	0.21
11/14/08	2/13/09	Feb 09	46.09	43.60	2.49	Mar 09	42.35	42.35	0.00	2.49
12/12/08	3/13/09	Mar 09	48.58	42.10	6.48	Apr 09	46.63	41.60	−5.03	1.45
1/16/09	4/9/09	Apr 09	43.44	38.30	5.14	May 09	41.20	39.90	−1.30	3.84
2/13/09	5/15/09	May 09	39.25	33.15	6.10	Jun 09	38.25	33.20	−5.05	1.05
3/13/09	6/12/09	Jun 09	38.20	28.35	9.85	Jul 09	37.30	29.95	−7.35	2.50
4/9/09	7/17/09	Jul 09	39.75	25.60	14.15	Aug 09	39.15	29.00	−10.15	4.00
5/15/09	8/14/09	Aug 09	33.20	25.20	8.00	Sep 09	33.40	28.30	−5.10	2.90
6/12/09	9/11/09	Sep 09	30.45	24.75	5.70	Oct 09	30.50	27.70	−2.80	2.90
7/17/09	10/16/09	Oct 09	30.40	22.35	8.05	Nov 09	30.15	25.30	−4.85	3.20
8/14/09	11/13/09	Nov 09	28.70	24.25	4.45	Dec 09	28.25	25.85	−2.40	2.05
9/11/09	12/11/09	Dec 09	27.95	22.10	5.85	Jan 10	28.70	26.00	−2.70	3.15
10/16/09	1/15/10	Jan 10	26.80	19.65	7.15	Feb 10	27.35	22.55	−4.80	2.35
11/13/09	2/12/10	Feb 10	27.80	24.45	3.35	Mar 10	27.75	24.90	−2.85	0.50
12/11/09	3/12/10	Mar 10	28.05	18.35	9.70	Apr 10	28.40	21.45	−6.95	2.75
1/15/10	4/16/10	Apr 10	24.05	18.20	5.85	May 10	24.30	19.95	−4.35	1.50
2/12/10	5/14/10	May 10	26.00	30.10	−4.10	Jun 10	25.95	28.75	2.80	−1.30
3/12/10	6/11/10	Jun 10	23.25	29.30	−6.05	Jul 10	23.55	30.90	7.35	1.30
4/16/10	7/16/10	Jul 10	22.55	28.10	−5.55	Aug 10	23.00	30.60	7.60	2.05
5/14/10	8/13/10	Aug 10	28.40	26.75	1.65	Sep 10	29.15	30.70	1.55	3.20
6/11/10	9/10/10	Sep 10	31.70	23.05	8.65	Oct 10	31.80	27.00	−4.80	3.85
7/16/10	10/15/10	Oct 10	33.75	20.95	12.80	Nov 10	33.70	24.05	−9.65	3.15
8/13/10	11/12/10	Nov 10	31.80	20.35	11.45	Nov 10	31.25	22.25	−9.00	2.45

future would have been shorted at 24.78 and the November 2008 future would have been purchased at 24.44. Even if the two contracts had the same price at expiration, the trade would have resulted in a small profit as the October contract was at a small premium to the November contract.

Fast forwarding to October 17, 2008, the Friday prior to October VIX expiration, shows a pretty disappointing outcome for this trade. Due to a spike in the VIX index, the October futures traded at a very high premium relative to the November contract for several days in October, including the exit date for this trade. With the October contract at 63.25 on October 17, a short position in this contract would have resulted in a loss of 38.47.

The November contract did react to the increase in the VIX index, just not as dramatically as the October contract, while the October contract was the front month contract. The long position in the November contract did result in a profit of 22.60 points, with November priced at 47.04 on October 17. However, the profit from the long November contract was not nearly enough to offset the loss of 38.47 from the short October leg of the spread. The net result was a loss of 15.87 points on this spread, which was actually the worst of the 46 potential trades.

A summary of the 46 trades using this initial method of trading calendar spreads appears in Table 12.8. Consistently applying this method results in a profit of 35.00 points over almost four years. The average trade is up 0.76 points, which with a $1,000 multiplier applied to a VIX futures contract comes to $760 excluding commissions. The maximum winning trade is 4.00 points or $4,000, and the maximum loser is the trade shorting the October 2008 and buying the November 2008 VIX contracts, resulting in a loss of $15,870.

TABLE 12.8 Summary of Trading VIX Futures Calendar Spreads

Number of trades	46
Profitable trades	36
Unprofitable trades	10
Win %	78%
Losing %	22%
Average trade	+0.76
Maximum gain	+4.00
Maximum loss	−15.87
Total profit	+35.00

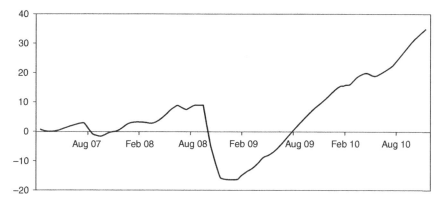

FIGURE 12.9 Running Profit and Loss from Trading VIX Futures Calendar Spreads

Figure 12.9 is a chart of the accumulated profit and loss from trading a VIX futures calendar spread consistently. Note the dramatic drawdown that occurs during the last quarter of 2008. This drawdown is associated with a period of high market volatility, a high level of the VIX index, and an inverted VIX curve. As the inverted curve has a negative impact on trading calendar spreads, a filter was developed to try to avoid these time periods.

A filter was explored in an attempt to avoid periods of time in which a typical curve was not in place. The trades that appear in Table 12.9 are the result of initiating a calendar spread only when the VIX index is at a discount to the VIX future contract that is to be shorted in the spread. The logic behind this very simple screen is that with the index at a discount, the future contract will move along a curve and approach the index over the next four months and do so at a more rapid pace than the next expiring contract.

Again this is a very simplistic screen, and more stringent screens are possible and probably worth exploring. This screen is just an example of narrowing down the trades to a typical environment. The result is actually pretty similar to the results from trading calendar spreads with no screen with one significant exception. Table 12.10 summarizes the results of this filtered system.

Of the 46 potential pairs, there are 33 occurrences that the screen was passed and a trade would have been initiated. The win percentage of 76 percent is pretty close to the previous result. The average trade results in a profit of 0.95 or $950, which is a bit better than the unfiltered system. The maximum losing trade is a loss of 9.15 points from the pair consisting of long one December 2008 and short one November 2008 contract. The filter

TABLE 12.9 Filtered Results of Trading VIX Futures Calendar Spreads

Entry Date	Exit Date	Short Future	Entry	Exit	P/L	Long Future	Entry	Exit	P/L	Trade P/L
11/10/06	2/9/07	Feb 07	13.16	11.23	1.93	Mar 07	13.75	12.20	-1.55	0.38
12/15/06	3/16/07	Mar 07	14.02	15.99	-1.97	Apr 07	14.26	15.79	1.53	-0.44
1/12/07	4/13/07	Apr 07	13.82	12.39	1.43	May 07	14.45	13.57	-0.88	0.55
2/9/07	5/11/07	May 07	13.74	12.77	0.97	Jun 07	14.14	13.94	-0.20	0.77
4/13/07	7/13/07	Jul 07	14.13	15.45	-1.32	Aug 07	14.28	16.50	2.22	0.90
5/11/07	8/17/07	Aug 07	14.46	30.07	-15.61	Sep 07	14.59	26.47	11.88	-3.73
6/15/07	9/14/07	Sep 07	14.91	24.80	-9.89	Oct 07	15.00	23.78	8.78	-1.11
7/13/07	10/12/07	Oct 07	16.70	17.95	-1.25	Nov 07	16.77	19.45	2.68	1.43
10/12/07	1/11/08	Jan 08	19.55	24.96	-5.41	Feb 08	19.76	26.15	6.39	0.98
11/16/07	2/15/08	Feb 08	25.98	26.07	-0.09	Mar 08	25.77	25.93	0.16	0.07
12/14/07	3/14/08	Mar 08	24.36	29.03	-4.67	Apr 08	24.47	28.52	4.05	-0.62
1/11/08	4/11/08	Apr 08	25.92	23.91	2.01	May 08	25.50	24.98	-0.52	1.49
2/15/08	5/16/08	May 08	25.50	17.15	8.35	Jun 08	25.36	20.14	-5.22	3.13
4/11/08	7/11/08	Jul 08	25.14	27.15	-2.01	Aug 08	24.72	25.25	0.53	-1.48
5/16/08	8/15/08	Aug 08	21.69	20.18	1.51	Sep 08	21.95	21.92	-0.03	1.48
6/13/08	9/12/08	Sep 08	23.89	24.68	-0.79	Oct 08	23.78	24.57	0.79	0.00
8/15/08	11/14/08	Nov 08	22.71	62.90	-40.19	Dec 08	22.47	53.51	31.04	-9.15

4/9/09	7/17/09	Jul 09	39.75	25.60	14.15	Aug 09	39.15	29.00	−10.15	4.00
5/15/09	8/14/09	Aug 09	33.20	25.20	8.00	Sep 09	33.40	28.30	−5.10	2.90
6/12/09	9/11/09	Sep 09	30.45	24.75	5.70	Oct 09	30.50	27.70	−2.80	2.90
7/17/09	10/16/09	Oct 09	30.40	22.35	8.05	Nov 09	30.15	25.30	−4.85	3.20
8/14/09	11/13/09	Nov 09	28.70	24.25	4.45	Dec 09	28.25	25.85	−2.40	2.05
9/11/09	12/11/09	Dec 09	27.95	22.10	5.85	Jan 10	28.70	26.00	−2.70	3.15
10/16/09	1/15/10	Jan 10	26.80	19.65	7.15	Feb 10	27.35	22.55	−4.80	2.35
11/13/09	2/12/10	Feb 10	27.80	24.45	3.35	Mar 10	27.75	24.90	−2.85	0.50
12/11/09	3/12/10	Mar 10	28.05	18.35	9.70	Apr 10	28.40	21.45	−6.95	2.75
1/15/10	4/16/10	Apr 10	24.05	18.20	5.85	May 10	24.30	19.95	−4.35	1.50
2/12/10	5/14/10	May 10	26.00	30.10	−4.10	Jun 10	25.95	28.75	2.80	−1.30
3/12/10	6/11/10	Jun 10	23.25	29.30	−6.05	Jul 10	23.55	30.90	7.35	1.30
4/16/10	7/16/10	Jul 10	22.55	28.10	−5.55	Aug 10	23.00	30.60	7.60	2.05
5/14/10	9/10/10	Sep 10	31.70	23.05	8.65	Oct 10	31.80	27.00	−4.80	3.85
6/11/10	10/15/10	Oct 10	33.75	20.95	12.80	Nov 10	33.70	24.05	−9.65	3.15
7/16/10	11/12/10	Nov 10	31.80	20.35	11.45	Dec 10	31.25	22.25	−9.00	2.45
8/13/10										
9/10/10										
10/15/10										
11/12/10										

TABLE 12.10	Filtered Results of Trading VIX Futures Calendar Spreads
Number of trades	33
Profitable trades	25
Unprofitable trades	8
Win %	76%
Losing %	24%
Average trade	0.95
Maximum gain	4.00
Maximum loss	−9.15
Total profit	31.45

did not manage to avoid all the unusual volatility from 2008, but it did avoid that 15.87-point loser.

Figure 12.10 shows the running profit and loss from the filtered system. The same scale is maintained for comparison sake with Figure 12.10; note that the drawdown is not nearly as dramatic as the nonfiltered drawdown. This is where the filtered system really stands out.

So far this method of trading calendar spreads has been approached only with a hard exit based on the Friday before VIX expiration. This is unrealistic as far as risk management goes, so in the following section, a couple of potential exit or risk management additions to these entry rules will be explored.

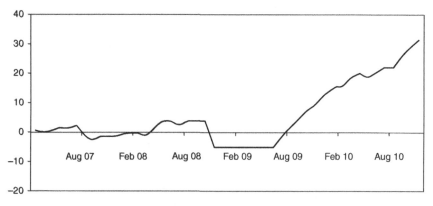

FIGURE 12.10 Running Profit and Loss from Filtered Results of Trading VIX Futures

TRADE MANAGEMENT

In the past, a few occurrences of high volatility have inverted the results in the VIX curve. A dramatically inverted curve may result in substantial losses for a calendar spread that is short the front month and long a further out month. When entering a calendar spread, or any trade for that matter, an exit strategy for when things do not work out should be in place. In a simple directional trade, a stop-loss order may be placed in order to attempt to limit losses. This section lays out a couple of exit strategies that may be useful when trading these spreads. Also, you'll see an example of how to use VIX options in conjunction with the calendar spread to help with risk management.

The first exit strategy is straightforward. Use a stop-loss based on the spread not working. Using both entry systems from the previous section, a trader seeking a viable strategy might establish a value applied to the spread where the trade is not working anymore or hold to the roll date.

Table 12.11 shows the results of using a variety of stop-loss levels based on the closing prices of the respective futures contracts. The results displayed start with a 1.00 point stop-loss and extend to 5.00 points in single-point increments. Also, for comparison sake, the original system, which did not use any stop and no screen, is included.

As a note of explanation, the maximum loss in each case is higher than the stop-loss prices that are in place. This is in order to account for using only closing prices to explore these stop-loss levels. Since only closing prices are used, cases of a system being stopped out assume that this is done on the close of the day. The result is that the recorded exit prices end up in a loss greater than the stop-loss level. Also, if the assumption is made that the stop were executed with no slippage during the trading day,

TABLE 12.11 Results Applying a Variety of Stop-Loss Levels

Stop	1.00	2.00	3.00	4.00	5.00	None
Number of trades	46	46	46	46	46	46
Profitable trades	26	34	35	36	36	36
Unprofitable trades	20	12	11	10	10	10
Win %	57%	74%	76%	78%	78%	78%
Losing %	43%	26%	24%	22%	22%	22%
Average trade	0.62	1.00	0.96	1.02	0.97	0.76
Maximum gain	4.00	4.00	4.00	4.00	4.00	4.00
Maximum loss	−3.68	−3.68	−3.84	−5.52	−5.52	−15.87
Total profit	28.39	46.20	44.33	46.83	44.47	35.00

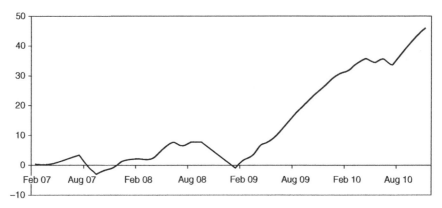

FIGURE 12.11 Running Profit and Loss from Trading VIX Futures Calendar Spreads Using a 2.00-Point Stop-Loss

the possibility of being stopped out during the day, when the closing prices would not dictate an exiting transaction, exists. This is another reason that the closing transactions are assumed to occur with prices on the close of the trading day.

Note with the exception of using a 1.00-point stop-loss, using a stop price actually improves the overall profitability of the system. The win percentage is pretty steady for 2.00 through 5.00 points' stop-loss levels when compared to the system with no stop. However, through limiting losses, the profitability is definitely an improvement. This is a great example of how even a basic risk management program improves trading and investing.

Figure 12.11 depicts the running profit and loss of the nonfiltered system using a 2.00-point stop-loss. There is a stark difference between this chart and the original chart, with a large loss attributed to the 2008 market difficulties.

Taking the filtered system and applying the same stop levels to it resulted in the summary of trades appearing in Table 12.12.

Figure 12.12 depicts a running profit and loss chart from taking the filtered entry system and combining a 2.00-point stop-loss. This is a diagram showing the consistency of applying this system mechanically.

Also, combining the stop with a target exit price is also worth exploring. Note that the maximum gain from holding to expiration was 4.00 points in the previous section for both entry methods. A target of 4.00 points or higher will probably not change much, but exploring levels below and above 4.00 points would be worthwhile. Table 12.13 shows the results of combining a variety of target prices with a 2.00-point stop-loss on the nonfiltered entry system.

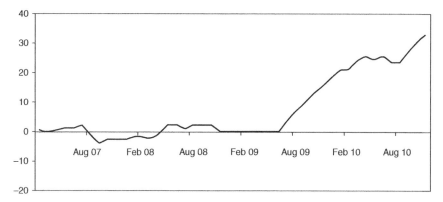

FIGURE 12.12 Running Profit and Loss from Trading VIX Futures Calendar Spreads Using a 2.00-Point Stop-Loss with Filtered Entry

TABLE 12.12 Results Applying a Variety of Stop-Loss Levels to Filtered Entry System

Stop	1.00	2.00	3.00	4.00	5.00	None
Number of trades	33	33	33	33	33	33
Profitable trades	20	24	25	25	25	25
Unprofitable trades	13	9	8	8	8	8
Win %	61%	73%	76%	76%	76%	76%
Losing %	39%	27%	24%	24%	24%	24%
Average trade	0.78	1.00	1.04	1.11	1.06	0.95
Maximum gain	4.00	4.00	4.00	4.00	4.00	4.00
Maximum loss	−3.68	−3.68	−3.84	−4.06	−5.46	−9.15
Total profit	25.82	32.94	34.27	36.54	35.14	31.45

TABLE 12.13 Results Applying a Variety of Targets to a 2.00-Point Stop-Loss System

Target	1.00	2.00	3.00	4.00	5.00	None
Number of trades	46	46	46	46	46	46
Profitable trades	37	35	34	34	34	34
Unprofitable trades	9	11	12	12	12	12
Win %	80%	76%	74%	74%	74%	74%
Losing %	20%	24%	26%	26%	26%	26%
Average trade	0.49	0.81	1.00	1.01	1.00	1.00
Maximum gain	1.70	2.35	3.85	4.05	4.00	4.00
Maximum loss	−3.68	−3.68	−3.68	−3.68	−3.68	−3.68
Total profit	22.37	37.12	45.90	46.40	46.20	46.20

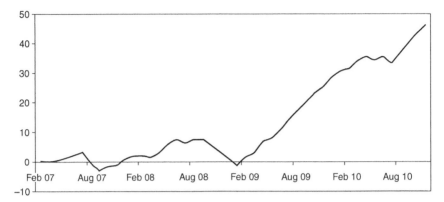

FIGURE 12.13 Running Profit and Loss from Applying a Variety of Targets to a 2.00-Point Stop-Loss System

Using a target combined with a stop-loss does not change the results too much, although combining a 4.00-point target with a 2.00-point stop-loss increases the profitability slightly along with a slight smoothing out of the running profit and loss as seen in Figure 12.13.

Finally, targets were tested using the filtered entry system. The summary of those results appears in Table 12.14. Since a 4.00-point stop-loss with the filtered system was the best of the filtered results with a stop, a variety of target prices was combined with this stop. Using a target with this filtered system had similar results to adding in a target with the previous system, or not much improvement. A 4.00-point target slightly improved profitability.

TABLE 12.14 Results Applying a Variety of Targets to a 4.00-Point Stop-Loss System

Target	1.00	2.00	3.00	4.00	5.00	None
Number of trades	33	33	33	33	33	33
Profitable trades	28	26	25	25	25	25
Unprofitable trades	5	7	8	8	8	8
Win %	85%	79%	76%	76%	76%	76%
Losing %	15%	21%	24%	24%	24%	24%
Average trade	0.62	0.93	1.10	1.11	1.11	1.11
Maximum gain	1.70	2.35	3.85	4.05	4.00	4.00
Maximum loss	−4.06	−4.06	−4.06	−4.06	−4.06	−4.06
Total profit	20.43	30.53	36.24	36.74	36.54	36.54

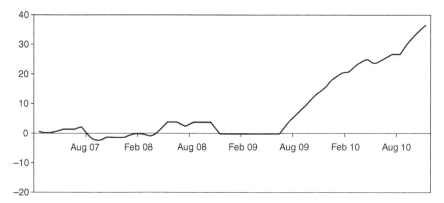

FIGURE 12.14 Running Profit and Loss from Applying a 4.00 Price Target to a 4.00-Point Stop-Loss System

Figure 12.14 depicts a running profit and loss based on using a 4.00-point stop and 4.00-point target using the filtered system. Note that the stop and target combined result in not too much of a drawdown during the 2008 period that dramatically impacted trading calendar spreads with no risk controls.

OTHER PARAMETERS

The previous example is a basic approach to analyzing and trading various VIX futures contracts against each other. Certainly, other approaches will likely yield superior outcomes on a back-tested basis.

Another potential exit or entry strategy could be based on where the VIX index is relative to the front month future. Remember, the whole idea behind being short a near month and long a further-out month is that the contract with less calendar to expiration will trend lower relative to long contract. The VIX futures contract prices approach the VIX index level as expiration approaches. If the index is at a premium to the future contract, the contract may trend higher instead of lower. When this occurs, the premise behind the trade is no longer valid, so the trade should be exited. Using this method as an exit may be a more valid prospect than just a target price.

The final thought behind the management of risk associated with calendar spreads involves using VIX options as a hedge. The situation that a calendar spread trader would be most concerned about would be when there is a dramatic increase in market volatility. Many institutions use out of the money VIX call options as a version of disaster insurance against a major market move to the downside. A similar approach may be implemented as a hedge against this occurring when trading futures calendar spreads.

CHAPTER 13

Calendar Spreads with VIX Options

C hapter 12 discusses trading two different VIX future contract expirations as a spread. These spreads take advantage of the effect of price changes over the passage of time on the relative values of the two contracts. The change in the relative values of two futures contracts also shows up in the pricing of VIX index options with different expiration dates. Remember, the proper underlying instrument used to value a VIX option contract is the VIX futures contract that shares expiration with the option. Being that the ability exists to benefit from the pricing differences of futures contracts, trading option contracts in this manner is also a trading strategy used by VIX option traders.

This chapter will begin with a quick review of VIX option pricing, specifically how the price of VIX futures contracts should be considered the correct underlying when valuing a VIX option contract. Then two option trading strategies will be discussed. These strategies would be implemented to benefit from a forecasted change in the corresponding futures prices. Versions of this strategy may be implemented with both put options and call options, so both will be demonstrated. After the introduction of this strategy, a time-based option spread strategy with the same fundamental thesis will be discussed.

VIX OPTION PRICING

As discussed in the introduction to VIX index option contracts in Chapter 4, there is a pricing relationship between VIX option contracts and VIX futures contracts with the same expiration. Specifically, the best underlying price to value a VIX option is the corresponding VIX future. A quick example involves VIX option contracts that expire in January 2011. In late November 2010 on a day that the VIX index was trading at 18.00, a VIX Jan 2011 20 Put was offered at 1.00. This price of 1.00 for the right to sell the VIX at 20.00, when the index is quoted at 18.00, appears to offer a mispricing. However, at the same moment the January 2011 VIX future contract was trading at 23.85. Using that pricing as the underlying for this VIX put option contract results in the 1.00 offer being a more reasonable price.

For example, take a look at the VIX option and future pricing from November 20, 2010:

VIX index = 18.00
VIX Jan 20 Put = 1.00
Jan VIX future = 23.85

Put options are used in this pricing example as the first example in which this chapter will utilize puts. Experienced option traders will automatically consider call options when a time or calendar spread using options is mentioned. However, due to the unique nature of VIX options combined with the pricing of VIX futures contracts moving along the curve in a normal environment, a VIX calendar spread that may be created using put options may benefit from the actual VIX index being unchanged at expiration. A common method for trading this outlook would involve a version of a calendar spread using put options.

CALENDAR SPREAD WITH PUT OPTIONS

This section starts out with a demonstration of how put options would be used to create a calendar spread on a stock or index. After a brief explanation of a calendar spread, this section will dive into using put options on the VIX index to capitalize from a pricing difference between two futures contracts.

When stock options with different expirations are compared, the comparison is based on the two expiration series sharing an underlying instrument. Using XYZ as an example of a stock, the January and March expirations for XYZ are both priced according to the current price for XYZ. The underlying price will also be the same for the two options series upon expiration of the January option contracts. Option calendar spreads on equities are constructed mainly to take advantage of time decay differences that impact the prices of options with different expirations.

TABLE 13.1 Put Calendar Spread
Example Quotes

	Bid	Ask
XYZ Jan 40 Put	1.00	1.05
XYZ Mar 40 Put	2.00	2.05

The option prices in Table 13.1 will be used to demonstrate how a calendar spread would work using put options. In this example, January options have 15 days until expiration while the March contracts expire in 75 days. With XYZ trading at 40.00, a calendar spread to benefit from time decay may be initiated by shorting the XYZ Jan 40 Put at 1.00 and buying the XYZ Mar 40 Put for 2.05. The net result is a debit or cost of 1.05 (2.05 – 1.00).

The entry trades are:

Sell 1 XYZ Jan 40 Put at 1.00
Buy 1 XYZ Mar 40 Put at 2.05

The goal for this trade is that XYZ will be trading at or very close to 40.00 on January expiration. This goal results in the value of the long Mar 40 Put to be at its maximum value relative to the value of the expiring short position in the Jan 40 Put. The quotes in Table 13.2 use the assumption that the best case scenario is XYZ closing at 40.00 on January expiration.

At January expiration, the XYZ Jan 40 Put would have lost all value expiring at the money. The result of a short position would be a gain of 1.00 with the option expiring. The time decay for the XYZ Mar 40 Put would have reduced the value to 1.85. The result would be a loss of 0.20 on the long XYZ Mar 40 Put. The net result would be a gain of 0.80. This profit is the result of benefiting from the difference in time decay between the two options.

The exit trades are:

XYZ Jan 40 Put expires at 0.00 (+1.00 profit)
Sell 1 XYZ Mar 40 Put at 1.85 (–0.20 loss)
Net gain = 1.00 – 0.20 = 0.80

TABLE 13.2 Put Calendar Spread Example
Quotes—January Expiration

	Bid	Ask
XYZ Jan 40 Put	0.00	0.00
XYZ Mar 40 Put	1.85	1.90

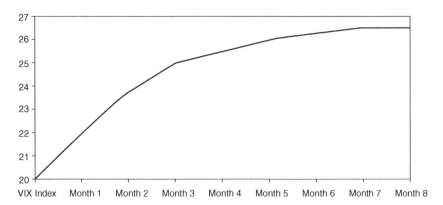

FIGURE 13.1 Typical VIX Index and Futures Pricing Curve

When using option contracts with different expirations on the VIX, the changes in values will be dependent on more than just the passage of time. VIX index options with different expirations are priced based on corresponding futures that have different expiration dates. With different contracts as the underlying pricing instrument, the relative futures' price changes come into play also. In fact, the relative future contract pricing changes may be more significant than the effect of time decay on a VIX calendar spread.

Figure 13.1 shows what is referred to as a typical or normal curve depicting the pricing relationship between the VIX index and actively traded VIX futures contracts. The previous chapter shows how in a normal environment, selling what is labeled at Month 4 and taking a long position in Month 5 results in a profitable trade if the curve holds up and the trade is exited when these two contracts become Month 1 and Month 2. This trade takes advantage of the price movement of futures along a curve using futures prices. This chapter shows how to use option contracts instead of futures in this situation.

Using the curve as a basis, it may also be possible to take advantage of this through the use of option contracts. Also, through the use of options instead of futures, the potential risk behind the trade has a different profile. This risk profile, under certain market conditions, may actually be favorable in comparison to a calendar spread using the futures contracts.

For an example, we will analyze trading a calendar spread using put options as opposed to VIX futures for a trade from August 31, 2010, to November 15, 2010. This trade will use the method of trading futures calendar spreads that was shown in the previous chapter. Table 13.3 shows the closing futures prices on August 31, 2010.

TABLE 13.3 Closing VIX Index and VIX Futures Prices, August 31, 2010

Contract	Close
VIX Index	26.05
Sep 10	27.90
Oct 10	31.25
Nov 10	32.05
Dec 10	31.70
Jan 11	33.20
Feb 11	33.20
Mar 11	33.45
Apr 11	33.30

These prices reflect the market's outlook for volatility changes over the next eight months. A graphical depiction of the curve based on these prices appears in Figure 13.2. This chart shows the plotted curve based on the VIX index and active futures prices on the close on August 31.

A potential calendar spread on this date could involve a short position in the VIX November 2010 contract and a long position in the December 2010 contract. The settlement prices on August 31 were 32.05 for the November future and 31.70 for the December future. The December contract is actually at a slight discount, which is a bonus based on the expectation of the November contract moving to a discount. The outlook behind this trade does not involve an outlook for the VIX, just the relative prices of the November and December contracts.

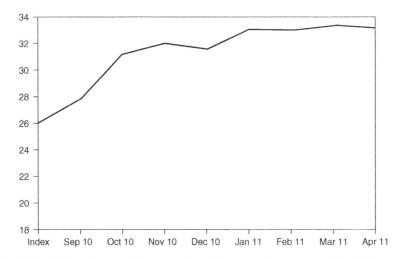

FIGURE 13.2 Closing VIX Index and VIX Futures Prices, August 31, 2010

TABLE 13.4 Closing VIX Index and VIX Futures Prices, November 15, 2010

	August 31	November 15	Change
Index	26.05	20.20	−5.85
Nov 10	32.05	19.75	−12.30
Dec 10	31.70	21.95	−9.75
Jan 11	33.20	25.05	−8.15
Feb 11	33.20	26.00	−7.20
Mar 11	33.45	26.75	−6.70
Apr 10	33.30	27.05	−6.25
May 10	N/A	27.35	N/A
Jun 10	N/A	27.65	N/A

The entry trades are:

Short 1 VIX Nov 2010 Future at 32.05
Buy 1 VIX Dec 2010 Future at 31.70

During the period that this position would be open, the overall stock market was in a steady uptrend. The result was lower market volatility than expected, and on November 15 the VIX index closed at 20.20, or 5.85 points lower than when this spread would have been entered. Table 13.4 shows the closing VIX index and active futures prices on November 12, 2010. In addition, the changes for contracts that were also active on August 31 are included.

The curve of VIX prices on the exit date is depicted in Figure 13.3. With a 5.85-point drop in the index price, there has been a drop in prices of all the VIX futures that were trading on August 31. The drop has been more dramatic based on the time to expiration. That is, the November 2010 contract has lost more value than the December 2010 contract.

To emphasize the changes in the VIX and futures contract, the scale that was used in Figure 13.2 is also used in Figure 13.3. This shows how dramatic was the price drop for both the index and the actively traded futures contracts. Exiting this trade just before November expiration, the short November VIX future could be covered at 19.75 and the long position in the December VIX future could be sold at 21.95.

The exiting transactions are:

Cover 1 VIX Nov 2010 Future at 19.75 (12.30-point profit)
Sell 1 VIX Dec 2010 Future at 21.95 (9.75-point loss)
Net gain = 12.30 − 9.75 = 2.55 Points

The same trade may be done by substituting put contracts for the futures. Using put options in place of the futures would require making a

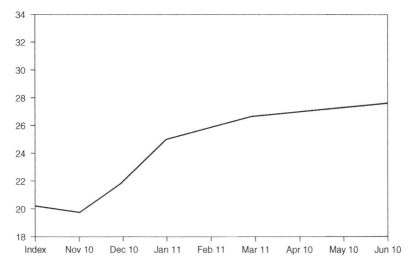

FIGURE 13.3 Closing VIX Index and VIX Futures Prices, November 15, 2010

decision regarding which strike prices to use. This decision would be based on a combination of factors including the current level of the futures, the option premiums, and an outlook for the direction of the VIX Index and futures. Table 13.5 shows quotes for November and December VIX put options on August 31, 2010.

To initiate a calendar spread using these two option series, the November purchased and the December contract will be sold. The individual transactions appear in Table 13.6.

As a reminder, on August 31 the VIX closed at 26.05, the November VIX future at 32.05, and December VIX future at 31.70. Part of the forecast behind a calendar spread using these put contracts would be an outlook

TABLE 13.5 November and December VIX Put Option Quotes, August 31, 2010

Contract	Bid	Ask	Contract	Bid	Ask
Nov 25.00 Put	0.65	0.80	Dec 25.00 Put	0.75	1.00
Nov 27.50 Put	1.45	1.60	Dec 27.50 Put	1.55	1.80
Nov 30.00 Put	2.55	2.70	Dec 30.00 Put	2.60	2.90
Nov 32.50 Put	3.90	4.20	Dec 32.50 Put	3.90	4.30
Nov 35.00 Put	5.60	5.90	Dec 35.00 Put	5.50	6.00
Nov 37.50 Put	7.50	7.80	Dec 37.50 Put	7.30	7.80
Nov 40.00 Put	9.50	9.80	Dec 40.00 Put	9.20	9.60

TABLE 13.6 Trading Cost and Credits for Potential Calendar Spreads

Long	Debit	Short	Credit
Nov 25.00 Put	0.80	Dec 25.00 Put	0.75
Nov 27.50 Put	1.60	Dec 27.50 Put	1.55
Nov 30.00 Put	2.70	Dec 30.00 Put	2.60
Nov 32.50 Put	4.20	Dec 32.50 Put	3.90
Nov 35.00 Put	5.90	Dec 35.00 Put	5.50
Nov 37.50 Put	7.80	Dec 37.50 Put	7.30
Nov 40.00 Put	9.80	Dec 40.00 Put	9.20

for the VIX index at November expiration. Also, a forecast based on the potential spread between the two futures contracts would be needed.

The forecast in this case will be for the VIX to be at 25.00 on November expiration and the December future contract to be at 2.00-point premium to the November contract. VIX futures contracts usually trade at a level that is very close to the underlying index when there are just a few days left until expiration. Using that historical norm, the outlook is for the November contract to be trading at 25.00 and the December VIX future to be at 27.00 when the trade would be exited. Those price forecasts for the two futures result in the outcomes shown in Table 13.7.

Using the assumptions, the higher the strike put options used for the calendar spread, the better the profit for the spread would be. Also, using this outlook, the lower strikes would actually result in a loss, even with a correct outlook for VIX and two futures contracts. The next two tables show the actual results for the various calendar spreads using puts. Table 13.8 is the closing bid ask quotes for the contracts on November 15, 2010.

The VIX dramatically overshot the target price of 25.00 and was at 20.20 on November 15. Both the futures contracts were also at a lower level than anticipated, with the November contract trading at 19.75 and the December

TABLE 13.7 Individual and Calendar Spread Results Based on Forecast

Long	Entry	Exit	P/L	Short	Entry	Exit	P/L	Net
Nov 25.00 Put	0.80	0.00	−0.80	Dec 25.00 Put	0.75	1.30	−0.55	−1.35
Nov 27.50 Put	1.60	2.50	0.90	Dec 27.50 Put	1.55	2.60	−1.05	−0.15
Nov 30.00 Put	2.70	5.00	2.30	Dec 30.00 Put	2.60	4.20	−1.60	0.70
Nov 32.50 Put	4.20	7.50	3.30	Dec 32.50 Put	3.90	6.15	−2.25	1.05
Nov 35.00 Put	5.90	10.00	4.10	Dec 35.00 Put	5.50	8.35	−2.85	1.25
Nov 37.50 Put	7.80	12.50	4.70	Dec 37.50 Put	7.30	10.70	−3.40	1.30
Nov 40.00 Put	9.80	15.00	5.20	Dec 40.00 Put	9.20	13.10	−3.90	1.30

TABLE 13.8 November and December VIX Put Option Quotes, November 15, 2010

Contract	Bid	Ask	Contract	Bid	Ask
Nov 25.00 Put	5.10	5.40	Dec 25.00 Put	4.40	4.60
Nov 27.50 Put	7.60	7.90	Dec 27.50 Put	6.50	6.80
Nov 30.00 Put	10.10	10.40	Dec 30.00 Put	8.70	9.00
Nov 32.50 Put	12.60	12.90	Dec 32.50 Put	11.00	11.30
Nov 35.00 Put	15.10	15.40	Dec 35.00 Put	13.40	13.70
Nov 37.50 Put	17.40	18.00	Dec 37.50 Put	15.80	16.10
Nov 40.00 Put	20.00	20.50	Dec 40.00 Put	18.40	18.70

VIX at 21.95. Using these option prices in the previous table, the profit or loss for each of the potential spreads appears in Table 13.9.

The 30.00, 32.50, and 35.00 strike spreads would all have resulted in a profit of 1.00 based on exiting the spread on November 15. This is a slight variation related to the estimated outlook, but then again the changes for the underlying did not match up to the original forecast.

This spread is a prime example of profiting from a normal curve holding up over the life of a trade. The trade is benefiting from the short contract gravitating more quickly to the index than the longer-dated long option. However, as seen by the volatility that occurred in 2008, this sort of outcome does not always hold up. Figure 13.4 is the curve based on the closing prices on November 17, 2008, which is the Friday before November expiration in 2008.

Figure 13.4 is an inverted curve with November 2008 expiration closing at over an 11.00-point premium to the December 2008 contract. The result would have been a loss of about $11,000 if a similar spike in volatility were to have occurred around the November roll date in 2010. In fact, a spread using the November 2008 and December 2008 futures would have resulted in a loss of 11.35 points or $11,350.

TABLE 13.9 Individual and Calendar Spread Results, November 15, 2010

Long	Entry	Exit	P/L	Short	Entry	Exit	P/L	Net
Nov 25.00 Put	0.80	5.10	4.30	Dec 25.00 Put	0.75	4.60	−3.85	0.45
Nov 27.50 Put	1.60	7.60	6.00	Dec 27.50 Put	1.55	6.80	−5.25	0.75
Nov 30.00 Put	2.70	10.10	7.40	Dec 30.00 Put	2.60	9.00	−6.40	1.00
Nov 32.50 Put	4.20	12.60	8.40	Dec 32.50 Put	3.90	11.30	−7.40	1.00
Nov 35.00 Put	5.90	15.10	9.20	Dec 35.00 Put	5.50	13.70	−8.20	1.00
Nov 37.50 Put	7.80	17.40	9.60	Dec 37.50 Put	7.30	16.10	−8.80	0.80
Nov 40.00 Put	9.80	20.00	10.20	Dec 40.00 Put	9.20	18.70	−9.50	0.70

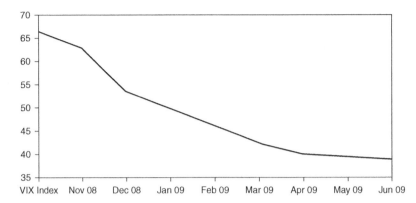

FIGURE 13.4   Closing VIX Index and VIX Futures Prices November 17, 2008

Hypothetical exiting transactions are:

Cover 1 VIX Nov 2010 Future at 67.95 (35.90 point loss)
Sell 1 VIX Dec 2010 Future at 56.25 (24.55 point gain)
Net loss = 24.55 – 35.90 = 11.35 point loss

Although based on the same underlying index and consisting of a long
and short position, calendar spreads using VIX futures contract have a high
level of risk. However, there is a method to using VIX index put options that
would have resulted in a gain in the case of the 2010 November–December
VIX spread, but would have not encountered the losses that would have
been incurred through the market volatility in 2008.

A calendar spread using put options on the VIX index would buy the
front month and sell the back month. Sticking with short the November
2010 future and long the December 2010 future, this would involve buying
a November VIX Put and selling the December VIX Put. The goal is for
the November VIX Put to benefit from a gain in intrinsic value above the
loss from the short December VIX Put option. However, in a case of a big
volatility spike where the near-term contract trades at a premium to the
following month, the outcome for a calendar spread with puts may not be
the same disaster that could occur using the futures.

The pricing that occurred in 2008 will be applied again to the put option contracts from August 31, 2010 to show the results of the near-term
future contract price running up to a much higher level than the farther out
contract. Using a pricing calculator, the following values and outcomes for
the calendar spreads are assumed to develop the scenarios in Table 13.10.

TABLE 13.10 Individual and Calendar Spread Results Based on 2008 VIX Futures Prices

Long	Entry	Exit	P/L	Short	Entry	Exit	P/L	Net
Nov 25.00 Put	0.80	0.00	−0.80	Dec 25.00 Put	0.75	0.05	+0.70	−0.10
Nov 27.50 Put	1.60	0.00	−1.60	Dec 27.50 Put	1.55	0.05	+1.50	−0.10
Nov 30.00 Put	2.70	0.00	−2.70	Dec 30.00 Put	2.60	0.05	+2.55	−0.15
Nov 32.50 Put	4.20	0.00	−4.20	Dec 32.50 Put	3.90	0.10	+3.80	−0.40
Nov 35.00 Put	5.90	0.00	−5.90	Dec 35.00 Put	5.50	0.10	+5.40	−0.50
Nov 37.50 Put	7.80	0.00	−7.80	Dec 37.50 Put	7.30	0.15	+7.15	−0.65
Nov 40.00 Put	9.80	0.00	−9.80	Dec 40.00 Put	9.20	0.25	+8.95	−0.85

Using put options for a calendar spread as opposed to a calendar spread with futures contracts has a dramatically different outcome based on a big spike in volatility. Both expiring put option series are out of the money to the point of there being very little value left in the contracts. The December 25.00, 27.50, and 30.00 puts actually have a value of 0.00 using a pricing calculator, but 0.05 was assigned to them to attribute some sort of cost to exiting the trade.

The worst result is a loss of 0.85 using 40 strike put options. This compares to the 11.35-point loss through using futures contracts instead of put options.

CALENDAR SPREAD WITH CALL OPTIONS

Most market-related outlooks have at least two choices when analyzing option positions. This holds true for a calendar spread as well as call options that may be combined in a similar manner as the previous example to benefit from changes in VIX futures prices.

A calendar spread using equity call options is initiated with the assumption that the near term contract will lose time value at a faster pace than the contract with more time to expiration. A calendar spread is generally held until expiration of the short call options. The profit will be based on no time value left for a short option and the long call contract still having some time value.

The option contract prices in Table 13.11 will be used to demonstrate a typical calendar spread using equity option contracts. In this table, January options have 15 days remaining until expiration while the March options have 75 days until expiration. The pricing is also based on the underlying

TABLE 13.11 Calendar Spread Example Option Quotes

	Bid	Ask
XYZ Jan 35 Call	1.05	1.10
XYZ Mar 35 Call	2.30	2.35

stock trading at 35.00. A calendar spread would be initiated with the expectation that the stock will be at 35.00 at expiration.

Using these quotes, the XYZ Jan 35 Call would be sold for 1.05 while the XYZ Mar 35 Call would be purchased at the offer of 2.35. The net result is a debit of 1.30 for this trade. Table 13.12 shows the same options with XYZ at 35.00 at January expiration.

This calendar spread could be exited by selling the XYZ Mar 35 Call and taking in 2.00. Subtracting the cost of the spread, 1.30, results in a profit of 0.70. This profit is due to the difference in time decay between the January and March option contracts.

In order to use call options to benefit from price differences that will emerge in the underlying VIX futures contract, the trade will involve shorting the call that has less time to expiration and putting on a long position in a call option with more time to expiration. The goal, as in a calendar spread constructed with call options, is for the short option with less time to expiration to lose more value than the long option that has more time left to expiration. However, this will occur through a combination of loss of time value for the short option and a loss of intrinsic value for the short call versus the long call.

As an example of a calendar spread using call options, a forecast for the VIX Index and VIX futures curve is made on August 31, 2010. Pricing for the index and futures contracts appears in Table 13.13.

A trade will be based on assuming the VIX index will approach 25.00 near November expiration and the shape of the curve will remain consistent with recent history. The forecast would result in the November contract at 25.00 and the January contract at about 31.00 when the trade is exited. Looking at these prices combined with these assumptions, the

TABLE 13.12 Calendar Spread Example Option Quotes

	Bid	Ask
XYZ Jan 35 Call	0.00	0.00
XYZ Mar 35 Call	2.00	2.05

TABLE 13.13 Closing VIX Index and VIX Futures Prices, August 31, 2010

Contract	Close
VIX Index	26.05
Sep 10	27.90
Oct 10	31.25
Nov 10	32.05
Dec 10	31.70
Jan 11	33.20
Feb 11	33.20
Mar 11	33.45
Apr 11	33.30

decision is made to use November and January options to create a calendar spread. November and January VIX index call option quotes appear in Table 13.14.

The November contracts have 77 days until expiration and the January contracts have 140 days until expiration. Table 13.15 contains data using the assumption that the November contract will settle at 25.00 and the January contract will be trading at 31.00. The table shows a projected result at November expiration for the profit or loss for short positions in each November call and long positions in the December calls. In addition, a combined time spread result is shown in the final column.

All combinations of a short November and long January call option with the same strike price result in a profitable trade based on the price projections that were the motivation for the spreads. The best of the possible trades involves taking a short position in the Nov 25 Call at 7.50 and buying the Jan 25.00 Call for a cost of 9.30. Based on a forecast of November settlement of 25.00 and the January VIX future priced at a 6.00-point premium to the November contract, the result of this trade would be a gain of 5.10. In reality, the pricing ended up a little different than expected.

TABLE 13.14 November and January VIX Option Prices, August 31, 2010

Contract	Bid	Ask	Contract	Bid	Ask
Nov 20.00 Call	11.80	12.40	Jan 20.00 Call	12.70	13.80
Nov 22.50 Call	9.60	9.90	Jan 22.50 Call	10.60	11.30
Nov 25.00 Call	7.50	7.90	Jan 25.00 Call	8.70	9.30
Nov 27.50 Call	5.80	6.10	Jan 27.50 Call	7.10	7.60
Nov 30.00 Call	4.50	4.70	Jan 30.00 Call	5.80	6.10
Nov 32.50 Call	3.40	3.70	Jan 32.50 Call	4.60	5.00

TABLE 13.15 Calendar Call Spread Trading Results Based on Forecast

Contract	Entry	Exit	P/L	Contract	Entry	Exit	P/L	Net
Nov 20.00 Call	11.80	5.00	6.80	Jan 20.00 Call	13.80	11.10	−2.70	4.10
Nov 22.50 Call	9.60	2.50	7.10	Jan 22.50 Call	11.30	8.90	−2.40	4.70
Nov 25.00 Call	7.50	0.00	7.50	Jan 25.00 Call	9.30	6.90	−2.40	5.10
Nov 27.50 Call	5.80	0.00	5.80	Jan 27.50 Call	7.60	5.20	−2.40	3.40
Nov 30.00 Call	4.50	0.00	4.50	Jan 30.00 Call	6.10	3.90	−2.20	2.30
Nov 32.50 Call	3.40	0.00	3.40	Jan 32.50 Call	5.00	2.80	−2.20	1.20

Table 13.16 shows the results of each calendar spread based on pricing on the close of November 16, 2010. This was the final trading date for November VIX futures and options. The November contract closed at 22.25 that day, and the January VIX future was trading at 25.85. The VIX index had fallen more than expected. Also, the spread between the futures contracts was narrower than projected.

Even though the projections were off, the result was still a profitable trade if the Nov 25 Call had been sold and Jan 25 Call had been purchased to create the calendar spread. In fact, none of the alternatives would have been losing trades, with the worst outcome being the spread using 32.50 calls, which has a breakeven result. The best choice if the outcome had been known ahead of time would have been a spread using the 22.50 strike options.

Finally, the pricing in Table 13.17 is a demonstration of the risk associated with creating a calendar spread with calls. This is theoretical pricing for these option contracts based on the near-term future spiking up and the longer-term future contract being at a significant discount. The volatile market environment in November 2008 is a perfect example of this. Using the November 2008 VIX and January 2009 VIX prices from November 17, 2008, the option values were determined. The closing price for the

TABLE 13.16 Calendar Call Spread Trading Results Based on November 16, 2010, Pricing

Contract	Entry	Exit	P/L	Contract	Entry	Exit	P/L	Net
Nov 20.00 Call	11.80	2.25	9.55	Jan 20.00 Call	13.80	6.20	−7.60	1.95
Nov 22.50 Call	9.60	0.00	9.60	Jan 22.50 Call	11.30	4.60	−6.70	2.90
Nov 25.00 Call	7.50	0.00	7.50	Jan 25.00 Call	9.30	3.40	−5.90	1.60
Nov 27.50 Call	5.80	0.00	5.80	Jan 27.50 Call	7.60	2.60	−5.00	0.80
Nov 30.00 Call	4.50	0.00	4.50	Jan 30.00 Call	6.10	2.00	−4.10	0.40
Nov 32.50 Call	3.40	0.00	3.40	Jan 32.50 Call	5.00	1.60	−3.40	0.00

TABLE 13.17 Calendar Call Spread Trading Results Based on November 17, 2008, Pricing

Contract	Entry	Exit	P/L	Contract	Entry	Exit	P/L	Net
Nov 20.00 Call	11.80	47.05	−35.25	Jan 20.00 Call	13.80	32.60	18.80	−16.45
Nov 22.50 Call	9.60	44.55	−34.95	Jan 22.50 Call	11.30	30.10	18.80	−16.15
Nov 25.00 Call	7.50	42.05	−34.55	Jan 25.00 Call	9.30	27.60	18.30	−16.25
Nov 27.50 Call	5.80	39.55	−33.75	Jan 27.50 Call	7.60	25.10	17.50	−16.25
Nov 30.00 Call	4.50	37.05	−32.55	Jan 30.00 Call	6.10	22.60	16.50	−16.05
Nov 32.50 Call	3.40	34.55	−31.15	Jan 32.50 Call	5.00	20.10	15.10	−16.05

November contract was 67.05, while the January contract closed at 52.60. This is a difference of 14.45, and this spread contributes to the loss of more than 16 points for any of the potential choices.

DIAGONAL SPREAD WITH PUT OPTIONS

A calendar spread with equity or index options is constructed with the same strike price and type of option, but different expirations. A strategy that is very similar is the diagonal spread. A diagonal spread uses two of the same type of options, but each has a unique expiration date and unique strike price. This type of spread may also be applied when using options to take a position based on VIX futures moving along the curve as time passes.

First, the option prices in Table 13.18 will be combined in a spread to demonstrate the mechanics and motivation behind a diagonal spread using put options on a stock or index.

As an example of a diagonal spread using put options, the near-term XYZ Mar 50 Put would be sold for a credit of 1.70 and the XYZ Apr 55 Put would be purchased for a cost of 5.70. The net result for this trade is a debit of 4.00. With the stock at 50.00 at March expiration, the two options would have the quoted prices in Table 13.19.

TABLE 13.18 Put Diagonal Spread Example Quotes

	Bid	Ask
XYZ Mar 50 Put	1.70	1.75
XYZ Apr 55 Put	5.65	5.70

TABLE 13.19 Put Diagonal Spread
Example Quotes

	Bid	Ask
XYZ Mar 50 Put	0.00	0.00
XYZ Apr 55 Put	5.25	5.30

The stock at 50.00 at March expiration is the best-case scenario for this trade. At that price the profit from the short position on the XYZ Mar 50 Put is the full 1.70 credit received for the trade. The long position in the XYZ Apr 55 Put has lost 0.45 for a net gain on the spread of 1.25.

There can actually be two benefits to creating a diagonal spread with put options. First, as with all spreads based on the difference in price changes between two different VIX futures contracts, using two put contracts may take advantage of this forecast. Also, as there is an option being sold, there may also be an added benefit of taking advantage of time decay differences between at the money and in the money options.

What's in the Name: Diagonal Spread

The diagonal spread is one of those option naming stories that originated on the trading floor. Before electronic trading took over the world, market makers would converge around a post where a handful of stock option series would be traded. Each post would be equipped with TV monitors (this is pre-LCD monitors) displaying market quotes for a variety of options. The method they were displayed for two different months would resemble this:

XYZ Jan 40 Call 6.30 × 6.35   XYZ Feb 40 Call 6.75 × 6.80
XYZ Jan 45 Call 3.30 × 3.35   XYZ Feb 45 Call 3.80 × 3.85
XYZ Jan 50 Call 1.50 × 1.55   XYZ Feb 50 Call 2.00 × 2.05

A market maker who wanted to determine the market for a spread involving the Jan 45 Call and Feb 40 Call would see that the quotes were diagonally located relative to each other on this screen. Hence the name, diagonal spread.

To demonstrate how a diagonal spread would work with VIX put options, the same quotes from the section on a put calendar spread will be used. The outlook is the same also with the expectation that the VIX index will move down by a point into November expiration, the November futures contracts will move along the curve and settle at 25.00, and the

TABLE 13.20 Individual Option Trading Results Based on Forecast

Long	Entry	Exit	P/L	Short	Entry	Exit	P/L
Nov 25.00 Put	0.80	0.00	−0.80	Dec 25.00 Put	0.75	1.30	−0.55
Nov 27.50 Put	1.60	2.50	0.90	Dec 27.50 Put	1.55	2.60	−1.05
Nov 30.00 Put	2.70	5.00	2.30	Dec 30.00 Put	2.60	4.20	−1.60
Nov 32.50 Put	4.20	7.50	3.30	Dec 32.50 Put	3.90	6.15	−2.25
Nov 35.00 Put	5.90	10.00	4.10	Dec 35.00 Put	5.50	8.35	−2.85
Nov 37.50 Put	7.80	12.50	4.70	Dec 37.50 Put	7.30	10.70	−3.40
Nov 40.00 Put	9.80	15.00	5.20	Dec 40.00 Put	9.20	13.10	−3.90

December contract will be trading at a 2.00-point premium to the VIX close to November expiration.

The diagonal spread in this scenario would again involve purchasing a near-term option and selling the longer-dated contract. Table 13.20 shows the payout for each individual option contract based on buying a November and selling a December put. These are based the same forecasts from the section on calendar spreads with put options.

Just considering a diagonal spread using these contracts can be over-whelming. There are 49 potential combinations of contracts, including potential calendar spreads. Table 13.21 shows the profit based on the forecast for those combinations, and the result of this matrix is 31 of the 49 potential spreads would yield a profit based on a correct forecast.

There are some potentially superior returns based on the anticipated prices for the November and December VIX futures contracts. The best result from the calendar spread example was a profit of 1.30. There are multiple instances of superior returns on the previous table.

One method to determine the potential risk for any of these potential spreads would involve applying the VIX option pricing based on November

TABLE 13.21 Diagonal Put Spread Trading Results Based on Forecast

	Nov 25.00	Nov 27.50	Nov 30.00	Nov 32.50	Nov 35.00	Nov 37.50	Nov 40.00
Dec 25.00	−1.35	0.35	1.75	2.75	3.55	4.15	4.65
Dec 27.50	−1.85	−0.15	1.25	2.25	3.05	3.65	4.15
Dec 30.00	−2.40	−0.70	0.70	1.70	2.50	3.10	3.60
Dec 32.50	−3.05	−1.35	0.05	1.05	1.85	2.45	2.95
Dec 35.00	−3.65	−1.95	−0.55	0.45	1.25	1.85	2.35
Dec 37.50	−4.20	−2.50	−1.10	−0.10	0.70	1.30	1.80
Dec 40.00	−4.70	−3.00	−1.60	−0.60	0.20	0.80	1.30

	Nov 25.00	Nov 27.50	Nov 30.00	Nov 32.50	Nov 35.00	Nov 37.50	Nov 40.00
Dec 25.00	−0.10	**−0.90**	−2.00	−3.50	−5.20	−7.10	−9.10
Dec 27.50	0.70	−0.10	−1.20	−2.70	−4.40	−6.30	−8.30
Dec 30.00	1.75	0.95	−0.15	−1.65	−3.35	−5.25	−7.25
Dec 32.50	3.00	2.20	**1.10**	−0.40	−2.10	−4.00	−6.00
Dec 35.00	4.60	3.80	2.70	**1.20**	−0.50	−2.40	−4.40
Dec 37.50	6.35	5.55	4.45	2.95	**1.25**	−0.65	−2.65
Dec 40.00	8.15	7.35	6.25	4.75	**3.05**	**1.15**	−0.85

2008 expiration. Using those option prices, the potential spread profit or losses shown in Table 13.22 were determined. In this table, the boxes that would have been profitable based on the original forecast have a bold font. This is to highlight the choices that may have been made when considering putting on the original spread trade.

Using theoretical results based on the market activity in November 2008 shows that using this method to initiate trades based on the normal VIX curve's holding up may result in significant losses. This unforeseen outcome would generally be the result of a market event that causes a short-term spike in market volatility.

DIAGONAL SPREAD WITH CALL OPTIONS

Finally, as there was a call option version of the calendar spread strategy, there is also a method to take advantage of shifting VIX futures prices with call options that have different expiration and different strike prices. Like the diagonal spread using puts, this version can benefit from both the calendar decay of differences of expiration and strike relative to underlying price.

A final example of benefitting from VIX future prices changing at different rates may traded with a diagonal spread using call options. A typical diagonal spread on a stock or index using call options involves a long position in a call with more time to expiration. This long-option contract is also deeper in the money than the short-call option in the spread. The short call also has less time to expiration. An example of a diagonal spread using call options uses the contracts that appear in Table 13.23.

TABLE 13.23 Call Diagonal Spread Example Quotes

	Bid	Ask
XYZ Jan 35 Call	1.45	1.50
XYZ Mar 30 Call	5.70	5.75

With XYZ trading at 35.00, January expiration is 30 days off and March expiration is 90 days in the future. A diagonal spread using these options would involve selling the XYZ Jan 35 Call at 1.45 and purchasing the XYZ Mar 30 Call for a cost of 5.75. The net cost of this trade would be 4.30.

The outlook for this trade involves a neutral to bullish outlook for XYZ over the next 30 days. The major motivation of the spread trade is to benefit from the calendar decay difference between the short position in the at the money XYZ Jan 35 Call and long XYZ Mar 30 Call.

Table 13.24 shows the pricing for the two options in the diagonal spread at January expiration. With the stock at the ideal price of 35.00 at January expiration, the long XYZ Mar 30 Call could be sold for 5.40 for a loss of 0.35 and the short Jan 35 Call would expire with no value for a profit of 1.45. The result would be a profit of 1.10.

A diagonal spread using call options is probably the most common method of benefiting from time deterioration of one option over another. It also may be applied to VIX options to benefit from the price change and time decay differences between two options. The example of a diagonal spread will use the example pricing from the section on the calendar spread using call options. The difference in this case is that the strike prices for the two options will be different creating a diagonal spread.

The example of how a diagonal spread using call options will use the same pricing dates and projections as were used in the call calendar spread example. To trade the outlook, a consideration is a diagonal spread that is long a January contract and short a November. Table 13.25 shows the results using the option pricing in the call calendar spread section.

In the example using the same outlook and option contract choices, the maximum potential profit is 5.30, which is not too much of an improvement

TABLE 13.24 Call Diagonal Spread Example at January Expiration

	Bid	Ask
XYZ Jan 35 Call	0.00	0.00
XYZ Mar 30 Call	5.40	5.45

TABLE 13.25 Diagonal Call Spread Trading Results Based on Forecast

	Nov 20.00	Nov 22.50	Nov 25.00	Nov 27.50	Nov 30.00	Nov 32.50
Jan 20.00	4.10	4.40	4.40	4.40	4.60	4.60
Jan 22.50	4.40	4.70	4.70	4.70	4.90	4.90
Jan 25.00	4.80	5.10	5.10	5.10	5.30	5.30
Jan 27.50	3.10	3.40	3.40	3.40	3.60	3.60
Jan 30.00	1.80	2.10	2.10	2.10	2.30	2.30
Jan 32.50	0.70	1.00	1.00	1.00	1.20	1.20

over the maximum gain of 5.10 from the calendar spread projection using the 25 strike calls.

Proceeding through the same exercise as with the put version of a diagonal spread, the outcome using market prices is shown in Table 13.26. The results in this case show dramatically better results for some of the potential diagonal pairs relative to the calendar spread example. The best

TABLE 13.26 Diagonal Call Spread Trading Results Based on November 16 Pricing

	Nov 20.00	Nov 22.50	Nov 25.00	Nov 27.50	Nov 30.00	Nov 32.50
Jan 20.00	1.95	2.85	3.65	4.55	5.45	6.15
Jan 22.50	2.00	2.90	3.70	4.60	5.50	6.20
Jan 25.00	−0.10	0.80	1.60	2.50	3.40	4.10
Jan 27.50	−1.80	−0.90	−0.10	0.80	1.70	2.40
Jan 30.00	−3.10	−2.20	−1.40	−0.50	0.40	1.10
Jan 32.50	−4.20	−3.30	−2.50	−1.60	−0.70	0.00

TABLE 13.27 Diagonal Call Spread Trading Results Based on November 2008 Pricing

	Nov 20.00	Nov 22.50	Nov 25.00	Nov 27.50	Nov 30.00	Nov 32.50
Jan 20.00	−42.85	−41.95	−41.15	−40.25	−39.35	−38.65
Jan 22.50	−42.55	−41.65	−40.85	−39.95	−39.05	−38.35
Jan 25.00	−42.15	−41.25	−40.45	−39.55	−38.65	−37.95
Jan 27.50	−41.35	−40.45	−39.65	−38.75	−37.85	−37.15
Jan 30.00	−40.15	−39.25	−38.45	−37.55	−36.65	−35.95
Jan 32.50	−38.75	−37.85	−37.05	−36.15	−35.25	−34.55

outcome from the calendar spread example using calls was a profit of 2.90 attributable to the Nov/Jan 22.50 Call Calendar spread.

As an example of the potential riskiness of this strategy, the November 2008 volatility market pricing was applied to these option prices. The risk is pretty apparent at the losses shown in Table 13.27. They range from a loss of 34 points to a loss of almost 43 points, depending on the spread chosen.

Using a diagonal spread with call options is a pretty risky trade when compared to the other alternatives in this chapter. The trades shown throughout this chapter assumed a normal curve structure, so this trade may be applied if something outside of the norm is the motivation for a trade.

CHAPTER 14

Calendar
Spreads with
VIX Options
and Futures

I n addition to trading the VIX curve using VIX futures or VIX options, it is possible to combine the two instruments into a calendar spread. Taking a position VIX index options with one expiration date and VIX futures with a different expiration date could result in a more favorable risk profile than a spread using all one or another type of option contract.

Remember, VIX options and futures do not match up one for one. VIX option contracts represent $100 times the VIX index, while VIX future contracts represent $1,000 times the index. This relationship will be covered before getting into a couple of strategies. Following this comparison, a variety of possible strategies using a combination of VIX options and futures will be introduced.

COMPARING OPTIONS AND FUTURES

VIX options and futures share the same underlying instrument at expiration, the VIX index. A major difference between the two is the multiplier or the dollar amount each contract represents. A VIX futures contract represents $1,000 times the index, so the dollar amount of a contract with a quote of 20.00 would be $20,000. The multiplier for a VIX index option is $100, so a VIX option with a strike price of 20 would represent $2,000. The VIX option is 1/10th the value of a VIX futures contract, so to keep things on a one-to-one basis, 10 option contracts would need to be bought or sold to match up to a single VIX future contract.

TABLE 14.1 XYZ and XYZ 40 Call Pricing and Delta

	Current Price	Delta
XYZ	40.00	1.00
XYZ 40 Call	1.50	0.50

In addition to a dollar-for-dollar matching, some traders match positions based on the Delta of the option. This price matching is more for a neutral position that would not be impacted by small price changes in the underlying security. Using a stock example, consider the securities in Table 14.1.

XYZ stock is trading at 40.00 with the XYZ 40 Call priced at 1.50. The Delta for the stock is 1.00 with the option having a Delta of 0.50. The meaning behind the Delta is the expected price change for the security based on a 1.00 point change in the underlying. The Delta for the stock is 1.00 by definition. For the option contract the Delta of 0.50 indicates that the option price should change by 0.50 if the stock moves from 40.00 to 41.00. A drop in the stock price from 40.00 to 39.00 would result in a loss of 0.50 in the price of the option. Admittedly there are many more moving parts in changing the value of an option, but the focus is on Delta in this section.

Using these examples, if a trader who is long 100 shares of XYZ wanted to be Delta neutral he would sell two of the XYZ 40 Calls. The combination of these two positions appears in Table 14.2.

Long 100 shares of XYZ is a position Delta of +100 or equivalent to long 100 shares. Short 2 XYZ 40 Calls position results in a Delta of −100 or equivalent to short 100 shares of XYZ. This position Delta for the short call is determined by multiplying the number of contracts (−2) times the shares per contract (100) times the option Delta (.50) with a result of −100.

Attempting to stay Delta neutral is an active strategy. Delta will change as the price of the underlying moves around and as time passes. For instance if the price of XYZ rises from 40.00 to 41.00, the price of the option is expected to rise by about 0.50, but also the Delta would move higher, possibly to something like 0.55. With this change and no other trades in

TABLE 14.2 Long XYZ–Short XYZ Call Option Positions Resulting in Delta Neutral Position

	Current Price	Position	Delta	Position Delta
XYZ	40.00	Long 100	1.00	+100
XYZ 40 Call	1.50	Short 2	0.50	−100

TABLE 14.3 Long XYZ–Short XYZ Call Option Positions Resulting in Delta Neutral Position

	Current Price	Position	Delta	Position Delta
XYZ	41.00	Long 100	1.00	+100
XYZ 40 Call	2.00	Short 2	0.55	−110

XYZ stock or options, the newly combined position would have a small short exposure to XYZ. This is shown in Table 14.3.

Note the Delta does not change for the stock position, but the Delta does increase for the XYZ 40 Call moving from 0.50 to 0.55. The result is the position Delta has gone from −100 to −110 for the short 2 Call Option position. In order to stay Delta neutral the trader would need to buy 10 shares of XYZ. Now, having a long position of 110 shares increases the long Delta exposure to +110 to offset the new short Delta of −110 that accompanies the 2 short call options.

The Delta of a VIX Index option would be determined relative to a single-point change in the VIX future that shares an expiration date. The examples in this chapter will match up a VIX future position with a VIX option position where the option has a different underlying pricing instrument. Due to this relationship, it is difficult to maintain a position that would be Delta neutral. However, it may be possible to create positions combining futures and options that have long or short exposure to the VIX index along with exposure to the difference in price changes between two futures contracts.

CALENDAR SPREAD EXAMPLES

The first calendar spread combining futures contracts and options will focus on benefiting from price movement along the curve of VIX futures prices. Instead of a position that involves being short a near-dated future contract and long a further-dated future contract, an option position will replace one of these positions.

In this initial example, the contract that represents a futures contract will be a short call in place of the short future. This may be a preferable alternative to a spread using purely futures contracts, depending on where the future contract is relative to the underlying index.

Short Call and Long Future

The VIX futures prices in Table 14.4 are from September 14, 2010. After checking these prices and with an outlook for steady implied volatility for

TABLE 14.4   VIX Index and Futures Prices,
                September 14, 2010

Contract	9/14/2010 Close
VIX Index	21.56
Oct 2010	25.70
Nov 2010	27.60
Dec 2010	28.40
Jan 2011	30.45
Feb 2011	30.70
Mar 2011	31.35
Apr 2011	31.45

the next few weeks, a calendar spread shorting the November 2010 VIX future and buying the December 2010 future is considered. This would involve selling the November contract at 27.60 and purchasing the December contract for 28.40.

Note the steepness of the curve in Figure 14.1. The expectations for the future price moves of November and December VIX derivative contracts will be based on this curve maintaining the same steep shape.

Before initiating this trade, the November VIX option contracts are considered, specifically the November VIX calls. These quotes appear in Table 14.5. Some extra columns are included in addition to the bid and offer prices for these November call options. The next two columns show what may be referred to as an equivalent future quote for the November VIX future. The key price to focus on is the Option Equivalent Future Bid column. This is the price determined by adding the option bid quote to the

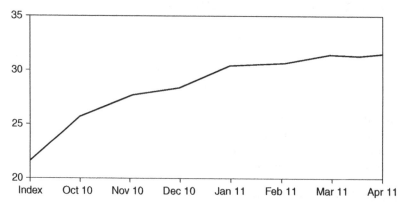

FIGURE 14.1   VIX Index and Futures Prices September 14, 2010

TABLE 14.5 November VIX Call Quotes, September 14, 2010

	Bid	Ask	Option Equivalent Future Bid	Option Equivalent Future Ask	Short Option-Short Future Improvement
Nov 20.00 Call	7.70	7.90	27.70	27.90	0.10
Nov 22.50 Call	5.70	5.90	28.20	28.40	0.60
Nov 24.00 Call	4.70	4.90	28.70	28.90	1.10
Nov 25.00 Call	4.10	4.30	29.10	29.30	1.50
Nov 26.00 Call	3.60	3.80	29.60	29.80	2.00
Nov 27.50 Call	3.00	3.20	30.50	30.70	2.90

strike price of the option. The final column shows that the selling amount of the option contract results in a higher equivalent short price on the future relative to the future close.

For example, if the VIX Nov 20.00 Call is sold at 7.70, then adding this price to the call strike of 20.00 results in a Option Equivalent Future Bid of 27.70. The November VIX future price is 27.60, so the option premium added to the strike price would result in an equivalent short price of 27.70, or 0.10 higher than the future price.

Calendar spreads using VIX futures require adding a couple pieces to the outlook. First, if the plan is to hold the spread to expiration, there should be an outlook for VIX expiration. The second piece to the puzzle would be an outlook for the future contract that will still be open upon expiration of the near month.

The outlook for this sample trade involves the following price assumptions at expiration:

VIX Expiration = 22.50—one point higher than current index.
December VIX Future = 26.70—consistent with current front month spread of 4.20 over the index.

If a spread were to be initiated through shorting the November VIX Future at 27.60 and purchasing the December VIX Future at 28.40, then the outcome based on these targets would be:

November VIX Future—Sold at 27.60 – Settle at 22.50 = +5.10
December VIX Future—Buy at 28.40 – Sell at 26.70 = −1.70
Net spread profit 5.10 − 1.70 = 3.40

The alternative to this trade may be the following trades:

Sell 10 VIX Nov 22.50 Calls at 5.70
Buy 1 December VIX Future at 28.40

Based on a target of 22.50, the outcome at November expiration:

VIX Nov 22.50 Calls—Sold at 5.70 – Settle at 0.00 = +5.70
December VIX Future—Buy at 28.40 – Sell at 26.70 = −1.70
Net spread profit 5.70 – 1.70 = 4.00

Note that this outcome is the best of situations for this trade. The target has been hit, and using the preceding comparisons combining short calls with longer dated long futures contracts outperforms a spread with two futures contracts. Two outlooks go into this trade. First, the December VIX future will be at a premium consistent with the current front month spread; second, the November VIX settlement will be at 22.50. Payout tables normally operate with a single assumption: the price at expiration of an underlying instrument. However, to account for the possibility that the price of the December VIX contract may not be consistent with assumptions, the payout table for this trade accounts for both assumptions.

Table 14.6 shows the potential payout of this trade using futures contracts. This would entail buying the December VIX future at 28.40 and shorting the November VIX contract at 27.60. The prices along the top represent the December VIX, while the column on the left of the table represents potential November VIX settlement prices.

The worst-case scenario on this table, but not the worst potential outcome, has November VIX settlement at 32.50 while the December VIX future is trading at 20.50. The cell on the table that shows this is in the bottom left. With November VIX settlement at 32.50 and the December VIX future trading at 20.50, the spread would lose 12.80. In this scenario, short-term volatility has moved up while there is an anticipation of lower implied

TABLE 14.6 Profit Loss Table for Calendar Spread Using Futures Contracts

	20.50	22.50	24.50	26.50	28.50	30.50	32.50
20.50	−0.80	1.20	3.20	5.20	7.20	9.20	11.20
22.50	−2.80	−0.80	1.20	3.20	5.20	7.20	9.20
24.50	−4.80	−2.80	−0.80	1.20	3.20	5.20	7.20
26.50	−6.80	−4.80	−2.80	−0.80	1.20	3.20	5.20
28.50	−8.80	−6.80	−4.80	−2.80	−0.80	1.20	3.20
30.50	−10.80	−8.80	−6.80	−4.80	−2.80	−0.80	1.20
32.50	−12.80	−10.80	−8.80	−6.80	−4.80	−2.80	−0.80

TABLE 14.7 Profit Loss Table for Calendar Spread Using Calls and Futures

	20.50	22.50	24.50	26.50	28.50	30.50	32.50
20.50	−2.20	−0.20	1.80	3.80	5.80	7.80	9.80
22.50	**−2.20**	**−0.20**	**1.80**	**3.80**	**5.80**	**7.80**	**9.80**
24.50	**−4.20**	**−2.20**	**−0.20**	**1.80**	**3.80**	**5.80**	**7.80**
26.50	**−6.20**	**−4.20**	**−2.20**	**−0.20**	**1.80**	**3.80**	**5.80**
28.50	**−8.20**	**−6.20**	**−4.20**	**−2.20**	**−0.20**	**1.80**	**3.80**
30.50	**−10.20**	**−8.20**	**−6.20**	**−4.20**	**−2.20**	**−0.20**	**1.80**
32.50	**−12.20**	**−10.20**	**−8.20**	**−6.20**	**−4.20**	**−2.20**	**−0.20**

volatility in the near future. The last half of 2008 and first quarter of 2009 resulted in this sort of price action for VIX futures contracts.

The best-case scenario, and again not regarding the outcome but relative to this table, would result from a drop in the November future and a rise in the December contract. The cell at the top right corner of the table shows this level. With November settlement at 20.50 and the December VIX future at 32.50, the spread would be up 11.20.

Table 14.7 shows the results when substituting the VIX November 22.50 Call position for the short November future position. The extreme case, where November settlement is low and December futures prices are high, results in a slightly better payout using the futures spread as opposed to the spread combining short November calls and long December futures. The price combinations that result in a better result than using futures have been highlighted on the payout table.

The consistent outperformance of selling the call option versus a short future position occurs through the benefit of the calendar value associated with the call. When this call was sold, there was about a month left until expiration and there was an extra 0.60 of time value associated with the contract. This extra 0.60 of value works to the benefit of the seller.

Long Put and Long Future

Combining a long put with a long future position is another interesting combination of VIX option and futures contracts. This combination may result in a payout that benefits from price moves along the VIX curve but that has a lower risk in case of a spike in volatility. The long position using VIX puts would replace the short VIX future trading in a calendar spread using only future contracts.

Long option positions have a limited maximum potential loss. This loss is limited to the premium paid for the option. A short future position has a theoretically unlimited potential loss. This difference in risk between a

TABLE 14.8 November VIX Put Quotes, September 14, 2010

	Bid	Ask	Future Bid	Future Ask	Put Option Extra Cost
Nov 30.00 Put	4.60	4.80	25.20	25.40	2.40
Nov 32.50 Put	6.50	6.70	25.80	26.00	1.80
Nov 35.00 Put	8.60	8.80	26.20	26.40	1.40
Nov 37.50 Put	10.80	11.00	26.50	26.70	1.10
Nov 40.00 Put	13.00	13.30	26.70	27.00	0.90
Nov 42.50 Put	15.40	15.60	26.90	27.10	0.70
Nov 45.00 Put	17.80	18.00	27.00	27.20	0.60

long option and short future position is a major reason to consider this version of a time spread in place of a short future, long future position.

This calendar spread example will use quotes from the same date as the previous example along with the same outlook for November VIX settlement. November VIX put quotes from September 14, 2010, appear in Table 14.8. As a reminder, the VIX index is trading at 21.56, the November VIX future is at 27.60, and the December VIX future is trading at 28.40.

These quotes include the bids and offers for several in the money put options. In addition, there are again columns that reflect the equivalent November VIX futures prices based on the bid and ask prices of the put option. The formula to determine this is a bit different than in the previous example.

Purchasing a put is a bearish position that can be thought of as the equivalent to being short a future contract. The future bid is based on subtracting the ask side of the put from the strike, while the future ask is based on subtracting the bid side of the put from the strike.

For example, the ask side of the VIX Nov 30.00 Put is 4.80. Purchasing that option could be thought of as being the same as shorting the future contract at 25.20. Therefore the future bid shows up as 25.20. The final column refers to the put option extra cost. As there is some time value in each of the put options considered, there is a little extra cost involved in using these contracts. Weighing the pros and cons of which put option would be best for this spread results in a purchase of the November 40 Put at 13.30.

The outlook for this sample trade involves the same price assumptions at expiration as the previous example:

VIX Expiration = 22.50—one point higher than current index.
December VIX Future = 26.70—consistent with front month spread of 4.70 over the index.

If a spread were to be initiated through shorting the November VIX future at 27.60 and purchasing the December VIX Future at 28.40, then the outcome based on these targets would be:

November VIX Future—Sold at 27.60 – Settle at 22.50 = +5.10
December VIX Future—Buy at 28.40 – Sell at 26.70 = −1.70
Net spread profit 5.10 – 1.70 = 3.40

The alternative to this trade may be the following trades:

Buy 10 VIX Nov 40.00 Puts at 13.30
Buy 1 December VIX Future at 28.40

Based on a target of 22.50, the outcome at November expiration:

VIX Nov 40.00 Puts—Paid 13.30 – Settle at 17.50 = +4.20
December VIX Future—Buy at 28.40 – Sell at 26.70 = −1.70
Net spread profit 4.20 – 1.70 = 2.70

Unlike the previous example, where selling a call option results in a superior payout, buying a put option instead of a short futures position actually results in a lower payout based on the target levels. With two moving parts, the November VIX settlement price and price of the December VIX future contract at November expiration, again a more elaborate payout table would be used. Table 14.9 shows the various potential profits or losses on this trade at expiration.

At all price levels on this table, using futures contracts together results in a better payout than creating the spread with a combination of a long put and long future contract. So why consider using this structure to create a calendar spread? The answer lies in times of extreme volatility.

TABLE 14.9 Profit/Loss Table for Calendar Spread Using Puts and Futures

	20.50	22.50	24.50	26.50	28.50	30.50	32.50
20.50	−1.70	0.30	2.30	4.30	6.30	8.30	10.30
22.50	−3.70	−1.70	0.30	2.30	4.30	6.30	8.30
24.50	−5.70	−3.70	−1.70	0.30	2.30	4.30	6.30
26.50	−7.70	−5.70	−3.70	−1.70	0.30	2.30	4.30
28.50	−9.70	−7.70	−5.70	−3.70	−1.70	0.30	2.30
30.50	−11.70	−9.70	−7.70	−5.70	−3.70	−1.70	0.30
32.50	−13.70	−11.70	−9.70	−7.70	−5.70	−3.70	−1.70

TABLE 14.10 October and November 2008 VIX Future Prices

	9/22/2008	10/22/2008
October 2008 VIX	26.55	63.04
November 2008 VIX	25.30	46.50

The best example of extreme volatility and how VIX futures prices re-acted relative to each other occurred during the latter half of 2008. It was only a single day, but as a highlight of what can happen, consider the set-tlement and front month futures prices in Table 14.10.

With respect to the prices in Table 14.11, on September 22, a month be-fore the VIX settlement, the October contract is actually trading at a slight premium to the November contract. The prices on October 22 represent October VIX settlement for the October contract and the market opening price for the November contract.

A calendar spread between the two would involve selling the October 2008 contract for 26.55 and buying the November 2008 contract for 25.30. The result of this trade would have been disastrous. A short position in the October contract would have settled at 63.04, while exiting the November long on the open October 22 would have resulted in an exit price of 46.50. Table 14.11 shows the individual and spread results for this trade.

If a put option had been purchased to represent the exposure gained from the short October VIX future contract, then the outcome for this trade may have been a bit different. Using the same pricing parameters as the example with 2010 prices, a VIX Oct 40.00 Put would be trading for about 13.95. Instead of shorting an October VIX future contract, 10 VIX Oct 40.00 Puts would be purchased at 13.95 each. Along with this purchase of options would be a purchase of a November VIX future contract at 25.30.

Using the settlement price for October VIX options and futures along with the opening price of the November VIX future on October 22, 2008, would result in the outcome in Table 14.12.

A losing trade turns into a winner due to the limited maximum poten-tial loss associated with the long option position. The most a trader may

TABLE 14.11 Results from Short October, Long November VIX Future Calendar Spread

	9/22/2008	10/22/2008	Profit/Loss
October 2008 VIX	Sell 1 @ 26.55	Settle Short @ 63.05	−36.49
November 2008 VIX	Buy 1 @ 25.30	Sell 1 @ 46.50	+21.20
		Spread	−15.29

TABLE 14.12   Hypothetical Results from Long Oct 40.00 Put, Long November VIX Future Calendar Spread

	9/22/2008	10/22/2008	Profit/Loss
Oct 40.00 Put	Buy 10 @ 13.95	Out of the Money	−13.95
November 2008 VIX	Buy 1 @ 25.30	Sell 1 @ 46.50	+21.20
		Spread	+7.25

lose when purchasing an option contract is the premium paid for that contract. This is not true for a short position in a future contract. There is theoretically an unlimited loss associated with a short future contract. This potential may play itself out in a detrimental outcome when there is a short-term spike in volatility.

CHAPTER 15

Vertical Spreads with VIX Options

C hapter 14 discussed combining VIX options to construct a time spread. This chapter is the first of two chapters introducing spreads that use VIX option contracts with the same expiration dates.

A wide variety of payoffs may be constructed when combining options. Due to the unique nature of VIX index options, with the pricing based on a future contract price but settling in an index calculation, spreads using VIX index options are a unique breed. In this and the following chapter, the spread will be introduced as it would be applied based on an outlook on a stock or index. Then the same spread will be shown using VIX index options displaying the differences between VIX and standard option contracts.

Although not encompassing all potential spreads that may be created with VIX index options, this chapter will take common bullish, bearish, and neutral option spreads and demonstrate how the risk reward of these spreads differs for the same strategies on other indexes or equities.

This is the first of two chapters that will introduce option spreads strategies and discuss how using VIX options may result in a slightly different risk reward by taking a look at vertical spreads. A vertical spread was already introduced in Chapter 11 as an alternative to a long call.

VERTICAL SPREAD EXAMPLES

A vertical spread involves two options that are the same type with the same expiration date. They differ in that each has a unique strike price and that

TABLE 15.1 Vertical Bull and Bear Spread Configuration

	Long	Short
Bull spread	Lower strike	Higher strike
Bear spread	Higher strike	Lower strike

the spread involves a long position in one contract and a short position with the other. Bullish and bearish versions of these spreads may be created through a combination of either all call or all put options. Depending on the combination of options and whether the trade is bullish or bearish, a vertical spread may be initiated with a credit or a debit to an account.

Regardless of the type of contracts, either call or put options, when bullish the lower strike is purchased and the higher strike is sold. If a bearish outlook is the motivation for a trade, then the lower strike option is sold and the higher strike option is purchased. A summary of this appears in Table 15.1.

Even though a bullish spread may be created with a debit or credit, the ultimate risk reward of the position is the same in either case. When each vertical spread is introduced, comparable debit and credit versions will be shown. The comparison of these two versions will also display how each has the same risk profile.

What's in the Name: Vertical Spread

The vertical spread is a name that originated on the trading floor. Before electronic trading took over the world, market makers would converge around a post where a handful of stock option series would be traded. Each post would be equipped with monitors displaying market quotes for a variety of options. Quotes for a single month would appear like this:

XYZ Aug 40 Call 7.35 × 7.45
XYZ Aug 45 Call 4.25 × 4.35
XYZ Aug 50 Call 2.40 × 2.45

If a market maker wanted to determine the market for a spread involving the Aug 40 Call and Aug 45 Call, the quotes were located vertically relative to each other on this screen. Hence the name vertical spread.

Vertical spreads are often considered alternatives to a bullish long call position or a bearish long put position. An example of this was shown briefly toward the end of Chapter 11. The next two sections introduce each bullish and bearish vertical spread in terms of a stock or index. Each example using standard options is followed by an example of the spread using VIX options. Along with each of the examples using VIX options will be a corresponding example of buying a VIX call or put option. The purpose of comparing vertical spreads with standard options to vertical spreads with VIX options is to highlight how the risk and reward of a spread with VIX options may differ greatly from those of a vertical spread with standard options.

Bullish Vertical Spreads

A bullish vertical spread will be created through buying an option contract that has a lower strike price and selling an option with a higher strike price. This is done through combining either two put options or two call options. If the spread is initiated with calls, then there will be a debit to an account; if initiated with put options, then a credit will be received on the trade.

The sample option prices in Table 15.2 are used to demonstrate how a bullish vertical spread may be created with either call or put options. The option prices in this table are based on XYZ, which represents a stock, trading at 37.25. The price target for XYZ by option expiration is 40.00, so bullish spread examples are created using the 35 and 40 strike options.

The vertical spread was created with call options; the XYZ 35 Call would be purchased for 3.00 and the XYZ 40 Call would be sold at 0.60. The result is a debit or cost of 2.40. At expiration, if XYZ closes at any price equal to or above 40.00, then the 35 strike call will have 5.00 more in value than the 40 strike call. The spread is long the 35 strike call and short the 40 strike call, so the spread will be worth 5.00. Subtracting the cost of the spread (2.40) from the value of the spread, 5.00 – 2.40, results in a maximum profit from this trade of 2.60.

With put options, the XYZ 35 Put would be purchased at a cost of 0.60 and the XYZ 40 Put would be sold for 3.20. Receiving 3.20 and paying out 0.60 results in a credit of 2.60 for initiating the trade. At expiration, with XYZ at or above 40.00, both put options will be out of the money and have no value. The result is a profit equal to the 2.60 credit received when the trade was initiated.

TABLE 15.2 Vertical Spread Quotes

	Bid	Ask		Bid	Ask
XYZ 35 Call	2.95	3.00	XYZ 35 Put	0.55	0.60
XYZ 40 Call	0.60	0.65	XYZ 40 Put	3.20	3.25

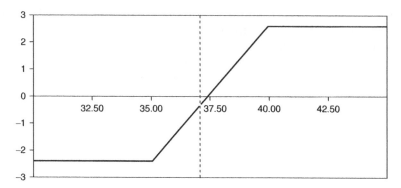

FIGURE 15.1 Vertical Bull Spread Payout

In both cases, creating the spread with call or put options, the risk and potential reward are the same. That is the maximum potential loss of 2.40 and maximum potential gain of 2.60 at expiration. The major differences between the two spreads are how they are created (credit versus debit), the process that may occur at expiration (exercise/assignment versus expiring out of the money), and how the profit is calculated (credit kept or value of spread minus debit paid). The payout diagram in Figure 15.1 shows the result of these bullish spreads at a variety of prices at expiration.

Note on the payout diagram that the price where XYZ was trading when the trade was initiated is highlighted with a vertical dashed line. The line is pretty close to the breakeven point on the diagram. The risk and potential reward of vertical spreads varies based on the price of the underlying security when the spread is initiated. This aspect of vertical spreads translates to VIX options in an unusual way.

As mentioned multiple times in this book, but worth repeating, VIX index options are not priced based on where the VIX index is trading. VIX index options are priced using the VIX future contract that expires on the same date as the option. As the futures may be at a discount or premium to the index, the payout of a vertical spread relative to the index may result in a risk reward profile that differs greatly when considering the future or the index as the underlying.

An example of a bullish vertical spread will use the option contract quotes in Table 15.3. These quotes are for November expiration and based on the November 2010 Future contract trading at 18.90. The VIX index is trading at 19.10 at a small premium to the November Future. These quotes are from November 9, with these option contracts expiring in eight days on November 17.

To stick with a realistic example of purchasing these contracts, the ask side of the quote is assumed to be a long entry price. With the exception

TABLE 15.3 November VIX Option Quotes, November 9, 2010

	Bid	Ask
Nov 15.00 Call	3.70	4.10
Nov 16.00 Call	2.70	3.10
Nov 17.00 Call	1.95	2.10
Nov 18.00 Call	1.25	1.35
Nov 19.00 Call	0.75	0.85
Nov 20.00 Call	0.50	0.60

of the 20 Call, taking a long position in any of these November call options results in profit at a VIX settlement level of 20.00. A quick comparison of these options to determine the best use of capital appears in Table 15.4. The key figures to focus on in this table are the percent profit along with the breakeven prices.

The best choice based on percent return is the VIX Nov 18.00 Call with a 48 percent return. However, taking a look at breakeven, the next three strikes down all have a breakeven level of 19.10. Taking the percentage return and breakeven levels into account for compromising between the two, and for vertical spread comparison purposes, the decision is to take a long position in the VIX Nov 17.00 Call at 2.10.

Often an alternative to a long call is to consider a bull spread. As discussed earlier in this chapter, a vertical spread may be created using put or call options. Many traders prefer creating a vertical spread and receiving a credit. As the risk reward for a vertical spread created with either a debit or a credit is the same, for easy comparison purposes a bull call spread is going to be used as the vertical spread example.

There are multiple potential bull spreads that can be created from the available options in Table 15.5. Bull call spreads that use the VIX Nov 17.00 Call as the long side combined with short positions in higher strike calls

TABLE 15.4 Outcomes for a Variety of Long Call Positions Assuming November VIX Settlement of 20.00

	Cost	Profit	% Profit	Break Even
Nov 15.00 Call	4.10	0.90	22%	19.10
Nov 16.00 Call	3.10	0.90	29%	19.10
Nov 17.00 Call	2.10	0.90	43%	19.10
Nov 18.00 Call	1.35	0.65	48%	19.35
Nov 19.00 Call	0.85	0.15	18%	19.85
Nov 20.00 Call	0.60	−0.60	−100%	20.60

TABLE 15.5 Outcomes for a Variety of Bull Call Spreads at November VIX Settlement of 20.00

Long / Short	Cost	Profit	% Profit	Break Even
Nov 17.00 / 18.00	0.85	0.15	18%	17.85
Nov 17.00 / 19.00	1.35	0.65	48%	18.35
Nov 17.00 / 20.00	1.60	1.40	88%	18.60

appear in Table 15.5. Each of these spreads show potential profits and breakeven levels based on VIX settlement at 20.00.

The cost of each of these potential spreads is based on paying the ask side of the 17 strike call and selling on the bid side of each of the options that are paired with this contract. Using the bid side of a contract as the sell price combined with the offer side as the purchase price results in a representation of a true entry price for the spread. For example, the VIX Nov 17.00 / 18.00 Bull Call Spread cost is 0.85. This is determined by paying 2.10 for the VIX Nov 17.00 Call and receiving 1.25 for selling the VIX Nov 18.00 Call.

Does Having Too Many Strikes Result in Too Many Choices?

Each VIX option series has an abundance of contracts available for trading. For example, the January 2011 contract has 28 strike prices listed ranging from 10 to 80. The result of having 28 contracts sharing the same expiration date is a potential of 756 vertical spreads.

This is stark comparison to 10 to 15 years ago when many stock option series had only 4 or 5 strike prices available at each expiration date. In those cases, the combinations would have resulted in 16 or 20 potential vertical spreads.

Two of the three potential spreads have a superior return with November VIX settlement of 20.00 relative to a long position in the VIX Nov 17.00 Call. The VIX Nov 17.00/19.00 Bull Call spread would cost 1.35 to initiate and have a profit of 0.65 with the VIX at 20.00 for a return of 48 percent. The VIX Nov 17.00/20.00 Bull Call spread would cost 1.60 to initiate and have a profit of 1.40 for a return of 88 percent. Based on percent return alone, the VIX Nov 17.00/20.00 Bull Call spread is the best choice with a target price of 20.00 for the VIX at November expiration. The percentage return for a long 18 call was 48 percent, so this is also a superior choice relative to that trade based on the VIX settlement target of 20.00.

TABLE 15.6 Payout Table for XYZ Oct 17.00/20.00 Bull Call Spread

VIX Settlement	17.00 / 20.00 Bull Call Spread	% Profit
15.00	−1.60	−100%
16.00	−1.60	−100%
17.00	−1.60	−100%
18.00	−0.60	−38%
18.60	**0.00**	**0%**
19.00	0.40	25%
20.00	1.40	88%
21.00	1.40	88%

Table 15.6 is a payout table showing the result of this bull spread at a variety of VIX prices at expiration. At any price from 17.00 and lower, the maximum potential loss of 1.60 would be realized. Between the lower strike price in the spread of 17.00 and the higher strike price of 20.00, there would be a partial gain or loss. Even if settlement comes in at 19.00, a point under the target, there would be a profit of 25 percent. From 20.00 and higher, the maximum gain of 1.40 would be realized.

A payout diagram for this spread trade appears in Figure 15.2. In addition to the profit and loss of this spread, note the two vertical lines. These lines represent where the VIX index and the November VIX futures are trading as the spread is initiated. The line on the right represents the VIX index, which is trading at 19.10, and the line to the left is the November VIX future contract, which is trading at 18.90, a slight discount to the index.

One of the first things that is apparent on this payout diagram is that both the index and future contract are trading at prices equal to the spread being a profit at expiration. This makes the outlook for this spread neutral to bullish, as even this spread trade can benefit from a neutral

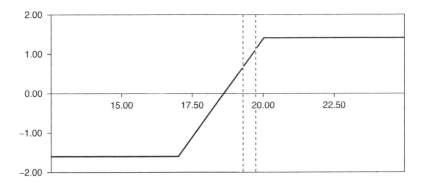

FIGURE 15.2 Payout Diagram for XYZ Oct 17.00/20.00 Bull Call Spread

TABLE 15.7 January VIX Option Quotes, November 9, 2010

	Bid	Ask
Jan 18.00 Call	6.30	6.60
Jan 19.00 Call	5.50	5.90
Jan 20.00 Call	4.90	5.20
Jan 21.00 Call	4.20	4.60
Jan 22.50 Call	3.40	3.80

outlook, it also can benefit from a stagnant stock or index. The spread is bullish in name, but it actually benefits from a neutral or bullish price change for the index between the date the trade would be initiated and its expiration date.

The outlook behind the bullish trades to be considered is for a VIX index settlement of 20.00 at expiration the following week. Commonly a long call option is the first consideration when there is a bullish outlook for a stock or index. Before analyzing the different bull spreads, a comparison with a position that may be created with these call options or a pure long call position would be considered.

It is more common for VIX futures contracts to be at a premium to the index than at a discount. When the VIX futures are at a premium to the VIX index, the options are being priced based on an underlying that is at a premium to the index. This pricing occurs while settlement will still be determined by the underlying instrument or the VIX index.

An issue arises when bullish on the VIX index when the VIX futures are at a significant premium to the index. This issue with this pricing characteristic between the index and the option pricing may result in a risk reward profile that is prohibitive. An example of long call options being too expensive will be developed using the option quotes in Table 15.7. On November 9, 2010, the same date as the previous bull call spread example, the VIX index was trading at 19.10. Using a further price outlook for the VIX index, maybe the belief is that the VIX index will settle at 22.50 on January expiration, which is 71 days off. This is 3.40 points higher than the current level of the VIX index. Using this outlook, the January VIX call option quotes are analyzed.

Before even considering the profit or loss of a bull spread using January options with the VIX settling at 22.50, the individual long option positions are considered. The outcome of purchasing each of these contracts with January VIX settlement at 22.50 is shown in Table 15.8.

None of these option purchases would result in a profitable trade, with the VIX settling 3.40 points higher than the current index level at January expiration. In fact, a trader would be better off selling these calls than

TABLE 15.8 Outcomes for a Variety of Long Call Positions at January VIX Settlement of 22.50

	Cost	Profit	% Profit	Break Even
Jan 18.00 Call	6.60	−4.50	−68%	24.60
Jan 19.00 Call	5.90	−2.40	−41%	24.90
Jan 20.00 Call	5.20	−2.70	−52%	25.20
Jan 21.00 Call	4.60	−3.10	−67%	25.60
Jan 22.50 Call	3.80	−3.80	−100%	26.30

purchasing them even though they expect a higher VIX settlement than the current index level. The reason behind this is due to the pricing of these options being based off the January 2011 Future contract which is trading at 24.10. This occurs on the same date that the November Future was at a slight discount to the index.

These contracts are combined to come up with the best Bull Call Spread resulting in what is referred to as being long the VIX Jan 18.00/22.50 Bull Call spread. The cost of this spread would be 3.20 through purchasing the VIX Jan 18.00 Call for 6.60 and selling the VIX Jan 22.50 Call for a credit of 3.40. A payout table for this bull call spread appears in Table 15.9.

A variety of price levels are included in this table. The first two include the lower strike price of 18.00, which results in a maximum loss of 3.20 on the spread. This is the price paid for the spread. As the long VIX Jan 18.00 Call has value, there is a partial loss or gain for the spread. Note that at 21.20 the spread is breakeven. At this price level, the value for the long option in the spread is 3.20.

A payout diagram for this trade appears in Figure 15.3. As in the previous example, the price levels for the VIX future contract and the VIX index are highlighted with vertical lines. Contrary to the previous bull spread

TABLE 15.9 Payout Table for VIX Jan 18.00 / 22.50 Bull Call Spread

VIX Settlement	18.00/22.50 Bull Call Spread	% Profit
16.00	−3.20	−100%
18.00	−3.20	−100%
19.10	−2.10	−66%
20.00	−1.20	−38%
21.20	0.00	0%
22.00	0.60	19%
22.50	1.30	41%
24.10	1.30	41%
25.00	1.30	41%

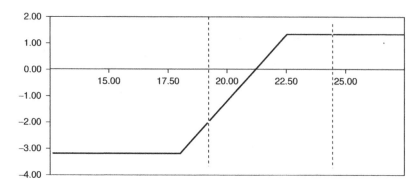

FIGURE 15.3 Payout Diagram for VIX Jan 18.00 / 22.50 Bull Call Spread

example, however, there is a significant difference between the index and future price. The line on the right indicates the January VIX futures price when the trade is initiated. The line on the left shows the price of the VIX index at the same time.

These two lines show different significant levels when the trade is initiated. The significance is that the trade will be settled if held until expiration and the index comes into play. When pricing, the futures contract is significant.

The spot VIX index line is at a level where this spread would be a losing trade at January VIX expiration. On the same date, the January futures contract line is at a point where this trade would be a winner. The maximum potential gain for this trade is 3.20 while the maximum potential loss is 1.30, which results in a potential gain of 41 percent of capital. Typically if the underlying is in the area of a maximum potential loss, the result is a payout that is close to if not higher than the cost or risk associated with the spread.

To illustrate the risk reward feature of a VIX index option spread, the VIX index is substituted for the VIX futures as the underlying instrument. Using the VIX index to determine option values and applying it as the underlying for this spread would result in the prices for the January VIX Call options. Table 15.10 compares the prices based on the futures with approximate option prices determined using a pricing calculator.

The method used to get these altered option prices involved applying similar inputs into a pricing calculator. The only change is the underlying price is 19.10 instead of 24.10. The outcome is much lower option prices, as the underlying price is 5 points lower.

Using these altered prices, a VIX January 18.00/22.50 Bull Call spread would cost 1.80. This debit is determined through buying the 18 strike call for 2.90 and selling the 22.50 strike call for a credit of 1.10. A comparison

TABLE 15.10 January VIX Calls versus Calls Prices with VIX Index as Underlying

	Future Bid	Future Ask	Future Midpoint	Index Bid	Index Ask	Index Midpoint	Midpoint Difference
Jan 18.00 Call	6.30	6.60	6.45	2.75	2.90	2.83	3.62
Jan 19.00 Call	5.50	5.90	5.70	2.25	2.40	2.32	3.38
Jan 20.00 Call	4.90	5.20	5.05	1.85	2.00	1.93	3.12
Jan 21.00 Call	4.20	4.60	4.40	1.50	1.65	1.58	2.82
Jan 22.50 Call	3.40	3.80	3.60	1.10	1.25	1.18	2.42

of the spread created with market prices and one created through prices determined with the index as the underlying combined with the use of a pricing calculator appear in Table 15.11.

Note the final two rows in this table. The vertical spread using market prices has a potential loss of 100 percent of capital and a potential maximum gain of 41 percent. The spread created based on the index has a potential maximum loss of 100 percent of capital and a maximum potential return of 150 percent. This difference of risk versus reward from the spreads is a direct result of the value of the quoted VIX index options deriving their value from the futures. Considering that the index needs to rise over 10 percent to reach a profit, this pricing may be prohibitive relative to the risk and reward scenario depicted by the payout.

Table 15.12 is a payout comparison at a variety of price levels for both bull spreads. Note at VIX index settlement prices below and including the lower strike price that there is a 100 percent loss of capital for this spread. This loss is incurred regardless of which series is used. The difference is still in a dollar amount, as the hypothetical spread is based on lower option prices. At all price levels above the lower strike, the spread that would be created with lower priced options has a superior percent profit based on the corresponding VIX settlement price.

TABLE 15.11 Key Levels for Bull Spread Based on Market Prices and Bull Spread Based on VIX Index as Underlying

	VIX Future	VIX Index
Underlying Price	24.10	19.10
VIX Jan 18.00 Call	6.60	2.90
VIX Jan 22.50 Call	3.40	1.10
Bull Spread	3.20	1.80
Max Profit	1.30	2.70
Risk	100%	100%
Reward	41%	150%

TABLE 15.12 Payout Comparison for Bull Spread Based on Market Prices and Bull Spread Based on VIX Index as Underlying

VIX Settlement	Spread with Market Quotes	% Profit	Spread Using Index as Underlying	% Profit
16.00	−3.20	−100%	−1.80	−100%
18.00	−3.20	−100%	−1.80	−100%
19.10	−2.10	−66%	−0.70	−39%
19.80	−1.40	−44%	0.00	0%
20.00	−1.20	−38%	0.20	11%
21.20	0.00	0%	1.60	89%
22.00	0.60	19%	2.20	122%
22.50	1.30	41%	2.70	150%
24.10	1.30	41%	2.70	150%
25.00	1.30	41%	2.70	150%

Another important comparison in this table is the profit or loss at 19.80 and 21.20. At 19.80, the spread that would be based on the index as the underlying would break even, while the breakeven for the spread based on market prices is 1.60 points higher at 21.20. This difference in breakeven levels is very apparent in the payoff diagram shown in Figure 15.4.

The diagram shows the two bull call spreads in this exercise side by side. The higher of the two lines represents a spread created with options based on the lower index price. This chart also shows the price for the index represented by the vertical line on the left and the January VIX Future shown with the line on the right.

This comparison of the two bull spreads is mostly an academic exercise, as the more attractive of the two spreads is not a trading possibility.

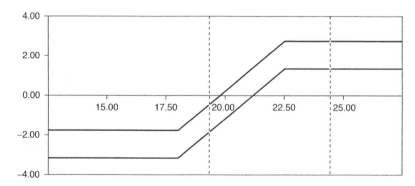

FIGURE 15.4 Payoff Diagram Comparison for Bull Spread Based on Market Prices and Bull Spread Based on VIX Index as Underlying

The goal is to depict what occurs with VIX index options due to the underlying pricing being based on futures. By showing the index versus futures option values, it illustrates that at times a vertical spread using VIX index options may not have a very favorable risk reward profile when the index is considered as the underlying. This occurs more often with a bullish spread than a bearish spread. In fact, as shown in the next section, sometimes this pricing difference may result in a very favorable risk reward scenario.

Bearish Vertical Spreads

A bearish vertical spread will have the opposite goal of a bullish vertical spread with respect to the target price for the underlying security associated with the trade. That is, the bearish version is initiated with the outlook that a stock or index will be below the lower strike price at expiration as opposed to above the higher strike price.

The goal is opposite for a bearish vertical spread, and so is the construction of the spread. When a bear spread is initiated, the lower strike price is sold and the higher strike option contract is purchased. If the spread is initiated with put options then a debit will be incurred, and if the spread is created with all call options then a credit will be received.

Using the option quotes in Table 15.13, a bearish spread with put options would be created through buying the higher strike XYZ 40 Put at 3.25 and selling the XYZ 35 Put for a credit of 0.55 with the result being a cost of 2.70 (3.25 – 0.55). If XYZ is at any price below the lower strike price of 35 at expiration, the long XYZ 40 Put would have 5.00 more in value than the short 35 strike put. The value of the spread is 5.00, while the cost of this spread was 2.70. With a cost of 2.70 and a final value of 5.00, the profit from the trade is 2.30 at these price levels.

On the call side, to implement a bearish spread the XYZ 40 Call would be purchased at a cost of 0.65 and the XYZ 35 Call would be sold for a credit of 2.95, with the result being a credit of 2.30 for implementing the spread. This credit is also the maximum potential profit for the trade if XYZ is at or below 35 at expiration. At this price level, both call options would expire out of the money.

TABLE 15.13 Vertical Spread Quotes

	Bid	Ask		Bid	Ask
XYZ 35 Call	2.95	3.00	XYZ 35 Put	0.55	0.60
XYZ 40 Call	0.60	0.65	XYZ 40 Put	3.20	3.25

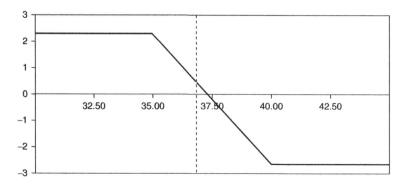

FIGURE 15.5 Typical Vertical Bear Spread Payout Diagram

Figure 15.5 shows the payout for both of the vertical bear spreads created with either put or call options. That is, they have an identical risk reward profile, so the payout diagram is also identical for the two. The dashed line shows where XYZ is trading when the spread would be initiated. The risk and reward associated with a vertical spread held to expiration is known when the position is initiated. This potential reward versus the risk taken on is based on the price of the underlying security when the trade is initiated.

Similar to the bullish version of the VIX spread, the bearish version also has option pricing based on VIX futures and a payout based on where the VIX index is trading at expiration. With pricing based on the futures and futures often being at a premium to the VIX index, a bear spread may consistently be an attractive trade.

The October VIX index option prices in Table 15.14 are from September 2, 2010, with the VIX index trading at 23.20 and the October VIX future contract trading at 29.15. October expiration is on October 20, or 48 days in the future.

TABLE 15.14 October VIX Option Quotes September 2, 2010

	Bid	Ask
Oct 24.00 Put	0.75	0.85
Oct 25.00 Put	1.05	1.10
Oct 26.00 Put	1.45	1.60
Oct 27.50 Put	2.20	2.30
Oct 30.00 Put	3.60	3.80
Oct 32.50 Put	5.40	5.60

TABLE 15.15 Outcomes for a Variety of Long Put Positions at VIX Settlement of 23.20

Long Option	Cost	Profit	% Profit	Break Even
Oct 24.00 Put	0.85	−0.05	−6%	23.15
Oct 25.00 Put	1.10	0.70	64%	23.90
Oct 26.00 Put	1.60	1.20	75%	24.40
Oct 27.50 Put	2.30	2.00	87%	25.20
Oct 30.00 Put	3.80	3.00	79%	26.20
Oct 32.50 Put	5.60	3.70	66%	26.90

This example is based on the outlook that the VIX index will be neutral to slightly bearish. Using this outlook, a trader considers a put purchase or possibly a vertical spread using put options. There is always a bearish vertical alternative of also using call options, but to keep the comparisons simple, a bearish vertical spread using put options will be presented in this case. Assuming a target price of 23.20, or the current VIX index price, a long put option results in the payouts and breakeven levels in Table 15.15.

The most attractive alternative on this table appears to be a long position in the VIX Oct 27.50 Put at 2.30. With VIX settlement at 23.20 the cash value of an Oct 27.50 put would be 4.30. A cost of 2.30 and a value of 4.30 would result in a profit of 2.00, or 87 percent. The breakeven is also pretty attractive at 25.20. This is almost 2 points higher than where the VIX index is currently trading. So even if the VIX moves a little higher, there would be a nice profit from the long put option.

An alternative to the long put is a bearish vertical spread. There are a large amount of vertical spread alternatives to choose from. The alternatives would involve pairing a long position in the 27.50 Put with a short position in a lower strike put. An overview of profits and breakeven levels for a few bear put spreads appears in Table 15.16.

This table shows the outcome with VIX settlement at 23.20 of buying the VIX Oct 27.50 Put and selling the 24.00, 25.00, and 26.00 strike put options against it to create a bearish spread. All three of these alternatives

TABLE 15.16 Outcomes for a Variety of Bear Put Spreads at VIX Settlement of 23.20

Long/Short	Cost	Profit	% Profit	Break Even
Oct 24.00/27.50	1.55	1.95	126%	25.95
Oct 25.00/27.50	1.25	1.25	100%	26.25
Oct 26.00/27.50	0.85	0.65	76%	26.65

TABLE 15.17 Payout Table for XYZ Oct 25.00/27.50 Bear Put Spread

VIX Settlement	25.00/27.50 Bear Spread	% Profit
20.00	1.25	100%
22.50	1.25	100%
23.20	**1.25**	**100%**
25.00	1.25	100%
27.50	−1.25	−100%
29.15	**−1.25**	**−100%**
30.00	−1.25	−100%

have a better breakeven point than the pure long option position and two of the three spreads has a superior percentage profit. After analyzing the various alternatives, a decision is made to not be terribly aggressive and go with buying the XYZ Oct 27.50 Put and selling the Oct 25.00 Put for a net cost of 1.25. Through being less aggressive, the breakeven point for the chosen spread results in a little higher level than the more aggressive Oct 24.00/27.5 spread. A payout table for this bear spread based on holding this spread through VIX expiration appears in Table 15.17.

In addition to equally spaced outcomes for VIX settlement, the two VIX prices that were in place when the spread was initiated are highlighted on the table in bold. Note that at 23.20, the price target and the VIX index quote when the bear spread would have been traded this spread has a maximum profit of 1.25. The outlook behind this trade was for the VIX index to remain in a narrow range from early September to expiration in mid-October so this also represents the target price. Although bearish by name, this spread is actually more of a neutral bet on the direction of the VIX.

Also, note the other bold level of 29.15. This is where the October VIX futures are trading when the spread is considered. This quote of 29.15 is also the price level that the pricing of the contracts would be based. This leads to an interesting observation regarding the risk reward of this spread when using an outlook for the index, but pricing based on the futures.

A payout diagram for the Oct 25.00/27.50 Bear Put Spread appears in Figure 15.6. To represent the significant index and future price levels at initiation of the trade this diagram has two price levels highlighted by a dashed line. The line on the right side of the chart represents the price of the October VIX Future contract when the spread was initiated. It is plainly falling in the area where the spread would lose the premium paid at expiration. On the left side of the chart the price where the VIX index is trading on this date is highlighted. At 23.20, the index is at a level of maximum profitability for this spread.

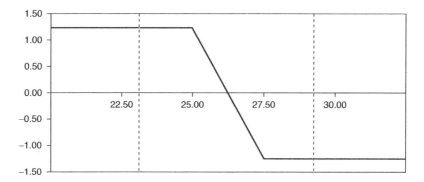

FIGURE 15.6 Oct 25.00/27.50 Bear Put Spread Payout Diagram

The two alternatives presented are to either purchase a VIX Oct 27.50 Put for 2.30 or initiate a bear spread through purchasing the VIX Oct 27.50 Put and selling the VIX Oct 25.00 Put for a net cost of 1.25. A payout table comparing a long put position and bear spread for this trade appears in Table 15.18. This table shows the payout for both strategies at a variety of price levels. The VIX index price and target price of 23.20 along with the October VIX Futures price of 29.15 are both highlighted on the table.

Comparing the two strategies on this table shows the vertical spread is a better alternative based on the target price of 23.20. However, the benefit of higher potential profitability from the long put is also displayed. Note that as the potential VIX settlement prices at lower levels are shown, the profit from this trade continues to increase. This potential difference is also highlighted on the payout diagram in Figure 15.7.

A benefit of the long put position relative to a bear spread is pretty apparent. Vertical spreads have a limited potential upside, while a long option position may continue to see an increase in profits with a stock moving in

TABLE 15.18 Payout Comparison of Bear Spread and Long Put

VIX Settlement	27.50/25.00 Bear Spread	% Profit	Long 27.50 Put	% Profit
20.00	1.25	100%	5.20	226%
22.50	1.25	100%	2.70	117%
23.20	**1.25**	**100%**	**2.00**	**87%**
25.00	1.25	100%	0.20	9%
27.50	−1.25	−100%	−2.30	−100%
29.15	**−1.25**	**−100%**	**−2.30**	**−100%**
30.00	−1.25	−100%	−2.30	−100%

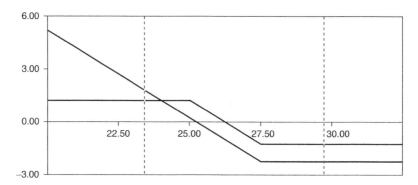

FIGURE 15.7 Oct 27.50 Put versus Oct 25.00/27.50 Bear Put Spread Payout Diagram

the correct direction. For this trade an assumption of a flat VIX index and the October VIX future drifting down to this level was the outlook motivating the transaction. Even though possibly missing out on additional profits, using an unchanged VIX index as a target does result in the bear spread being a superior choice of strategies.

Due to the pricing of VIX options being based on VIX futures pricing, but settling in a calculation of the VIX index, the risk reward of options spreads may differ from that of spreads based on stocks or other indexes. The vertical spread in this example has a 50–50 payout when initiated or a potential gain of 100 percent and a potential loss of 100 percent. The maximum potential loss of this trade was 1.25 with a maximum potential gain also of 1.25. A comparable vertical spread would have a different potential payout. The vertical spread created by applying the VIX index as the underlying results in a much less favorable payout scenario. The maximum

TABLE 15.19 Key Levels for Bear Spread Based on Market Prices and Bear Spread Based on VIX Index as Underlying

	VIX Future	VIX Index
Underlying price	29.15	23.20
VIX Oct 25.00 Put	1.05	3.45
VIX Oct 27.50 Put	2.30	5.25
Bear spread	1.25	1.80
Max profit	1.25	0.70
Risk	100%	100%
Reward	100%	39%

TABLE 15.20 November VIX Option Quotes September 14, 2010

	Bid	Ask
Nov 20.00 Put	0.25	0.30
Nov 22.50 Put	0.70	0.75
Nov 24.00 Put	1.15	1.35
Nov 25.00 Put	1.65	1.75
Nov 26.00 Put	2.10	2.25
Nov 27.50 Put	2.90	3.10
Nov 30.00 Put	4.60	4.80

potential gain is 0.70 based on a cost of 1.80, which results in a gain of about 39 percent versus a potential loss of 100 percent of capital.

In the previous section an academic comparison between a spread created with market prices and one created with hypothetical prices resulted in showing how using the index would result in a better risk reward. The opposite is true in this example as the risk reward is superior using futures prices instead of options that may be created using the index as the underlying.

Finally, a truly bearish outlook will be examined. On September 14, 2010 the VIX index closed at 21.55 with the November VIX futures contract at 27.60. The November contract was at a 6-point premium based on the anticipation of increased volatility over the next 60 days or so. Specifically, November expiration is 63 days in the future. The outlook for the VIX index is a target of 20.00. The November put option quotes appear in Table 15.20.

Based on these prices and a target November VIX settlement of 20.00, profit or loss levels were determined assuming these options were purchased at the prevailing market price. These outcomes appear in Table 15.21. Considering that the VIX index closed at 21.55, the only option on this table that would not realize a profit at this price level at expiration

TABLE 15.21 Outcomes for a Variety of Long Put Positions at November VIX Settlement of 20.00

Long Option	Cost	Profit	% Profit	Break Even
Nov 20.00 Put	0.30	0.00	0%	20.00
Nov 22.50 Put	0.75	1.75	233%	21.75
Nov 24.00 Put	1.35	2.65	196%	22.65
Nov 25.00 Put	1.75	3.25	186%	23.25
Nov 26.00 Put	2.25	3.75	167%	23.75
Nov 27.50 Put	3.10	4.40	142%	24.40
Nov 30.00 Put	4.80	5.20	108%	25.20

TABLE 15.22 Outcomes for Long 22.50 Put and Long 20.00/22.50 Bear Spread at a Variety of VIX Settlement Prices

	Long 22.50 Put Profit	Percent Return	Long 20.00/22.50 Spread Profit	Percent Return
17.50	4.25	567%	2.00	400%
18.75	3.00	400%	2.00	400%
20.00	1.75	233%	2.00	400%
21.75	0.00	0%	0.75	150%
22.50	0.00	0%	0.00	0%
23.75	0.00	0%	0.00	0%

would be the Nov 20.00 Put. All other option purchases have breakeven levels higher than the prevailing price of the index.

The VIX Nov 22.50 Put is the best choice based on percent profit with this outlook for the VIX index. Also, as stated previously, even if the VIX index does not move at all there would be a profit based on a long position in this option. The only choice using a long Nov 22.50 Put in a bearish spread would involve selling the Nov 20.00 Put at 0.25 to create a bear put spread.

Paying 0.75 for the VIX Nov 22.50 Put and purchasing the VIX Nov 20.00 Put for 0.25 results in a cost of 0.50. The resulting spread is commonly referred to as being long a VIX Nov 20.00/22.50 Bear Put spread for 0.50. The maximum potential value of this spread would be 2.50 if the VIX is at 20.00 or lower on November settlement. At 20.00 or lower the result would be a 2.00 profit based on a cost of 0.50 for a return of 400 percent. This is clearly a better return than the long 22.50 Put, but there is an opportunity cost associated with this better return.

Table 15.22 shows the return for the bear spread and long put option at a variety of November VIX settlement levels. If the VIX settles at 18.75 or 1.25 lower than the target price, there is also a 400 percent return for the long put position.

What needs to be weighed when deciding between a vertical spread and long option position is if the extra return sacrificed through selling an option is worth giving up potential upside. In this example, if the VIX is under 18.75 at settlement, the better trade would have been purchasing the VIX Nov 22.50 Put and not selling the 20.00 strike put to create the bearish spread. A payout diagram that shows this a little better appears in Figure 15.8.

Two significant points emanate from this example. First, as in the other payoff diagrams in this chapter, two price levels are highlighted on the chart. However, in this case they do not represent the VIX index and corresponding futures contract. On this diagram the line on the right shows the

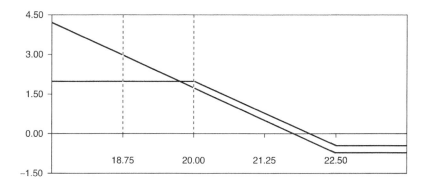

FIGURE 15.8 Nov 22.50 Put versus Nov 20.00/22.50 Bear Put Spread Payout Diagram

target price and maximum potential profit level for the bear spread. The second line shows the price level at which the percent profit from the long put option would match the percent profit having traded this opinion with a bear spread. At any price below 18.75, the long put is a better choice than the bear spread.

Also, focusing on the bear spread, the breakeven level for this trade is very close to where the index was quoted when the trade would have been initiated. Note the payout of 2.00 relative to the risk of 0.50 or a 4-to-1 risk reward profile. This is another of those payouts that occurs with VIX options that would not be available using standard stock or index options.

CHAPTER 16

Iron Condors and Butterflies with VIX Options

T his chapter addresses the use of traditionally neutral option spreads with VIX options. A common use of these two strategies is to target a specific price or range of prices at option expiration. The pricing of each of these strategies and resulting risk reward is based on where the underlying security is trading in relation to the strike prices of the option contracts that are used to construct the spread. What makes these two neutral strategies attractive when traded using VIX options is that very relationship. That is when the VIX future price is at a premium or discount to the VIX index, a favorable risk reward may be available when a neutral outlook exists for the VIX index.

This chapter will follow the same format as the previous chapters describing the application of option spreads using VIX options. Each strategy will be introduced with an example of how it may be used in conjunction with traditional equity or index options. Then the same spread will be shown using VIX options. For this chapter, the two neutral spreads are an iron condor and iron butterfly.

WHAT IS AN IRON CONDOR?

An iron condor is a combination of a bull put and a bear call spread. Both of these strategies were discussed in the previous chapter. Recall that these two spreads are the credit versions of vertical spreads. A bullish vertical spread is initiated with the outlook that a stock will trade above the higher strike price, while a bearish vertical spread has a goal that is achieved if the

TABLE 16.1   Quotes to Create Iron Condor

	Bid	Ask		Bid	Ask
XYZ 30 Call	7.60	7.65	XYZ 30 Put	0.20	0.25
XYZ 35 Call	3.80	3.85	XYZ 35 Put	1.45	1.50
XYZ 40 Call	1.50	1.55	XYZ 40 Put	4.10	4.15
XYZ 45 Call	0.30	0.35	XYZ 45 Put	8.05	8.10

stock is below a lower strike price at expiration. By combining these two spreads, the targeted outcome is for a stock or index to land in a certain price range at expiration.

The common use of an iron condor is with a range-bound stock or market. The spread is entered as a credit, and the goal is for the underlying instrument to stay in this range until expiration. The option pricing in Table 16.1 is used to demonstrate an iron condor on a stock.

The pricing in this table is based on a stock, XYZ, trading at 37.50. An iron condor is put on with an outlook that the stock will be in a range between 35.00 and 40.00 on option expiration. An iron condor combines a bullish spread created with put options and a bearish spread created with call options. The put side of the iron condor would be initiated by selling the XYZ 35 Put at 1.45 and purchasing the XYZ 30 Put for 0.25. The result of this part of the spread is a credit of 1.20. On the call side the XYZ 40 Call is sold for 1.50 and the XYZ 45 Call purchased at 0.35 for a net credit of 1.15. By placing the trades the net credit for the XYZ 30/35/40/45 Iron Condor is 2.35.

Again, the outlook that this trade is based on has XYZ closing between 35.00 and 40.00 at expiration. In this price range all option contracts in the spread expire out of the money. This best case scenario results in the profit from the trade being equal to the credit of 2.35 that was taken in when the trade was initiated. Table 16.2 is a summary of the outcome for this spread at expiration based on a variety of prices.

TABLE 16.2   XYZ 30/35/40/45 Iron Condor Profit—Loss at Expiration

XYZ	Long XYZ 30 Put	Short XYZ 35 Put	Short XYZ 40 Call	Long XYZ 45 Call	Credit	Iron Condor Profit Loss
25	5.00	−10.00	0.00	0.00	2.35	−2.65
30	0.00	−5.00	0.00	0.00	2.35	−2.65
35	0.00	0.00	0.00	0.00	2.35	2.35
40	0.00	0.00	0.00	0.00	2.35	2.35
45	0.00	0.00	−5.00	0.00	2.35	−2.65
50	0.00	0.00	−10.00	5.00	2.35	−2.65

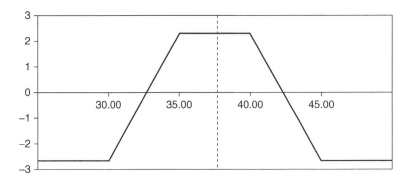

FIGURE 16.1 XYZ 30/35/40/45 Iron Condor Payout Diagram

The worst possible outcome is if the stock is at or below the lower strike put option or at or above the higher strike call option. At either of these pricing points the spread will result in a maximum loss. With XYZ at 30.00 or lower, both put options in the spread will be in the money. The short 35 strike put option will have 5.00 more in value than the long 30 strike put. The result here is a spread with a negative 5.00 in value for the holder.

To the upside, if XYZ is at 45.00 at expiration, then both call options in the iron condor will be in the money. The XYZ 40 Call will have 5.00 more in value than the XYZ 45 Call and as there is a short position in the 40 strike call and a long position in the 45 strike call, the spread will again be worth negative 5.00 points. This negative value is offset by the credit of 2.35 to result in a loss of 2.65 at expiration.

A payout diagram for this iron condor appears in Figure 16.1. Note the dashed line down the middle of the chart. This line represents where XYZ is trading when the spread is initiated. This is typical of iron condors constructed with option on indexes or stocks, where the underlying instrument is often trading within the range of maximum profitability when the trade is entered.

The risk reward associated with this iron condor involves a maximum potential loss of 2.65 and a potential gain of 2.35. This sort of gain versus loss is typical of an iron condor initiated when the underlying is trading in the price range. The next example is an iron condor that is initiated when the underlying stock price is outside the area of profitability at expiration. The quotes in Table 16.3 are based on XYZ trading at 45.00 instead of 37.50.

Using these quotes, a credit of 3.40 would be taken in to put on a 30/35/40/45 Iron Condor. This credit is a result of selling the XYZ 40 Call for 6.15 and selling the XYZ 35 Put for a credit of 0.25. The XYZ 45 Call

TABLE 16.3 Quotes to Create Iron Condor

	Bid	Ask		Bid	Ask
XYZ 30 Call	15.10	15.15	XYZ 30 Put	0.05	0.10
XYZ 35 Call	10.35	10.40	XYZ 35 Put	0.25	0.30
XYZ 40 Call	6.15	6.20	XYZ 40 Put	0.95	1.00
XYZ 45 Call	2.85	2.90	XYZ 45 Put	2.80	2.85

TABLE 16.4 XYZ 30/35/40/45 Iron Condor Profit—Loss at Expiration

XYZ	Long XYZ 30 Put	Short XYZ 35 Put	Short XYZ 40 Call	Long XYZ 45 Call	Credit	Iron Condor Profit Loss
25	5.00	−10.00	0.00	0.00	3.40	−1.60
30	0.00	−5.00	0.00	0.00	3.40	−1.60
35	0.00	0.00	0.00	0.00	3.40	3.40
40	0.00	0.00	0.00	0.00	3.40	3.40
45	0.00	0.00	−5.00	0.00	3.40	−1.60
50	0.00	0.00	−10.00	5.00	3.40	−1.60

would be purchased for 2.90 and the XYZ 30 Put would be purchased for a cost of 0.10. Table 16.4 shows the profit and loss of this trade at a variety of price levels.

Note the maximum potential gain and loss from this iron condor are a gain of 3.40 and a loss of 1.60. This is the result of this trade being initiated with XYZ at a price level that is outside the area of maximum profitability. This is illustrated further in the payout diagram in Figure 16.2.

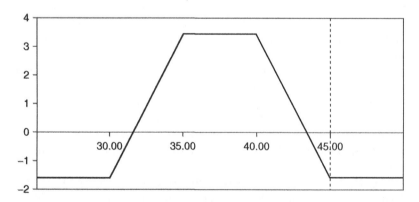

FIGURE 16.2 XYZ 30/35/40/45 Iron Condor Payout Diagram

TABLE 16.5 Iron Condor Comparisons		
	IC @ 37.50	**IC @ 45.00**
Max gain	2.35	3.40
Max loss	2.65	1.60
Down break even	32.65	31.60
Up break even	42.35	43.40

This payout diagram shows the profit or loss at expiration for the second iron condor example. The price level of XYZ when the trade is initiated is highlighted and is actually at a level where the maximum potential loss would be incurred at expiration. With the stock at 45.00 when the trade was initiated, the risk reward of this trade is different than the same trade with the stock at 37.50. A comparison appears in Table 16.5.

Both spreads would have a maximum gain if XYZ is between 35.00 and 40.00 at expiration. The iron condor created with XYZ trading at 45.00 would have a much better result at a gain of 3.40 relative to the gain of 2.35 for the other iron condor. The maximum potential loss favors the second iron condor also at a potential loss of 2.65 versus a potential loss of 1.60. Finally, the breakeven levels are wider for the second iron condor relative to the first one. However, there is a key difference that is not included on the table. This is the XYZ price movement that needs to happen for the second iron condor to make a profit.

XYZ would need to move 5 points lower to reach a level of maximum profitability, while the first iron condor would need no movement from XYZ to realize a maximum profit. There is more reward from the second iron condor because there is more risk that the trade will not be a profit.

This example also relates to the unique nature of using VIX options to create spreads. If VIX option contracts are being priced off of a future price that differs greatly from the index level, then a very favorable risk reward could exist when creating an iron condor with VIX options.

IRON CONDOR WITH VIX OPTIONS

As with the vertical spread examples in the previous chapter, when considering an iron condor using VIX options the pricing of the option contracts will be based on futures contracts and not the spot VIX index price. In fact, when there is a wide difference between the VIX index and VIX future prices an iron condor may only make sense when a trader has a directional outlook for the VIX index. That is, the risk reward profile of a spread may not justify a trade based on a neutral outlook.

TABLE 16.6 November VIX Option Pricing

Contract	Bid	Ask	Contract	Bid	Ask
Nov 15.00 Call	13.30	13.80	Nov 15.00 Put	0.05	0.10
Nov 20.00 Call	8.70	8.90	Nov 20.00 Put	0.10	0.15
Nov 22.50 Call	6.50	6.80	Nov 22.50 Put	0.55	0.65
Nov 25.00 Call	4.80	5.10	Nov 25.00 Put	1.40	1.45
Nov 27.50 Call	3.50	3.70	Nov 27.50 Put	2.50	2.65
Nov 30.00 Call	2.65	2.75	Nov 30.00 Put	4.00	4.20

On September 10, 2010, the November VIX future contract was trading at 28.55 and the VIX index was at 22.00. The November future contract is at a 6.55 point premium to the spot index. In addition, the November option contracts prices appear in Table 16.6. Also, November expiration is 65 days in the future.

Assuming a neutral to slightly bullish outlook for the VIX index over the next two months, a trader considers initiating an iron condor. Using the available strike prices, an iron condor is created with a target range for the VIX index of 22.50 to 25.00. The put side of the spread involves buying a Nov 20.00 Put at 0.15 and selling a Nov 22.50 Put for a credit of 0.55. There is a net credit of 0.40 for this side of the transaction. On the call side, a Nov 25.00 Call is sold at 4.80 and a Nov 27.50 Call is purchased for 3.70 for a net credit of 1.10. This iron condor is initiated for a net credit of 1.50.

The payoff for this iron condor at expiration for a variety of prices appears in Table 16.7.

With a net credit of 1.50 and a spread of 2.50 between the outside strike prices and the middle strike prices, a maximum potential loss is 1.00 for this spread. Risking 1.00 for a 1.50 reward makes for a pretty attractive

TABLE 16.7 November VIX Option Pricing

VIX	Long Nov 20.00 Put	Short Nov 22.50 Put	Short Nov 25.00 Put	Long Nov 27.50 Call	Credit	Iron Condor Profit/Loss
17.50	2.50	−5.00	0.00	0.00	1.50	−1.00
20.00	0.00	−2.50	0.00	0.00	1.50	−1.00
22.50	0.00	0.00	0.00	0.00	1.50	1.50
25.00	0.00	0.00	0.00	0.00	1.50	1.50
27.50	0.00	0.00	−2.50	0.00	1.50	−1.00
30.00	0.00	0.00	−5.00	2.50	1.50	−1.00

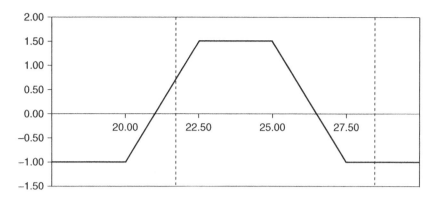

FIGURE 16.3 VIX Iron Condor Payout Diagram

iron condor, especially when the profit is based on very little change in the VIX index. The payout diagram in Figure 16.3 depicts the potential outcome for this trade.

This payout diagram has two prices, indicated by vertical lines. The line on the left shows where the VIX index was trading when the spread was initiated. The other line on the far right shows the pricing for the November VIX future. Note the future contract price is at a level where the spread would result in a maximum loss of 1.00 at November expiration. The index is at a price level that is very close to the maximum gain range of 22.50 to 25.00.

WHAT IS AN IRON BUTTERFLY?

An iron butterfly is very similar to the iron condor as far as the goal of the trade and the construction of the spread. A major difference between the two is that the iron butterfly held to expiration is targeting a specific price, as opposed to the iron condor which targets a range of prices.

The iron butterfly is constructed through purchasing a call and put along with selling a call and put. The contracts share the same expiration date and underlying. The more expensive put and call are sold and the less expensive versions of each are purchased. Finally, the short put and call contracts that are sold share a strike price. The result is a specific price where a maximum profit will be realized as opposed to a range.

These two spreads are often grouped together as the winged spreads. The naming of the spreads and the two being called "winged" stems from the appearance of their payoff diagrams. With a little imagination, the form of a bird may be seen in the iron condor diagram, and the shape of a butterfly may be seen in an iron butterfly diagram.

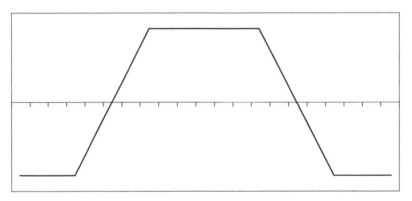

Iron Condor

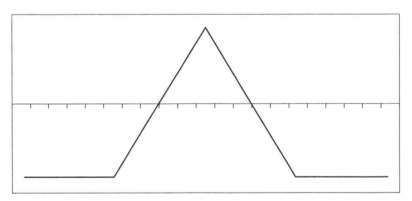

Iron Butterfly

Table 16.8 contains price quotes that will be used to create an example of an iron butterfly. The underlying pricing for these options have XYZ

TABLE 16.8 Quotes to Create an Iron Butterfly

	Bid	Ask		Bid	Ask
XYZ 45 Call	5.30	5.35	XYZ 45 Put	0.20	0.25
XYZ 50 Call	1.80	1.85	XYZ 50 Put	1.75	1.80
XYZ 55 Call	0.30	0.35	XYZ 55 Put	5.20	5.25

trading at 50.00, which is also the best case scenario for this trade. The 50 strike call and put options are sold, with the wings then being purchased.

The XYZ 50 Call at 1.80 and XYZ 50 Put at 1.75 are sold for a net credit of 3.55. The iron butterfly spread is completed through purchasing the XYZ 45 Put at 0.25 and XYZ 55 Call at 0.35 for a cost of 0.60. The net result is a credit of 2.95 (3.55 – 0.60) for initiating the trade.

Table 16.9 shows the payout for the iron butterfly at a variety of prices for XYZ at expiration. At 50.00 the spread actually has a maximum profit of 2.95, based on the credit received when the trade was put on. From 45.00 and lower or 55.00 and higher, this spread would incur a loss of 2.05. Between those two outer strike prices this trade would have a partial gain or loss at expiration.

The payout diagram appears in Figure 16.4. The vertical line represents the price of XYZ when the trade was implemented. The point where the maximum gain is realized results in a different look to the diagram when compared with an iron condor in the previous example.

Table 16.10 contains price quotes that will be used to create a second example of an iron butterfly. The underlying pricing for these options has XYZ trading at 55.00, which is at a price at expiration where the maximum potential loss of this spread would be incurred.

Using these prices, an iron butterfly targeting a price of 50.00 would be initiated at a credit of 3.60. This results from selling each of the 50 strike options for a credit of 5.75. The XYZ 50 Call would be sold at 5.45 and a credit of 0.30 would be received for selling the XYZ 50 Put. An XYZ

TABLE 16.9 XYZ 45/50/55 Iron Butterfly Profit-Loss at Expiration

XYZ	Long XYZ 45 Put	Short XYZ 50 Put	Short XYZ 50 Call	Long XYZ 55 Call	Credit	Iron Condor Profit Loss
40	5.00	−10.00	0.00	0.00	2.95	−2.05
45	0.00	−5.00	0.00	0.00	2.95	−2.05
50	0.00	0.00	0.00	0.00	2.95	2.95
55	0.00	0.00	−5.00	0.00	2.95	−2.05
60	0.00	0.00	−10.00	5.00	2.95	−2.05

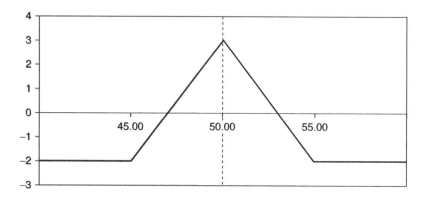

FIGURE 16.4 XYZ 45/50/55 Iron Butterfly Payout Diagram

TABLE 16.10 Quotes to Create Iron Butterfly

	Bid	Ask		Bid	Ask
XYZ 45 Call	10.10	10.15	XYZ 45 Put	0.05	0.10
XYZ 50 Call	5.45	5.50	XYZ 50 Put	0.30	0.35
XYZ 55 Call	2.00	2.05	XYZ 55 Put	1.90	1.95

45 Put would be purchased for 0.10 and an XYZ 55 Call would cost 2.05 for a net debit of 2.15. The results at a variety of prices at expiration appear in Table 16.11.

This table shows that the maximum potential profit is 3.60 while the maximum loss is 1.40. On the surface, this appears to be a better potential trade than the previous example. However, the current pricing for XYZ is an obstacle that needs to be overcome if this trade is to result in a maximum profit. The stock would have to drop by 5 points from 55.00 to 50.00 at expiration for the full 3.60 to be realized.

TABLE 16.11 XYZ 45/50/55 Iron Butterfly Profit-Loss at Expiration

XYZ	Long XYZ 45 Put	Short XYZ 50 Put	Short XYZ 50 Call	Long XYZ 55 Call	Credit	Iron Condor Profit Loss
40	5.00	−10.00	0.00	0.00	3.60	−1.40
45	0.00	−5.00	0.00	0.00	3.60	−1.40
50	0.00	0.00	0.00	0.00	3.60	3.60
55	0.00	0.00	−5.00	0.00	3.60	−1.40
60	0.00	0.00	−10.00	5.00	3.60	−1.40

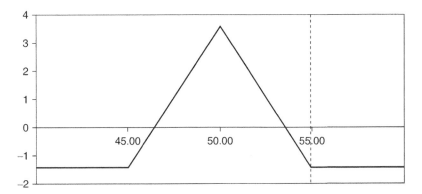

FIGURE 16.5 XYZ 45/50/55 Iron Butterfly Payout Diagram

TABLE 16.12 Iron Butterfly Comparisons

	Iron Butterfly XYZ @ 50.00	Iron Butterfly XYZ @ 55.00
Max gain	2.95	3.60
Max loss	2.05	1.40
Down break even	47.05	46.40
Up break even	52.95	53.60

Figure 16.5 shows the potential profit or loss for this iron butterfly based on prices at expiration. As in other diagrams, the pricing level for the underlying is depicted by a vertical line. In this case, the vertical line falls right on the 55.00 price level, which would result in a maximum loss of 1.40 for this trade.

Finally, Table 16.12 is a good comparison of the two iron butterfly spreads. The less risky iron butterfly, which is priced off XYZ at 50.00, has a lower potential gain and higher potential loss than the spread priced off XYZ at 55.00. Also, note the range of prices where the two spreads fall between break even. The spread created with the stock trading at the center strike price has a narrower range of profitability than the riskier trade. However, the stock is priced within this range, indicating the higher likelihood that it will be in the range at expiration.

IRON BUTTERFLY WITH VIX OPTIONS

A favorable payout structure may be created using VIX index options when the target is equal to the index but the corresponding future contract is at

TABLE 16.13 January VIX Index Option Quotes, September 27, 2010

	Bid	Ask		Bid	Ask
Jan 20.00 Call	10.10	10.50	Jan 20.00 Put	0.25	0.30
Jan 22.50 Call	8.10	8.40	Jan 22.50 Put	0.65	0.70
Jan 25.00 Call	6.30	6.50	Jan 25.00 Put	1.35	1.45

a premium or discount. This is similar to the iron condor, where the risk reward may be favorable when the outcome of the trade is based on the VIX index level and not the VIX future pricing.

VIX pricing from September 27, 2010, is used to demonstrate an iron butterfly. On this day, the VIX index closed at 22.54 and the January 2011 VIX future contract closed at 30.15. An iron butterfly is going to be initiated based on a neutral outlook for the VIX index over the next $3\frac{1}{2}$ months. Due to the pricing difference between the January contract and the index, the iron butterfly will have a very favorable risk-reward scenario based on the neutral outlook. The January VIX index option pricing appears in Table 16.13.

The put side of the iron butterfly would involve buying the Jan 20.00 Put at 0.30 and selling a Jan 22.50 Put for a credit of 0.65. The net result is a credit of 0.35 for this side of the spread. On the call side, the Jan 22.50 Call would be sold for a credit of 8.10 and the Jan 25.00 Call would be purchased for a debit of 6.50. The net result for this side of the spread would be a credit of 1.60, and when combined with the 0.35 credit from the put transactions, the net result is a credit of 1.95.

The outcome for this trade at a variety of VIX index settlement prices appears in Table 16.14. At 22.50 all contracts in the spread have no value, and the maximum profit for the trade of 1.95 would be realized. As the settlement value moves higher or lower from this price point, the profit will be lower until turning into a loss with a move of more than 1.95 in either direction.

TABLE 16.14 VIX Iron Butterfly Profit-Loss at Expiration

VIX Index	Long Jan 20.00 Put	Short Jan 22.50 Put	Short Jan 22.50 Call	Long Jan 25.00 Call	Credit	Profit/Loss
17.50	2.50	−5.00	0.00	0.00	1.95	−0.55
20.00	0.00	−2.50	0.00	0.00	1.95	−0.55
22.50	0.00	0.00	0.00	0.00	1.95	1.95
25.00	0.00	0.00	−2.50	0.00	1.95	−0.55
27.50	0.00	0.00	−5.00	2.50	1.95	−0.55

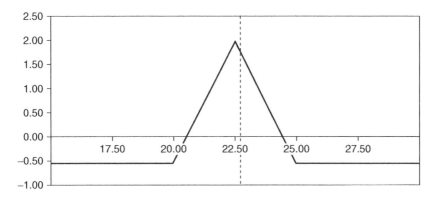

FIGURE 16.6 VIX Iron Butterfly Payout Diagram

Figure 16.6 is a payoff diagram for this iron butterfly based on January VIX settlement prices. The dashed line on the diagram indicates where the VIX index was when this trade would have been put on. The VIX index was trading at 22.54, just a hair above the maximum potential payout price of 22.50. Also, the breakeven levels show up on this diagram. If the index is at any level between 20.55 and 24.45, there will be a profit for this trade.

What is unique for this trade is the risk reward for a neutral strategy that involves very little price movement out of the underlying security. The maximum profit is 1.95 with a maximum potential loss of 0.55. The reward is almost four times the risk involved in this trade. A similar trade with the underlying pricing instrument being this close to the maximum profit level would have a less favorable risk reward than this 4-to-1 ratio.

About the Author

R ussell Rhoads, CFA, is an instructor with The Options Institute at the Chicago Board Options Exchange. He joined the Institute in 2009 after a career as an investment analyst and trader with a variety of firms. He also is a financial author and editor, having contributed to *Technical Analysis of Stocks and Commodities* magazine and edited several books for John Wiley and Sons. In 2008 he wrote *Candlestick Charting for Dummies* and in 2010 authored *Option Spread Trading*. He is a double graduate of the University of Memphis with a BBA (1992) and an MS (1994) in Finance and also received a Master's Certificate in Financial Engineering from the Illinois Institute of Technology in 2003. Also, he instructs a graduate-level options course at the University of Illinois–Chicago and an undergraduate-level derivatives class at Carthage College in Kenosha, WI.

Russell lives in Hinsdale, Illinois, with his wife, Merribeth, and their two daughters, Emmy and Maggie. In addition to his job and writing books, he serves on the Board of Education for Community Consolidated School District 181, which covers five suburban Chicago communities.

Index

Printed and bound by CPI Group (UK) Ltd, Croydon, CR0 4YY

16/04/2025

14658451-0005